Longman's Charity

Longman's Charity

*A Novel about Landscape and Childhood,
Sanity and Abuse, Truth and Redemption*

P. H. Brazier

www.longmanscharity.net

RESOURCE *Publications* · Eugene, Oregon

LONGMAN'S CHARITY
A Novel about Landscape and Childhood, Sanity and Abuse, Truth and Redemption

Copyright © 2014 P. H. Brazier. All rights reserved. Except for brief quotations in critical publications or reviews, no part of this book may be reproduced in any manner without prior written permission from the publisher. Write: Permissions, Wipf and Stock Publishers, 199 W. 8th Ave., Suite 3, Eugene, OR 97401.

Resource Publications
An Imprint of Wipf and Stock Publishers
199 W. 8th Ave., Suite 3
Eugene, OR 97401

www.wipfandstock.com

ISBN 13: 978-1-62564-845-7

Cataloging-in-Publication data:

Brazier, Paul

Longman's charity : a novel about landscape and childhood, sanity and abuse, truth and redemption / P. H. Brazier.

xviii + 254 p. ; 23 cm.

ISBN 13: 978-1-62564-845-7

1. Childhood—Novel. 2. England—Social life and customs—20th century—Novel. 3. Dysfunctional families—Novel. 4. Child Abuse—Novel. 5. Family violence—Novel. 6. Psychiatric hospital patients—Novel. I. Title.

PS3603 B639 2014

Manufactured in the U.S.A.
Typeset by P. H. Brazier, Ash Design
Minion Pro 10 pt. on 13.5 pt.

For Hilary

"Paul Brazier describes a Dantean personal journey
from the living hell of his childhood and adolescence through the purgatory
of finding forgiveness for those who wronged him to the paradise
of his faith and loving devotion to his wife.

Guided by his Virgil, the natural beauty of the world,
he comes to see that the world is, indeed, fused
with 'the beauty and grandeur of God.'
A moving and, ultimately, uplifting story of the triumph of love over evil."

—SUZANNE M. WOLFE, WRITER IN RESIDENCE, SEATTLE PACIFIC UNIVERSITY

"Paul articulates his powerful story in a beautiful profound way.
It is a powerful story that compels readers to consider the presence of God
in the midst of terrible lifelong circumstances.

It was helpful for me as a fellow victim of child abuse
and other life circumstances that he suffered (along with the after effects
of relatives that committed suicide). Thank you, Paul, for bringing me hope
through the presence of Christ as your hope."

—JULIE WOODLEY, RESTORING THE HEART MINISTRIES, INC., SETAUKET, NY

Contents

Acknowledgements   xi
Preface   xiii

LONGMAN'S CHARITY

Prologue—A Welcoming   1

PART ONE—THE LAND AND THE CHILD

Chapter 1. Creation: Fruitfulness and the Serpent   7
Chapter 2. Town: People and Family   23
Chapter 3. Beginnings: Infancy and Quietude   41
Chapter 4. Love: Sickness and Death   62
Chapter 5. Summer: Vibrancy and Joy   82

PART TWO—THE VILLAGE IDIOT

Chapter 6. Abuse: Sanity and Dis-ease   103
Chapter 7. Winter: Christmas and Survival   129
Chapter 8. Realization: Fear and Depression   149

PART THREE—THROUGH FIRE AND WATER

Chapter 9. Captivity: Sanctity and Sanctuary   181
Chapter 10. Deception: Terror and Dread   197
Chapter 11. Sanity: Emptiness and Escape   212
Chapter 12. Exile: Desperation and Return   231
Epilogue—A Leave-Taking   248

This story, in its setting and landscape, culture and town,
is considered here to be evocative of England.

Therefore the spelling conventions used by the writer—
those of his indigenous language, British English—are retained.

The landscape, town, setting for this story is real:
the Vale of Evesham, on the borders of Worcestershire
and Gloucestershire, England.

The author has attempted where relevant to reproduce the dialect often referred to as Ayssum (or Asum), that is the local dialect spoken around the Vale of Evesham. Most locals born since the Second World War either spoke standard English or used some fragments of this dialect. Many, even of an older generation, would mix traditional pronouns (thees and thous) with their modern equivalents (you) in the same sentence. The word "bist" was often used simply for "is" or "are", sometimes "been!" Truncation of words, or elision, was often personal, and varied from village to village. The dialect around the village of Badsey to the east of Evesham was often purer, unadulturated, and more guttural than used by gardeners around Elmley Castle to the south west. Often men exhibited a variation of the dialect different from women; often mothers used a subtly different dialect when talking to their children. However flawed the writer's attempts may be, he has attempted to reproduce the nuances of dialect he heard and observed as a child, with the multiple regional variations
evident in the Vale of Evesham.

There is a complementary website to this book,
which has photographs (landscape, town, and family), maps,
explanatory background, details about the cover photographs and paintings,
the author, the psalms used, and more, which readers may find of use:

www.longmanscharity.net

Acknowledgements

My thanks must go to my parents. For all the difficulties of my childhood, and despite their attempt to abort me, they gave me life, and for that life I give thanks to them—and to God, in Christ. To my sister Christine who looked after me in our early years, and throughout our childhood kept me sane, I likewise give thanks.

Secondarily I thank Hilary, my wife—for I did not start living till I started loving you. Hilary has severe epilepsy, we met when she was in hospital after the first episode of *status epilepticus*, and married in 1983. For half that time I have been and continue to be her full-time carer. I did not start living till I started loving her, and for that I thank the Lord. For there is no safe option, there is no escape from the pain and torment of life. To love at all is to be vulnerable. Hide away and you may think you are safe, indeed you will appear not to suffer, but you will become impassable, shut-off and inaccessible, irredeemable: to avoid the pain of love is to risk of damnation—self-damnation. C. S. Lewis once commented that the only place outside heaven where we can be perfectly, indeed absolutely, safe from all the dangers of love, indeed the cost, the risks, the trepidations of truly loving, along with the disquiet and self-denial of caring, is hell. If we refuse to love we condemn ourselves to hell when confronted with the absolute purity of love.

I give acknowledgment and thanks to Anthony Dyson, who, more than thirty years ago, listened, as this story began to unfold, and helped immeasurably down the years. Likewise to Revd Peter Hughes, University Church of Christ the King (University of London), who generated in me an objective assessment of what had happened to me in my childhood years. Likewise, key members of the Anglican religious community of The Sisters of the Love of God at Fairacres, Oxford, must be thanked for prayer and support down the years, and for simply being there.

My thanks go to Robin Parry who carefully went through the initial manuscript to assess it objectively and recommend some editorial changes.

My thanks also go to Brendan N. Wolfe, a linguist and friend, from the University of Oxford, for proof reading.

The extracts from the psalms are my own translation from the *Septuagint*, the Greek edition of the Hebrew Bible (the Old Testament) from the late second century BC. The edition consulted here was Sir Lancelot C. L. Brenton, *The Septuagint with Apocrypha*, London: Samuel Bagster and Sons, 1851 (eighth printing, Hendrickson Publishers, 1999). The numbering of the Psalms here is from modern translations; for those interested the two systems are used on the complementary website where the Greek text can be found (*Septuagint* number, followed by modern number in parentheses): http://www.longmanscharity.net/psalms.html.

Preface

This story has taken the best part of a third of a century to write. No, the writing was not spread out evenly over thirty-three years. The first period of writing was in April 1981. I was staying on a solitary silent retreat at Fairacres in Oxford—the Sisters of the Love of God, an Anglican religious order. Approximately 14,000 words were sketched out, and much of the scenes in Powick was written at that time. However, I was aged twenty-seven years and I was still much too close to the events of my childhood to be able to write about, let alone fully understand, what had happened to me. Furthermore, many of the memories were still locked away. These sketches were relatively formless, but confessional (in the Augustinian sense); they were written in an attempt to try to remember objectively what had happened, record, and as a result move on. There were further sketches written around 1988–89, however, much of the book *Longman's Charity* as such was written between October 1990 and August 1994. Yet much was still locked away: it is quite daunting and even fearsome how the human mind will blank out certain memories until the person is ready to face, fully, certain events. The work seemed incomplete so I put it to one side.

My parents died in October 1993 and February 1994. Memories came back after their deaths—in particular, the full recollection of what happened in my childhood only started to impress itself on me after my mother's suicide (February 1994). However, the full admittance and realization was complete in my mind and memory from the year 2000. The admission of what had happened in my childhood was alluded to in other personal writing at that time; the events were then revised in sketches in 2001. Christine, my sister, died of cancer in December 2003. I began the restructuring and rewriting of *Longman's Charity* in the second half of 2005. The final writing happened in 2013: thirty-two summers after the original sketches written at Fairacres. From 1981 on I knew that there would one day be a complete single volume that told this story. I had no idea at the time that it would take so long to write, however, the development of the structure of the narrative, the recovery and recollection of key events, the writing all demanded such a period of gestation: it was in God's good time.

Preface

Recovered memory has a bad press. Therapists who try to help people recover memories may inadvertently sow the seeds of false memories in a patient; or they may indeed tease out and help someone to confront memories of events they have repressed. Fortunately I have had no contact throughout my adult life with psychiatrists, psychologists, or therapists of various persuasions. The memories of abuse and suffering I endured as a child gradually surfaced of their own accord in middle age, from the age of forty years. The test, as such, of their veracity was in how the inkling of an idea came, the flavour of that memory and the feeling that it was something I had felt and experienced before came seemingly from nowhere, but, crucially, the way in which different details of events that resurfaced hung together—they cohered with each other and made sense. There was no sudden revelation, but a gradual reclaiming of details and moments of the memories. I say there was no sudden revelation, but I believe that this gradual dawning and realization was generated by the whispering influence of the Holy Spirit: only when the time was right did the sublimated memories—memories that had been sublimated for good reason—gradually resurface. I doubted, and tested the memories, but noted how they related to each other and cohered, and displayed their form, like missing pieces of a jigsaw puzzle. This was particularly so in the way a sublimated memory would confirm the truth of an existing remembered event: reasoning was as much a part of the recovery as the seeming emergence of a memory from nowhere.

Six months before her death my sister, Christine, gave me some papers that our mother had given her for safekeeping decades before. They were papers about our maternal grandfather's professional work in the early decades of the twentieth century, they were about his masonic—high-ranking masonic—status, work, and connections, all of which began to point to details relating to the abuse that my mother, as a young girl, had received at the hands of a business associate of her father. I was in my early fifties by the time I read these papers, so evidence came after the memories relating to the past had gently resurfaced.

Longman's Charity is therefore autobiographical; as such, it can be seen as an illustration of the realities of human life as portrayed in the Biblical book of Psalms, therefore each chapter opens with a highly pertinent quotation from the Psalms, which complements the content of each part and its chapters (the translations are my own, essentially from the Septuagint Bible, with a heavy influence from the Book of Common Prayer). The psalms illustrate the crises people face, wrestling with the situation they find themselves in, struggling to find the way forward, to do good, aware they are responsible to God for their lives, crying out to God. Furthermore, this work can be seen as an exposition of Milton—there was a serpent in that garden, that market garden; a dark force, animated and conscious, that beguiled and seduced, flattered and corrupted, that merely whispered thoughts into the minds of men and women; a dark strength that deluded, wilfully; personified evil that seduced men and women to corrupt children; an evil that convinced responsible adults of the vanity of their thoughts. A person finds he (or she) can do something, an act or action that initially he might have regarded as repugnant, even abominable; then he finds he enjoys this act, then he realizes he can no longer stop doing it. Such a person then develops justification for this act, even religious theories to justify such fallen wilfulness; such an action is often abuse, whether physically violent or sexual. Often, the person's involvement in these actions cannot be reconciled with the beliefs—religious or otherwise—that he has held, and with the perception of an external morality, so that the tension may lead to suicide. All sins can be forgiven; but suicide is perhaps the worst manifestation of the sin against the Holy Spirit that Jesus warns us about. Suicide rejects God's forgiving judgment; the person simply passes judgment on itself with all the consequences of that action. Therefore, this story is about the dark side of humanity, the dark side of desire, but above all this story is about the corruption of love.

Longman's Charity is therefore autobiographical but also parabolic: characters are renamed, in some cases combined, but the events are all factual. The key family, the Broadley's, is the family I was raised in. Why change the name?—because by resituating I could somehow distance myself from the events and try to present them, in literary form, objectively. The Prophet Nathan could expose King David to the truth of his actions by resetting the king's adultery and the wasting of Bathsheba's husband in a parable. Thus, Nathan could identify a deeper level of truth than he could by merely stating the bare facts: such deeper truths are by their very nature theological, and truthfully mythological.

Fact or fiction? Everything that happens to Paul Broadley in this story happened to me. But, we see "in a glass darkly." What is presented here is as accurate as I can make it. I have endeavoured to be true to the memory, and therefore to the facts as I remember, know, and understand them. On the one hand, the human can all too often be imperfect, frail and mortal, yet, it is uncanny how memories from years ago can be accurate when measured against external data (this is especially true as we grow old). We are often divinely inspired, fallible knowers. Therefore, everything that happens to Paul Broadley in this story I experienced. The presentation of my sister, parents, and grandparents is also an honest recollection; likewise, what is presented of their characters and motivations, their weaknesses and flaws, is as accurate as my memory serves. This is also the case with regard to the people with power, status, and authority who exercised a profound effect on my childhood—for example, the doctors,

Preface

social workers, and psychiatrists. Therefore outside of my immediate family circle I have changed the names of characters, sometimes amalgamating real-life characters for artistic reasons (and to distance from the real person), also for reasons of narrative and economy. For example, the characters in Powick are all accurate portraits—though given pseudonyms—some, especially in the staff, are amalgamations. Some characters around Evesham are accurate portraits (for example, Chowskie—no one knew his real name). Others—for example Jim and Doris Beason—are a fictitious portrait drawn from accurate observations of around half a dozen real-life characters that I knew. As such Jim and Doris are, I believe, typical of the rural working class Protestant market gardeners, often deeply Christian, who survived just above the poverty line, and as such exhibited a righteousness before God generated by their restraint, though they were not flawless. Such righteousness the wealthier market gardeners often lacked. Did the conversations between Jim and Paul happen? Yes, but not with "Jim"; the conversations were with a man who drove a black-and-white lorry for a gardener—a market gardening firm—with large dealings, land, whom Paul would go and talk to when he was out walking down the Corn Mill Road, or when the driver came to collect produce from Paul's father. "Jim," however, is a composite.

What is presented in this story should not be seen as a criticism of anyone, simply a portrait of fallen humanity (Genesis 3), who, in trying to do good so often get it wrong, doing the evil they hate, who have the desire to do what is good, but cannot carry it out (Romans 7). I would confidently assert that *Longman's Charity* is theologically charged, perhaps in sweep, intention, and meaning because it reflects a true understanding of the human condition and dilemma before God and the profound cry from humanity—however corrupt and guilty, stained and broken—for forgiveness and redemption. If that cry is lacking or stifled then the result is despair, and all too often suicide.

Paul Brazier
January 2014

There was a Serpent in that Garden

MILTON, *PARADISE LOST*, BOOK IX

Prologue—
A Welcoming

~ *"Have mercy on me, O Lord, for I am weak;*
O Lord, heal me, for my very bones are troubled."
PSALM 6:2

The sky was clear, bright, sharp. It was early March. The air was cool, the frost had cleared, and the sun was strong for the time of year—its light was bright, piercing, but it gave no heat. The land was bare. The trees were bare. A rabbit sat nervously twitching on the furrowed earth, looking, ever looking. A crow cawed from the nearby copse, startling the rabbit as though it expected something to swoop and tear its flesh with beak and claws. The crow cawed again. The rabbit shot across the field, hopping over the brown furrowed ridges, weathered down now by winter rains and frost. The crow cawed once more. Then, falling more than flying, it flapped its way down from the top of the ivy-strangled naked elm on which it stood, landing on the bare earth. It hopped clumsily over the soil to a stone. Picking up a snail from the earth in its beak it hopped its wide-legged drunken gait this time to the stone. Twitching its eyes and head for a second or two it struck the snail against the stone. Stopping for a moment to move its head from one side to another, then, crack, it brought the snail down again. Crack, it turned to pecking at the flesh through the opening in the shell. Peck, peck, peck, shake, hop, peck; soon the crow had finished. Looking around from side to side, it lurched itself upwards, flapping its wings clumsily, gaining a little height, then touching the ground, flapping with tremendous effort against the cold air.

The boy had seen it all. He had seen the rabbit, he had watched it slowly, fitfully, making its way across the ground. Saw its nervous terror as the crow cawed. Paul watched its panic, sensed its fear. Felt for it. The boy felt the same fear, often fearing his fellow humans. The boy had seen the crow, watched its clumsy flight earthward. He listened to the cracking of the snail shell, he flinched as with each smash the struggle seemed more and more hopeless. The boy seemed to shrink back nervously, his face twitching as if he were the snail, as if he were being broken, eaten. He twitched his mouth, nose, nodded his head involuntarily. This often happened when he was being teased by other children, when he was being set upon by a group of other boys and girls—teasing, taunting, pillorying him. It wasn't just the names that hurt, but the loneliness, having no friends, being called mental, being made to feel different, odd, not wanted. His head nodded, twitched, particularly when his father was rowing, storming about the kitchen, banging the stove, thumping down saucepans. He could usually stop this nodding, twitching, but the terror in him returned as he watched his father's face screw up with the pain and hurt following some despicable comment his mother would say, the child not fully realizing or understanding what was said. But then when his mother was hit! The terror was too much, he would curl up tight on the floor and cry quietly to himself, his head nodding, slightly to the left, hung slightly over to his left shoulder. Sometimes he would run out of the house, across the smallholding he lived on, into the hedgerows and curl up into his own little world.

Today he had gone further, through several smallholdings, along the lane, through Longman's Charity, to a small hideaway that was precious to him. It was in the centre of a small copse nearly two miles away from home. No more than four hundred yards long, by about sixty wide, tapering to a point at the far end. It consisted mainly of rowan, ash, and elm, with holly and bramble at ground level. This, coupled with the barbed wire fence that surrounded it, made the copse quite difficult to penetrate. However, at one point, near where the brook emerged from the trees, there was a small hole through the wire, and by lying on his stomach he could crawl under the holly bushes, through the brambles, for about ten yards, to find himself clear of the undergrowth, and inside. Inside! He felt like he was in another world. If he then clambered still further through the thinner undergrowth, heading south towards the centre of the copse, the struggle abated.

The tallest trees were in the centre, and their crowns allowed little light through. As the undergrowth thinned the ground opened up. Near the centre there was even thin, pale, grass, with the brook trickling gently over the stony earth. This was the boy's favourite spot. No one else knew of his secret. No one else had ever ventured into here—or so he believed. He had run and walked, and walked then run from the house, wanting the security of this, his secret hideaway. The peace was almost magical, the stillness was complemented by the trickling of the water over the stones, with the light dappling through the bare

Prologue—A Welcoming

branches overhead. The boy flopped down on the grass, desperately trying to get his breath. No other house was near. No other person was in sight. It was his own little world, his sanctuary. He was safe. He sat up. Hooking his arms around his knees, he looked around. The grassy glade he sat on was about four yards by two, with the brook gently traversing from south to north, widening a little to form a shallow pool. He looked at the tall, smooth trunks of ash, with their black buds swelling, preparing to burst forth into spring in a matter of days. He looked around at the holly bushes, the brambles that created an enclosure around the glade. He was happy. But then his head started to spin, the high-pitched squeal in his ears got worse. He listened to the stream, lay back . . . and slept.

Paul woke to the sound of men's voices, men shouting, calling—calling his name. He soon realized two things: first, that he must have slept for quite a long time, and secondly, that if they found him here his secret refuge would be lost. They would know about it. Even if they never came back to it, they would know: it would no longer be his secret. So, quietly he left the peace, the still quietude of this inner sanctuary. The shouts sounded closer, so he quickly darted through the holly and brambles, out west to the edge of the copse, pausing for a few minutes to observe the frightened rabbit, and the crow with the snail, watching in empty pain, wishing in one sense that he was the crow, getting his own back, yet much deeper, deep down, sensing an affinity with the snail in its pain, its brokenness, its loss, its fate. Quickly regaining his senses he dashed across the muddy field to the hedge that formed the boundary between this part of the farm, and the Charity. Moving up the hedge about fifty yards, he crawled through, then lay low in the ditch between the hedge and the lane.

"Here's ee!"

It was the voice of Alan, one of the hands who worked for his father on the smallholding.

"Come here you little. . . . Your father 'ul kill 'ou if he gits 'is 'ands on 'ee!"

The boy crawled out of the ditch. His secret was safe. It was not that this small wiry ten-year-old boy got up to anything in the copse; he didn't kill any animals, did not collect birds' eggs, did not steal and store like other boys. No, this was one of the few safe havens, a sanctuary for the boy, living as he did in a world dominated by violence and abuse: by bitterness between his parents: of anger, frustration, and sexual taunts between those who had brought him, albeit accidentally, into this world. But there was worse, this safe haven masked out the near daily memory of abuse, of the touch and feel of abuse; of intention and touch that a child will sense and want to run from so that the memory is locked away, lost, and escaped from. But however much the memory of being touched in ways no child should experience could be escaped from, the effect on his personality and behaviour remained. At its most explicit this disturbance exhibited itself when the child nodded his head involuntarily, repeatedly, screwed up his eyes, repeatedly, could not keep still, moving his limbs, repeatedly. . . .

His father walked up the lane from the Red Barn. He could see the boy with Alan, walking down towards them.

"Your mother's been tearing her hair out don't you know! Come here. Where you 'bin? If it wer'n't for old Jim Beason having seen 'ou running down 'ere about an 'our gone, then, then, I don't know." His father turned and clasping his cap, tore it from his head, hurling it at the boy's feet.

They were stood near to a pigsty, itself behind a small ramshackle shed. The boy looked longingly at the pig, shut as it was in this small concrete sty, with barely enough room to turn around.

"You're not listening to me, bist thee? You're not even listening!" And with one sweep he grabbed the boy by the arm and dragged him back down the lane to where an old Austin lorry was parked. Throwing the boy into the cab, he started up the engine; Alan jumped onto the rear end of the flat bed of the lorry to help guide the boy's father as he carefully reversed the vehicle back up the lane to Gypsies' Corner.

Longman's Charity

Part One
The Land and The Child

"Behold, I was brought forth in iniquity,
and in sin my mother did conceive me."

PSALM 51:5

Chapter One
Creation: Fruitfulness and the Serpent

> ~ "He sends the springs into the valleys,
> they flow among the hills.
> They give drink to every beast of the field. . . .
> He causes the grass to grow for the cattle,
> and vegetation for man,
> that he may bring forth food from the earth. . . ."
>
> PSALM 104:10–11a & 14

One

The lane led down a shallow gradient to a brook. The land, as far as one could see, was green: grey-greens, rich forest-greens, light pea-greens, beige-greens, blue-greens, brown-greens, sandy-greens, yellows, occasional orangey flecks, but everywhere shades of green. The colours were moulded by shape and texture: tall thin shapes, short tight curly shapes, blue-grey wispy shapes, full round beige-greens, tight excited shapes with a multiplicity of shades, or plain flat textures: like a gentle dusting of green snow on the soil. The land was covered with crops. Crops growing. Vegetables growing in short rows, in long rows, in patches, in large rectangles, in isolated strips, in groups: and all in this beautiful cadence of greens and related shades or flecks of yellow, sand, blue, grey, red, purple, and orange; underlined everywhere by the rich dark brown soil. They formed a patchwork. The crops were no more than two feet in height, interrupted only by occasional scrubby trees, stunted through being cut for firewood. Most of the crops were separated by small embankments, with occasional hedgerows of hawthorn and brambles. Everywhere there was a low undulating flatness, with, in the distance, the hazy pattern of a small, ancient market town on the horizon. If one looked closer, many of the grey patches one took for hawthorn or blackthorn scrub were tiny ramshackle sheds made from old weathered, irregular grey timber, or rusted corrugated tin. Some had a thin trickle of smoke coming from them. Most had a small but substantial wooden barrow, timbers grey with age parked next to the shed—the sole means for getting produce out and into the market town. The lowliest were single-wheeled barrows; others boasted four steel-rimmed wooden wheels mounted on leaf springs, steered by means of the bar used for pulling it at the front. Others, a rare few, had pick-ups parked next to them: small half-lorry half-car vehicles—some being converted from a Ford Model T, others being a newer Austin with a small wooden bed about five feet by four behind the single seat cab, with the four cylinder engine, headlights, and bonnet in front. Only one of the men working the Charity had such a luxurious vehicle for transporting the goods to market. Most relied on the sturdy old barrows, or the larger market gardening firms to come and collect the produce for them in lorries.

The sky was a clear blue-grey, with occasional wisps of white cloud. There was no breeze, and the slight chill in the air showed how it was now quite late in the year. Over to the west the sky was leaden, the blue-grey indicating, as this was the direction for the prevailing weather, that there might be rain later. Along the centre of this landscape, as if to echo the darker blue-grey sky over to the west, ran a darker green—the sides of the brook. The landscape was thin, fragile, made of multiple patches and textures of green with the occasional grey swatches from sheds, pick-ups, or scrub; indeed, it was an entirely manmade landscape. The only apparently natural line was the brook snaking through the mêlée of textures made by the crops, despite their confinement into rows, strips, patches.

Ordinarily the brook would have run clear, northwards to the River Avon about two and a half miles away. The condition of the brook was no longer natural. If one walked along its length, in this part of the vale, then shallow dams, ponds, railings, scoured deeps—all made by men and women—interrupted its course. It was a working brook. Many who worked the land grumbled that it was not fuller, faster flowing. They grumbled that many took water out upstream, put in too much silt, impeded its flow: it was a working brook. The accusation was true to a degree. If one followed the lane as it divided, branched, multiplied, over the distance of about two miles through this landscape (but always following upstream the shallow depression where the brook flowed) then one would come to a copse, a small deciduous wood—the remnant of a much larger natural wood that several hundred years ago had covered most of the vale. If one continued

Chapter One, Creation: Fruitfulness and the Serpent

to follow the brook upstream, crawling through the barbed wire surrounding the copse where the brook emerged from the trees, and if one crawled on all fours through the undergrowth into the wood, to a small glade where the brook widened out to form a small pool—no more than a few feet in diameter—then one found cool, clear water. If one walked, crawled, further through the wood, following the brook upstream, it became smaller, narrower, faster, and as one came to the wire fencing on its furthest perimeter, one saw—in the distance—a farm surrounded by wheat fields. The brook skirted its edge. Beyond lay more wheat fields and pastures, across the flat vale, leading within a couple of miles to the foot of the North Cotswold escarpment. The scarp slope rose within one half mile to the height of just under one thousand feet above sea level; it stood like a pale hazy green-grey wall on the horizon.

It was here, on the face of the Cotswolds, that so many of these brooks and streams rose. They would start as a tiny spring, usually marked by a rock on the limestone scarp, on a windswept face, where the covering of beige-green grass thinned to allow the rock to erupt. Here the water flowed readily. The water dribbled and trickled lightly through the thin grass of this rough, steep, ancient pasture, eventually finding a course for itself and flowing under ancient dry-stone walls—often through small neat stone arches made to accommodate the trickling streams centuries earlier—then to flow through small hamlets standing at the foot of the escarpment. In some villages the waters ran down the side of the main street in open culverts made of finely cut limestone. These tiny villages, a handful of cottages and a church, nestled into the small sculpted valleys, gleaning whatever protection they could from the winds that tore up the side of the scarp from the prevailing west. The villages were enclosed by old yew and ash trees, which, along with most of the buildings, came from an era when monks and nuns regularly walked the yellow limestone roads, to and from Hailes Abbey. The streams flowed on through marshy patches in the corner of fields, then crossed under by-roads serving and connecting many of the small hamlets and villages nestled into the foot of the escarpment. On flowed the streams, keeping strictly to the field boundaries and hedgerows they had been designated to, then trickling over the white-yellow limestone of occasional farm tracks, till the waters reached the richer, darker soils of the Vale of Evesham. There were many such streams. Our brook first appears near to Hinton Green, draining the flat arable land at the foot of the escarpment. It skirted Long Acre farm, then flowing through hedgerows and past wheat fields till it entered the copse.

As the brook emerged out from the copse it flowed into a long rectangular pool—quite perfectly rectangular, for it was kept so. About four feet in depth it provided water for the pig, soaking for the onions, and washing for just about anything and everything. Next to the rectangular pool was a redbrick barn—light entered the building through tiny gaps between the bricks, which overall formed a diamond pattern about five feet by four. About thirty feet in length, it was built of Midlands red brick with characteristic curved bricks around the entrance—the door itself, in two halves, was about ten feet tall, by eight feet wide. Running over the whole structure was a large pitched roof of clay tiles. The barn had been built during the middle of the nineteenth century—surrounded by acres of orchards—before the land had changed use. The barn stood at right angles to the rectangular pool so that the entrance served a dirt yard, itself flanked by the pool, the whole being set about fifteen yards from the lane.

Around the barn, and growing up to its edges, as if to scale its walls, were grasses, rye and wild, along with tall hollyhocks and, depending on the seasons, harebells, ox-eyed daisy, and primrose. But this was a verge, and not practical to maintaining the land, and so the wild flowers were never allowed to invade the land reserved for vegetables, but at various times of the year, along the narrow banks of grassy earth that separated plots, corn marigolds, vetches, poppies, stitchwort, knapweeds, daisy, and many more could all be seen, with primrose and foxglove around the copse, and ragged robin in the wetter parts. The one exception to this were the yellow flags, which were tolerated along the banks of the brook. In season they could run along its length, but in fact were patchy: some growers tolerated them, others pulled them out.

In amongst this wild growth, around the edge of the barn, were the twisted remains of ancient and obsolete agricultural implements—equipment all of which was for hand use, or to be pulled by a small horse. None was of a size and scale for use in a farm field. Seemingly inexorably trapped by couch grass, was a small hand push-hoe. Made from two steel strips, each the size and thickness of a man's thumb, both strips ran parallel for about two feet before turning up to travel two feet further to form handles. The pair of metal strips was set apart by thin steel rods, with a metal-shod wooden wheel between the front of these runners. Similarly set to the rear of the strips, before their turn towards the handles, was suspended a hoe—a metal strip about six inches by two, set to cut the entire width of a soil between two rows of seedlings, thus dislodging any weeds growing. The entire was now a rusty black in colour, with no portion of smooth metal remaining—the whole, pitted with sweat and work, and the erosion of innumerable grains of soil and grit, and finally rust. Similarly, if one penetrated the bindweed and hawthorn at the rear of the barn, one found chipped white-blue enamelled basins, with the steel rusted right through wherever the enamel was missing; buried even deeper was an old beige earthenware butler sink. Scattered broadly throughout the undergrowth were innumerable bits of

Chapter One, Creation: Fruitfulness and the Serpent

wood and metal, some with ornate Edwardian tracery, but with their discernible purpose now sadly rusted and rotted away.

Two

A couple approached. A man and a woman in their fifties, bent double. They were carrying crates, one each filled with onions, spring onions, neatly trimmed, outer skins removed, in bunches of about five or six onions, tied with fine string; each crate containing about one hundred and fifty bunches. The crates were wooden, held together with wire, grey black, with the edges to each plank worn smooth, indeed eroded and sculpted by water. The couple put the crates down on the side of the pool. As they stood, straightening their backs, their features revealed a coarseness that for centuries has been the hallmark of land workers. They both wore old overcoats, tied tight around the waist with the same string. Both wore Wellington boots, worn almost white in places, with a smooth moulded look reminiscent of a well-rounded pebble from a streambed. The man took hold of the crates, first one then the other, and slid more than dropped them into the cool clear water of the pool. They floated down stream to the neck of the pool, where they joined three more crates of onions, their path halted by a section of park railing thrust many years earlier into the silt at the bottom of the brook, and secured with twine to posts on either side.

"Let'um sow'k."

The remark came from the man, as much a part of his breathing out, as was the exhalation of air. So tired was he that he did not waste precious energy and breath exhaling, inhaling, and then passing comment: all became one action. He slumped down by his wife, drew out a packet of Woodbines, carefully removed one, examined it with minute attention, placed it in his mouth, paused, and with a conservation of energy unknown to those unfamiliar with working, let alone living on the land, he slowly lit a match, drew in on his cigarette, let the match drop into the pool, took out the cigarette, and let his head fall into his hands:

"'Bout three'a'pence, I reck'n—sor'l we'll git."

"Nev'r mind dear, never mind," his wife offered, "we'se done it. We'se got'um. They're awl in. They're awl in."

"Yes. Yes, but three'a'pence," he drew on his Woodbine.

"But we got the land," she said, pressing her point, "they can't tak'it, they can't, the church, not so long as we pays our bit."

"Aye", he conceded "and s'long as we look after et, so long as we is right by et, they can't take et."

"Besides, we'as got each other, we'as, we been through worse." She added, with

11

a slight hint of triumph, loving triumph, in her voice, "you think on, we'as seen worse."

True, on reflection the man could see she was right. She knew it—for he did not answer back. The winter of 1947, six years earlier, was one example, the frost and snow that winter, the hardest that century, lost them over half of their crops; over thirty pounds in seed and labour was lost—not to mention the lost income that would have come from the crop. Four years before that, when the war was at its height, she had lost her Jim; he had been in a Japanese prisoner of war camp, but she had not been informed. They had no children, had tried, but never really minded. He had his job to go back to. True it was not much of a job, but as secure a job as was possible in market gardening, with prices and demand up and down. Men were taken on and laid off at monotonous regularity, but because he was a charge hand, looking after the loading, seeing orders were got from the fields and allotments, he knew that whatever the prevailing economic climate, he had a job. And he had his land: one and a half acres, to the south of the town of Evesham. It was leased on a secure tenure for a set rent of one guinea per quarter, and provided it was looked after and kept in order then this was as safe as owning it. The smallholding, the one and a half acres, near to the Red Barn, and access rights down both lanes, provided them with a second income. It also gave them a sense of independence. Some years, this one in particular, he fretted that he would not have the rent. It was due, and the rains were wreaking havoc with the crop of onions and cabbage.

The Charity consisted of more than one charity—Hampton Charity, Christchurch Charity (Christchurch, that is Cathedral and College, in Oxford from whom Jim rented his plot), the John Martin Charity, and several more, all occupying the flat undulating land just to the south of the town. All of this land had once belonged to Evesham Abbey and its monks, but then the land was split up with the Reformation. In the nineteenth century all of this area was covered with orchards. After the First World War, Hampton Parish, the principal owner, set aside one acre of the land for each man of the parish returning from the trenches. Over the intervening thirty years many of the men had died, or relinquished their right to hold their acre, and so now the holdings varied in size from some of the original one-acre plots to some that were three acres in size, plots having been amalgamated. Jim and Doris both knew that they had one of the best holdings in the Charity: it was upstream of the others (good when it came to using the brook for washing out crops, such as onions, leeks, and so forth); it had good drainage; and it had access to the Red Barn. There was good access for when lorries or pick-ups came to collect goods, and it was protected from the prevailing westerlies by the copse, from which the brook flowed. There were

Chapter One, Creation: Fruitfulness and the Serpent

about one hundred and thirty holders in all—many of whom tried to hide the fact that they held charity land, particularly in the company of more prosperous landowners.

The brook wound its way for nearly two miles through The Charities. By the time it flowed round the skirts of the local council estate, it was a thick murky khaki-brown. The one factor the holders never complained of was the smell—they were so use to it that they either did not notice it, or pretended it was not there. They smelt of it when they went home or drove to the market. The tenants of the newly built council estate houses complained vociferously (except for the stony silence from those tenants who either worked the land or were holders): the smell could be sensed day and night, through spring, summer, and into autumn—only relieved by the first frosts. The smell was an aromatic mixture of putrefying onions and rank vegetable matter. The brook was so full of vegetable debris from crop washing that the smell was overpowering to strangers. This was bad enough at most times during the onion growing season; but worse was to come when the brook flooded: a welcome sight to the holders, for it rejuvenated their meagre holdings with rich nutrients from this soup, but for anyone living near, the situation became desperate. After passing through the estate, the brook joined a much larger stream where the added waters diluted the debris; it flowed past the building site for a local secondary modern school. Then flowed through older parts of the town, finally to divulge its remaining contents into the river Avon. In the height of the spring onion season, a thick khaki-brown delta-shaped web could be perceived in the dark grey-black of the river, where the Charity Brook joined. Although many holders bickered and moaned that it was always "sumun else," not them, who fouled the Charity Brook, and although it was holders near top end (like Jim and Doris), who got most stick, there was one sight to bring them all back together, to form an impenetrable wall of obstinate silence and prevarication: a "Minstry-Ag" (a health inspector from the Ministry of Agriculture)—who needless to say got nowhere fast, particularly as it was usually some young green sapling of an officer sent down from Birmingham.

Since the early nineteenth century the area had been developing as a centre for market gardening, and men were eager for land to start a business—however small. For some holders this land formed the staple, or sole income, to others a second, or parallel income. The plots, or holdings, were no more than a few acres—some only a half-acre. Not only were the holders at the whim of the market away in the great northern cities as to the price of their produce, and hence their labour, but they were also, by and large, subject to the whim and discretion of the next level of land workers/gardeners in the hierarchy: those who owned the let on a large piece of land, or even the freehold of the land they worked, and had established links with customers away in the cities. There was a very strictly defined hierarchy amongst those working the land. It was, of course, dominated by men.

Woman were in large evidence on the land, but only for menial tasks. Women had kept the farms and smallholdings going during the war—the Land Army had carried out all the tasks that the men had done as well as, if not better. But they had by and large returned to their kitchens with the peace, only to come out to tie onions, pick runner beans, or gather plums and apples, tend and bind asparagus, indeed the hundreds of jobs there were in neatening and presenting fruit and vegetables for sale, packaged either loose or tied, in an assortment of chips (thin wood baskets with a pressed tin handle), trays, boats (deep, heavy wooden trays for leeks), crates, nets, boxes, bags, and so on. The women did most of the fine, finicky, and tedious work. This was always considered "ooman's werk," even during hard times when many of the regular men were used for these tasks—to keep them in work.

Three

This hierarchy of land-use and land-ownership was essential to the local economy, and was in essence somewhat feudal. On the bottom rung were the landless workers, many of them migrant labourers, most living in barns, sheds, or tied accommodation on large market gardening estates or farms. They owed their livelihood, and hence their loyalty to their employer. Some stayed with one gardener for many years—family commitments were often the cause of this degree of allegiance—others moved every few months around different gardeners according to demand, still others moved over to the rich plains in Herefordshire, or to gardening in Somerset or Kent, and would return years later looking for work. For those whose family commitments kept them in the Vale there was always the temptation of better-paid work on another farm or holding. Business was volatile, changeable, and subject not just to market forces, but the weather. If there was better-paid work elsewhere, or another gardener had a better crop, and hence there was more casual work in harvesting, then they had a stiff choice: stay put on a low basic wage or leave and lose house and home; tied accommodation was endemic. Such was the lot of the landless labourer.

On the next rung were those who held charity land: most often too little to provide more than a subsistence income, or a valued second income to a job as either a land worker or employment in one of the small factories in the town. Those who grew on church land considered themselves better than those who worked charity land. But then those who worked one of these larger church holdings were considered lesser people by those who actually owned the freehold of the land they worked. In addition there was a sense of privilege and status even amongst holders: a gardener working a small half-acre plot was considered a lesser individual than someone who worked a plot of say two or three acres. However, holders had a degree of independence that was valued—however large or small the plot they grew. What they grew was their own. It belonged to them, and not to whoever was employing them. They could—and many did—use some of the land to grow their own food (many of the holders down the Charity kept a pig in a brick or concrete sty, and several chickens), and were nigh self-sufficient in a modest sort of way. Money was generated by selling a surplus. Holders had a choice: prepare and take the produce to one of the two daily fruit and vegetable markets and trust to the best bid, or sell through word of mouth to another gardener who sent his produce away.

On the next rung of the ladder stood those who actually owned some land. Many of these men and women were also merchants who earned a living buying produce from charity landholders, or from the local fruit and vegetable markets, or from the big estates. They would then send the produce by rail to the great northern cities, either to wholesale markets, or direct to shops and customers who had been established over a number of years: these activities were referred to as a gardeners' dealings. During the height of a crop's season, many lorries could be seen labouring to the railway sidings with several hundred chips of plums or beans stacked meticulously. Running a lorry or a pick-up was considered an essential part of the status and responsibility for this group of gardeners. They worked long hours, growing crops and trading as merchants, and considered themselves much more respectable, and somehow more beholden of God's grace, than charity holders. That success was sometimes short lived as it was subject to the vagaries of a market economy. The social status attributable to any freehold gardener was in direct proportion to the land owned, the size of his dealings, and the number of men employed: they were the direct descendants of the yeoman class of freemen, with their small plots of land and their independence which no man could take from them. However large and prosperous such an individual's dealings and holdings might become, such a gardener could never cross the Rubicon to the next, and final, group within the hierarchy.

Finally, there were the farm and market garden estate-owning classes, whose wealth and status was effectively inherited. These were long-established land-owning families, who sent their sons and daughters to public school, who employed estate managers for everything, and owned large businesses dealing with all aspects of farming and market gardening, from seeds, through machinery, to land management. Many owned large fruit estates—orchards—or tracts of land growing vegetables, though they never really admitted to being market gardeners: they really aspired to be gentleman farmers—wheat or livestock was somehow more respectable. Outside of the church, this group was the largest landowner in the vale, but their contribution to the local economy—their direct contribution—was arguably the smallest, though they had heritage, tradition, and social cultivation to compensate, which was an essential ingredient in the rural lifestyle.

Outside of this hierarchy were the gypsies and travelling classes who not only were apart from the social aspiration of many, but they also kept themselves very much to themselves. At the appropriate time within the growing season they would appear, as it were from nowhere, always to the day or within a few days. Many growers relied upon them; a landowner could raise five acres of runner beans, sowing in the early spring, with the crop to be harvested between late June and early August, or later. If that landowner had a long-established tradition with a group of travellers or gypsies, then he knew that they would turn up, by tradition on a particular day, or week, come what may, year in year out. It was an unwritten agreement; it was a tradition. He knew that for the established period they would come, camp with their lorries and caravans in the same place each year, usually a little-used corner of a field; they would require water, nothing else, save privacy, and no interference, and for that few weeks they were the best workforce on God's earth. With care they would pick through and harvest, taking each day what was just at the right stage of growth and ripeness, leaving others to grow on. They knew best, and any landowner who valued his crop and income, acknowledged it. They cropped what was ready from a field; they did not pick to meet orders. If the landowner had too little, then he could buy in from other growers or from the markets; likewise, if he had too much, he could sell, within the markets.

All the members of a travelling family worked, except nursing mothers. Children did their bit, except when being schooled by the elders—schooled in what was necessary for their lives and within the tradition of travelling families; state education was too much in its infancy in the early 1950s to bother travelling families about their children's conformity to national standards. They spoke little to either land workers or to bosses. They relied upon one from their midst to act as spokesman. He would talk to the gaffer, come to terms, discuss their thoughts on the crop, how they wanted to go about picking it, how much they would earn, any other work that might be around, and so on. This was usually a fair arrangement, after all, market and social forces ruled—if they stung a grower, they knew their livelihood was in jeopardy: it was a two-way relationship, reliant upon trust.

Chapter One, Creation: Fruitfulness and the Serpent

If some of the men went drinking, it was usually to just one of two pubs in the town, and they usually held their drink impeccably. Those who were likely to cause trouble stayed at the ground, or so the elders would believe when it came to reassuring local people. Trouble there was—but not always from the gypsies or travellers. It was usually from either land workers or townsfolk. Land workers were often jealous of the gypsies' mobility, their freedom to dictate terms, and their immunity from local authorities. Townsfolk were the worst. Many were jealous of the travellers' independence, but they also despised the gypsy traditions, their culture, their song and dances, and worse still, the rugged, sallow complexion, their dress, their language, even allegedly their smell: in a word, prejudice—it amounted to racial prejudice.

The gypsies' roots were Irish and East European. Many around the vale in the early 1950s were Romanian, or from the southern Russian republics; they had intermingled with those of Irish descent, and they shared a culture. They shared religion: many caravans had ornate crucifixes within, and on many an occasion the local Catholic priest was seen visiting; but they were not seen in the local Catholic church—at least, only on a couple of occasions. Although many of the young men went along to the local dance hall, to swing to the big band sound, they were equally as at home listening to, and accompanying, the elders with their fiddles, squeezeboxes, tabors, and dances. A sound blended from Moorish, oriental folk tunes, wedded with English Morris, Irish airs, and scraps of music hall and modern songs: a rich cosmopolitan, yet historic, tradition. A sound culture fed during the day by the sound of work being carried out on diesel engines, and the air waves from occasional wireless sets, with an aerial precariously placed in a tree, its wire leading into the smokey interior of a caravan.

During the summer and autumn seasons, they could be seen camped in lay-bys, on wide grass verges, in fields, on the edge of woods; a migrant workforce without which the vale's economy, based as it was on fruit and vegetables, would have ground to a halt. Hundreds of tons of plums, apples, pears, runner beans, peas, dwarf beans, onions, carrots, cabbage, and more, were carefully harvested and packed by them. No one really knew what happened to this workforce in the winter and spring. Many children of land workers grew up with the notion that they were magical, had deep ancient powers; that they slept in the hillsides in winter, or disappeared to some far-flung oriental lands. Then they would reawaken as the earth brought forth and was ready for harvest. There were stories of young woman going away with them to be gypsy queens, though these stories were becoming scarce. There were still stories of children running away with the gypsies, or worse, of babies being kidnapped and carried away, to grow up to be a proud gypsy warrior; there were still families prepared to claim that their baby had died or that the wife had miscarried due to a spell cast by the gypsies.

Many did return to Ireland. Most earned enough in the summer to keep them going through the winter and spring. If there was a bad year, or a poor harvest, many would stay on, to work root crops, or fields of frozen leeks and sprouts in winter, but that impinged on the staple work for local land workers. Then there were real arguments. Local land workers argued that they should take the rough with the smooth, they took the lion's share of work of the big summer crops, and then they should go, leave in the autumn, and see what they could find elsewhere. There was only a limited amount of winter work. These winter crops were earmarked for local labour; in addition there was a marked increase in poaching if many of them stayed on and were hard up: first the rabbit and fish population was decimated, then if the winter was tough, local poultry. But the gypsies provided a scapegoat. Sometimes vicious fights broke out. A proud people, the travelling gypsies always steered clear of contact with the authorities, and once matters had degenerated thus, it would not be long before health inspectors, school inspectors, or the police would be round, just to look and chat of course. So they left. And if there was no work, they still kept together, and struggled through. Most in the early 1950s were too independent to approach the authorities for benefit, and relied upon the extended families they were born into. Ironically many growers would have liked to keep a group of families based on their land permanently, with more than enough work to go round, but they were a fiercely independent people, and always moved on when they felt they were putting down roots. They'd be back, at Whitsun, or the last Monday in June, or whatever the tradition was.

When it was time to leave, move on, they cleared away the ground they camped on, tidied up, and then early in the morning, while it was still dark, the first lorry would leave, pulling a large caravan. Within the train were still some old wooden caravans, but very few still used horses; they kept the horses, for local journeys, but when the caravan train was on the move, they carried the horses in their wagons—they were part of the family. Some small groups of gypsies could still be seen travelling by horse-drawn van, but for long journeys, most large troops used lorries, many dating from the early 1930s, and everyone in impeccable order mechanically, with gleaming polished panels. Once they had left, there was a scorched grey charred patch about six feet wide on the ground where the campfire had been, there was flattened grass where the vans had been parked, but nothing else, save an eerie silence, and an emptiness, where colour, vibrancy, and excitement had flown.

It was easy to see how the folklore of their magic still lived on in the imaginations of the children of land workers in this period: before television, and when radios were for grown-ups, and cars were still not that common-place.

Chapter One, Creation: Fruitfulness and the Serpent

There was very little mechanization, the soil was worked with hand tools, small implements, or sometimes, if the land really needed breaking up, a small Fordson tractor was brought in. Many growers still used horses, they bought them in from farriers to plough small patches, or strips. The whole agriculture of the Charity and of market gardening on this scale was almost a reverting to medieval strip farming; the hills, the vale, the glorious fecundity of God's creation was clothed in a pre-chemicalization, small-scale, almost Biblical, agrarian economy (the mass use of expensive pesticides and fertilizers was a generation away). The world revolved around sun and water, soil and fields, strips of crops, greens and browns of every hue and texture, rain, and the sky: the never-ending sky in all its moods, and seasons, and changes. A child could lie on his or her back on the low grass and wild-flower-clothed embankments that separated holdings, gazing into the sky, listening to the wind, eavesdropping on the birds, and watch the changes in clouds, the colours of the sky, or the larks as they rose and danced on the air, singing incessantly. Lying on these grassy banks, with the minutest of life teeming within it, gazing to the sky, it would seem to many a small child that heaven could not be more perfect.

Four

Jim drew on the Woodbine stump in the corner of his lips, the hot smoke from the remains of the cigarette caused him to catch his breath; with the fit of coughing, he sharply flicked the stump into the pool, caught his breath, and stood up.

"Aye, well, suppose we is best on our way," came out between coughs.

Doris gathered together the few remains from their tea—eaten within minutes of their arrival that afternoon. Jim had been at work since 6.00am, home mid-afternoon, whereupon they both walked from the small Victorian terraced house they lived in, between Merstow Green and the Bewdley, walked the three and a half miles to their charity plot, had a light meal of cheese, cold potatoes, ham, and bread, with tea from a rather battered thermos, then set-to tying the onions that had been pulled the previous evening, and had been stored in the barn. It was now 7.30 in the evening and the two trudged wearily along the lane from the barn heading West to the Cheltenham Road, the yellow-beige of the lane's limestone chippings levelled out as they approached Gypsies' Corner. Here they met the main road running south to Gloucestershire.

Jim and Doris walked along the grass verge, north along the Cheltenham Road, towards the town of Evesham. They stopped after a couple of hundred yards to buy some fresh eggs from a roadside stall, before walking on, past an assortment of houses on the edge of the town. Some of the houses were new, built in the late 1940s for those working in offices, or commuting to Worcester or Gloucester. Other houses were much older, a row of eight narrow Victorian cottages or a pair of Edwardian semi-detached houses from the early years of the century, but everywhere the houses were broken by narrow lanes or a dirt track, linking the road to smallholdings, orchards, or the Charity. Some of the houses, on both sides of the road, were set well back from the line of building, indeed set back within a smallholding. None of the Charity land actually met the road. Those holdings next to the road, particularly those with a house were freehold. The land, the house, the living, were owned lock-stock-and-barrel by those who worked the land.

Jim and Doris stopped by one such holding. Behind the tall hawthorn hedge, set back about sixty yards from the road was an unpretentious post-war detached house, plain brick, with even plainer metal window frames, all within a pitched tiled roof. A lane ran down the side, which served the holding within which the house stood. At the bottom of the lane stood a tall shed made of a timber structure covered with corrugated sheets of metal. Half way down the lane stood a lilac bush, next to the lilac bush stood a young woman in her late twenties holding a young child in her arms. The woman was also pregnant. She held her back with the remaining free arm, shuffled around, wondering where to go, or what to do. She seemed conscious of the possibility of other people around. She noticed Jim and Doris at the top of the drive, turned and went back behind the house.

"Shouldn't we do som'it?"

"No" answered Doris, shaking her head, "there's nowt any un can do wiv'em, you know, young Harry Broadley un'es missus. You saw, you saw...."

"Aye, aye, she was crying, fretting, and she was bleeding—from her head," interrupted Jim.

"Yes but you know that family, the Broadleys; they's trouble, trouble back from when they come here. They're trouble, trouble. No one can help."

"But..." persisted Jim, "but with the little one, and another on the way, and she should git that head seen to..."

"I know, I know, but you try—don't forget his father lives just over there, you know, old Jack Broadley. And if you want to take on Jack Broadley, you got another think coming, you have Jim Beason, that you have, you mark my words, you don't tackle old Jack Broadley!"

With that, they moved on, continued on their way home; shortly after the road dropped sharply down an incline, turning a sharp bend, descending about one hundred feet, with old Victorian houses on one side, and a tall yew hedge on the other, down to the river Avon. Jim and Doris turned right at the foot of the hill

Chapter One, Creation: Fruitfulness and the Serpent

and walked northeast, with the riverbank on their left, and the old Oxford Road on their right. Within half a mile, they came to the Workman Bridge, which they crossed, they then walked up Bridge Street, rising steeply again, but less overall height than they had descended. They walked along the old Bridge Street, past half-timbered Tudor buildings, across to Bewdley Street, finally walking down through the Bewdley. They stopped shortly for Jim to buy some more cigarettes from the shop on the corner of Littleworth Street. Then they continued on down, turning left after the Bewdley Mission, and along a pathway to the terrace that was home.

Five

The young woman, Margaret Broadley, still not knowing what to do with herself, sat outside the back of the house. Harry Broadley, her husband, had left—she could tell from the slamming of the back door. It was now safe to go back in. He had gone across the road to his father's—he would be there till late, till she had gone to bed, and the baby was asleep. Margaret, or Meg as she had been known for years, quietly got up, went in through the back door, placed the young girl carefully on a chair, and then set-to to bathe the cut on her forehead, the blood still flowing. The child started to cry. The baby was encased from the waist down in plaster—a congenital hip disorder, now set in place with plaster with the legs set wide apart by a rod. Normal bodily functions were restricted to small openings in the plaster, the child, about eighteen months old, only ceased crying when she had been cleaned and attended to. She was then placed on a large settee in the rear living room. Meg returned to bathing her head, then holding her back as she stretched, holding the womb that held the developing child. Slowly she moved across the kitchen, and sat down on a chair—only then did she place her head in her hands, and weep. Weep, with convulsions, but in silence. She wept.

Harry, having slept over the road at his parents, had risen at five to take the men and women to fields south of Dumbleton, and to Badsey and Bretforton to harvest spring onions. Harry walked in to the kitchen just after nine to sit down to breakfast with Meg. Having eaten he slammed down a paper bag on the table—

"Take that. Now. Go on."

Meg took the bag, opened it, and took out a small round card tub—a medicine box, no bigger than a half-crown coin. She removed the lid. Inside were two tablets.

"They cost me good money, damn good money."

Meg said nothing. Closed the box and looked at Harry.

"We can't afford another babby. Take 'um."

Harry always slipped into an Evesham accent when he got annoyed at situations he could not control.

"I got 'um from him in town—you know, the chemist."

"And you want me to take them."

"Yes—it'll get rid of it. Damn thing. We can't afford it."

Meg threw the box into the sink and walked out. Harry went after her—

"You agreed. You did. Damn it, take 'um."

Still smarting from the row and being struck the evening before, Meg relented and took the two tablets, swallowing them with a cup of cold tea.

A few weeks later when nothing had happened and Meg was clearly still pregnant Harry visited the pharmacist again, and arranged to buy more "under-the-counter" drugs to abort. He went round to the pharmacist's house to collect them, paying an exorbitant amount of money for now three little tablets. Again Meg, after complaining for a time, took the tablets. This time she woke in the night with appalling abdominal pains, cramps, and found she was passing a small amount of placental blood. The cramps lasted for just under three days, and Meg continued to pass blood irregularly. Then the cramps abated. She was still with child: a human being that had been assaulted, attacked by the chemical weapons that were the tablets, weapons aimed at Paul that had almost killed him. But he had survived, just. Despite her intentions, and those of Harry, Meg's body had defended Paul, fought-off the attack, although Paul had not survived unscathed. Harry was more concerned at the money wasted on the tablets—a point he would taunt the boy with as he grew up.

Chapter Two
Town: People and Family

～ *"Behold, I was brought forth in iniquity,
and in sin my mother did conceive me."*
PSALM 51:5

One

Jim and Doris settled into their home. Doris busied herself getting the supper things out from the scullery. Jim sat down; thinking on things. Doris noticed from the kitchen as his head fell to one side; she left him sleeping in his chair, in front of the cold, ash-grey grate. Jim and Doris could have walked a shorter route: instead of turning right when they met the river, and walking along to the Workman Bridge, they could have crossed immediately along the New Bridge and the viaduct across the Crown meadows, the flood meadow of the River Avon, then across Merstow Green and down the side of the Trumpet Inn, along the pathway to the terrace of five narrow houses, placed as it was between two roads, only accessible by foot. But they did not. Jim and Doris had walked their way for years, long before the New Bridge had been built between the wars. They walked their way. They were fiercely independent: if they had bad times, and sure enough there were bad times, if work was scarce, if crops were middling, they suffered through. They were Vale folk, Evesham folk: no one would be left wanting, but each to his own, each to look after their own needs—charity was for poor folk, not them. The trouble was that however poor they got, they were never *that* poor. This philosophy was rooted in that of the English working class: indeed many market gardening families had migrated, come from Lancashire in the early to mid-nineteenth century, leaving the industrial towns to try their own at this new agriculture of market gardening, servicing the very cities they left. The commitment to going it alone was ruthless. You didn't cross any one; you did not take or upset their living. The morality was rooted in a Protestant work ethic and in respect for another's bit. But no one owed you a living; if you were doing badly, you had no one to blame but yourself.

By comparison with other towns, Evesham was really quite small. Even in the 1950s it had escaped almost intact the ravages of industrialization, development, and modernization. There was a hub to the town, raised on the shallow hill in the centre of a loop of the River Avon, with Bengeworth, Hampton, and Greenhill almost as satellite villages. The population was still under ten thousand when men were returning from the beaches of Dunkirk. The town was central in the vale, bordered by hills. The hills were open, stark, surrounded by dry, sparse, arid fields and slopes; by comparison the valley was rich and green, small and intimate. Market gardening was the sole economic life of this town, save for one or two small examples of light industry—and of course the railway, which served to ferry the fruit and vegetables away to towns and cities. Evesham was an agrarian community; close knit and friendly, yet as unfriendly as poor folk living on top of one another can be. The town consisted of nineteenth-century redbrick terraced houses and shops, punctuated by older Georgian buildings around the High Street, Bridge Street, and Vine Street. Interspersed amongst this were remains of the medieval town: the Bell Tower, Abbey Gardens, Abbey Gateway, the Round House, and an assortment of medieval buildings around the north side of Merstow Green.

Parts of buildings, constructed after the Reformation (which saw the destruction of Evesham Abbey), had bits of the old medieval town wall within their structure. One could find masonry and tiles from the Abbey intertwined with Georgian brick and window. Sprout fields coexisted side by side in the town with the Police Station, the remains of the Abbey, the Almonry Museum, and the Crown Meadows: brown earth and red brick, grey yellow crumbling limestone, tiny shops and alleyways, fruit and vegetable markets, a stone and timbered Norman gateway, the local council infants and junior school, the railway yard, gypsy caravans, spring onions and apple blossom, plums in summer, and above all rose the Bell Tower—all that remained of the once glorious Evesham Abbey. The town had changed little in character since the dissolution of the monasteries—simply grown a little bit, within limits. Those limits were defined by the River Avon. The neck of the loop being less than a mile, and bearing an obelisk to Simon de Montfort, killed in the Battle of Evesham, 1265.

Chapter Two, Town: People and Family

Two

Harry Broadley had been born at the end of the First World War. He was an only child, his parents in their early twenties: Jack Broadley and May Willows having married a few years earlier. Jack Broadley's father, Henry John Broadley, had come from Manchester—arriving in the early 1880s. He met Alice, loved her, married her. Alice came from a family going back a long way in the Vale. Jack was born, in 1893, to be followed by Rose, Norma, Fred, Bert, and Beryl—six children before Henry John died of rheumatic fever. Alice bore his last child, Beryl, a matter of months after his death. Alice married again bearing two more children (Ralph and Alice). Jack Broadley, the oldest of this mixed tribe of children, was named John Henry, just as his father had been Henry John, as his father (back in Manchester) had been John Henry, as tradition was wont. Alice's roots were in the town, the vale, and in market gardening. She would often walk amongst the orchards of neat plum trees, covered as they were with pink blossom in the spring, stepping carefully between the two neat rows of spring onions, each flanked by a row of parsley, growing down the centre between the trees. All was neat, ordered, exhibiting the fullest use of the land.

Jack set himself up in market gardening, buying and trading in produce and renting land from Christchurch Charity. He rented land when prices were high, buying land when it was cheap, slowly built up links with customers away in northern cities and so developed a business. His younger brothers, Fred and Bert, set up in Harvington and Badsey respectively, creating new clans of Broadley's; while the sisters and step sisters (from Alice's second marriage) married into the tribal make-up of Evesham folk. Jack Broadley planted and grew, built and bought, sold and traded, establishing a solid and respectable, if small, fruit and vegetable business. While invalided out of the First World War he married young May Willows. May came from Aston Magna, a small hamlet in the North Cotswolds between Chipping Camden and Morton-in-Marsh. The Willows, a farm-labouring family, had been in Aston Magna for generation upon generation, living, loving, laughing, dying, cut off from the world in the security and seclusion of a Cotswold hamlet. They courted and married; Henry John—or Harry—being born in April 1918. They lived in a small redbrick Victorian house in Boat Lane. Their happiness did not last. Appendicitis, leading to severe peritonitis, nearly killed her, rendering her unstable. She would often be found wandering by the river, muttering, lost. Often Harry would arrive home from school to find her gone back to her family in Aston Magna, only to return, weeks later as if nothing had happened. As time went on she became more and more withdrawn. Harry joined his father in the business.

The family moved out of the small redbrick Victorian house in Boat Lane, buying a detached Edwardian house on the Cheltenham Road, opposite some of the ground they rented, and near the orchard Jack had bought just after the First World War in Corn Mill Lane. Harry enlisted in the army when war broke out in 1939, but whilst training on Salisbury Plain, his father brought him back home, arguing with the Ministry that it was a protected occupation. He was needed on the land to feed the war effort. Harry was considered something of a ladies' man. After the war he began going steady with Meg Riley. However, this was not a romance. They liked each other's company, but there was not much love. Within a few years they got engaged, delaying marrying again for a few years.

Meg Riley, by contrast, was not local. She was born in South London—Anerley—in the early 1920s. Meg's father, William, was from the East End: he had been born in the 1880s to an Irish dockworker and an English mother. The family lived in a back-to-back in Shadwell. William was born in 1887—the youngest of thirteen children, and the only boy. His mother, a large strong woman, brought the family up in the God-fearing tradition of the Victorian working class, framed by her husband's Catholicism. She could just manage, especially with the eldest daughters out at work. In an East End terrace, with poverty round every corner, this was not easy. As a young man William worked in a variety of administrative and secretarial duties (going to night school in the evenings). By his mid-twenties he was working with Lord Beaverbrook on the Investiture of the Prince of Wales; then during the First World War working for the Bank of England in West Africa. After many years he returned due to failing health in the tropics. While holidaying in Bournemouth, he met Renée (christened Irene) Prior, a milliner by trade and the daughter of a teacher, from Bristol. They married, and settled in Anerley, South London. Their first child, Anthony, died shortly after birth; their second child Margaret Irene was born in 1923. Meg's earliest memories were of the neat streets of Crystal Palace and Anerley and of firework displays at the top of the park by the famous palace.

Then the depression came. William got work as Company Secretary for Stokes Bomford in Evesham—a firm of high reputation in agricultural implements, land management, estates, market gardening, and farming that was spread across the Vale of Evesham, through Worcestershire, into Herefordshire. The family moved to Hampton, a small village to the southwest of Evesham, just a short ferry ride across the river. William cycled each morning to Stokes Bomford's office, while Meg attended Miss Alice Otley's Preparatory School for Young Ladies, housed in rooms above a shop in Bridge Street. Meg was something of a tomboy, or so some of her teachers said, often preferring to go exploring down Pewitt Lane with other children in the village, rather than indulge some of the pastimes other

Chapter Two, Town: People and Family

girls at Miss Otley's Preparatory School were encouraged to partake in. William and Renée had intended to return to London once things got better, but the depression continued in the 1930s, Meg was settled and growing up in Hampton, and, most important, William had a good secure job. Then, of course, the war came. That changed everything. Meg wanted to join the Women's Royal Air Force, with her friend Susan, but she was too young: she was only just sixteen when the war broke out. They worked together on blackout duty on top of a department store in nearby Worcester; then Susan joined the WRAF. Meg thought she would do her bit by joining the Land Army for a couple of years, and then she could go on and join the WRAF when she was old enough. But she never did. She became settled into a routine.

Meg worked on Mount Pleasant Farm near Childswickham (about two miles south of The Charities). It was not what her parents had expected of her—but it was war service. Months passed, seasons passed: harvest, ploughing, Christmas, sowing, harvesting. One day Tony arrived; he was being held with several other prisoners of war—Italians—who were to help on the farm. They were billeted at Childswickham. Tony would proudly show Meg a photograph of his wife and child. Meg and Tony talked often. Weeks turned into months, months into seasons; in the summer they spent long evenings, by oil lamp, mowing and harvesting. Michael—a much older Italian, short, stocky, well liked—often used to arrange matters so that Meg and Tony could talk, share, work together. Meg was troubled. She felt a warmth, a wholeness she had not known. Tony looked at her; he knew how she was feeling, but was a gentleman. She sensed in him a same troubled spirit. She wrestled in her mind—he was a prisoner of war, her parents would never approve. Her father was now a leading professional in the town, also on the church council in Hampton, and all importantly, a high-ranking stalwart of the lodge—he would not disapprove, she knew that, but he would look hurt, sad. She could not put him through the pain and taunts from the locals, not in his position now that he was Manager of Stokes Bomford in Evesham.

Time passed, Michael saw to it that they passed a little time in idle chat, but they were all too busy: Mrs. Braband ran the farm with a cool efficiency which would have put the army to shame. She never trusted the Italians, insisting they suffer the degradation of body searches each evening before returning to Childswickam, fearing they might take a handful of corn. Mrs. Braband had noticed things developing between Tony and Meg. She spoke to Michael. She did not believe him, would not believe him, that they had not even kissed, that it was really no more than a lovely warm friendship. Tony disappeared. Meg often thought of Tony. No other man would ever make her feel the way she had felt in his company.

27

Three

After the war Meg worked in Boots, working in the library upstairs from the chemist. She had friends to chat with, and went to church regularly with her parents. William and Renée were planning for their retirement. Meg had known Harry Broadley in passing. They walked together, talked together, went out together. Harry was, after all, tall; he cut a dashing figure, certainly when on the dance floor, or in the bar of the rowing club. A relationship was growing. The sort of relationship that is not characterized by passion, by overwhelming love; it was the kind of relationship where two people just get used to spending time together. Many of their friends, their peers, had been killed in the war, or had moved away. Ten years earlier they would not have considered going out together—both being from different social spheres, but now, after the war had brought irrecoverable changes, times were different. Meg wanted something for her life. The years passed and their relationship grew. Sexual attraction grew—but love? They got engaged. They planned to get married in a couple of years, or three: Jack Broadley insisted that the land opposite his house would be purchased, and a reasonable house built. The land backed onto Hampton Charity, and was prime agricultural land; with the addition of a house and some sheds it would make a neat smallholding. A mortgage was raised from the Town Council, on a very low rate of interest (as it was, after all, to be a "farmhouse," a working residence).

Slowly the years passed as the couple remained engaged. Was it one night of passion that made Meg feel she must go ahead with the marriage, despite her growing reservations? Or was she determined not to take any notice of her parents' comments? Her mother's comments rang in her ears: if it had not been for the war, she would not have fallen in with a family like the Broadleys. She wondered to herself, was she going ahead out of sympathy for Harry?—his father soaking up the whisky, and his mother a recluse. She could give Harry a home life, a secure base. They married on a cold damp February morning; the house and smallholding being ready.

The couple boarded the express to London that afternoon, later to book into the Strand Palace Hotel—Jack Broadley was not going to see things done on the cheap. Harry grumbled and rowed that evening about the cost and how much money was being spent. Meg spent the evening and early night walking the streets around the Strand trying to convince herself she had not made a mistake, a dreadful mistake. The couple saw out their honeymoon, returned home to Evesham, to the pink brick, metal windows of post-war frugality: Meg making a home, Harry working the land. By June they had separated. Meg had returned to her parents in Hampton village, Harry was to be found with his, or in the new

Chapter Two, Town: People and Family

house. Jack Broadley had decided he was the one to sort this out! He called on William Riley, wanting to know what was happening. He walked stiffly up the garden path with his stick supporting his bulk. He knocked firmly on the door. He pushed Renée aside as she opened the door, only to stop and stare. He found only an empty hall.

"Come on then," he demanded in a loud drawl, "what's been going on here? I've got a reputation in this town; we've all got reputations to think of. What's been going on between these two?"

Jack was doing his best to disguise his Evesham dialect—but still bawled and spat the words out. Renée just stood placidly, while Jack turned,

"Err, yes, sorry, er yes, well. Where is Mr. Riley? I've come to see Mr. Riley," he said, drawing out the vowels.

A quiet but firm voice came from the staircase, words spoken impeccably,

"Good afternoon Mr. Broadley, and what can I do for you?"

The voice was William Riley's. He was standing near the top of the staircase. Indeed he had been all the time, having moved to the stairs when he heard the knock at the door.

"Oh, Oh, yes, well . . ."

Jack had been caught unawares. He turned towards the voice, losing his balance as he pivoted around on his war-wounded bad leg, but in an instant as he regained his balance he noticed William's right arm bent so that he made a secret society sign against the centre of his chest that they both understood . . .

"Well, er, well, . . . if you're going to be like that, well, well. There bist nowt more to say. Bist there?"

Falling back into his Evesham accent he turned, stumbled towards the door, paused briefly to touch the brim of his hat to Renée, then disappeared down the path. Meg's tears could be heard from an upstairs room as the front door closed.

Meg walked round Hampton churchyard, amongst the trees at the foot of the bank behind the vicarage, where the River Avon lapped the roots. She walked along the bank, northwards towards Hampton ferry, thinking. Thinking on the separation, thinking of what was to happen, thinking of her parents. They were planning to move next spring to Weston-super-Mare. All they wanted was her happiness. They were doing their best to stay out of her marital problems. They were right. But what should she do? Harry had times when he was charming, pleasant, but he had such a foul temper. She had seen hints of it in their years of courting. But she had convinced herself that he would change, all he needed was a home, a marriage; that it was simply the domination of his father that caused the temper—it was frustration. To a degree she was right: Harry had always been dominated by his father—he had allowed him to get him out of the army

29

during the war, back on the land, working, driving, running things, while he, Jack Broadley, spent his days in the ex-servicemen's club, drinking. May was at home, cooked for Jack and Harry, but hid in her room day and night. If only Harry would not spend so much time over the road at his father's. How could a marriage work if he was still tied to his father's apron strings? Surely he should be with her!

Meg crossed the footbridge to Glover's Island. She listened to the water lapping around the island; she watched the swans moving silently, gracefully, and thought on her childhood. She had been happy, the village of Hampton was small, but she felt secure, happy at home, taking the two West Highland dogs out, going to church, exploring with her friends. She thought on those days, thought on the field by the bridge over the River Isbourne, covered as it was with cowslips in springtime. Thoughts drifted to her childhood friends, how they explored round Hampton Mill, down by the old tithe barn near the railway bridge. Yes, the railway, they used to climb through the fence and down to the track. She thought of her time at school—she was always scared of the Headmaster at Prince Henry's Grammar School. She was always being told off for sitting on the stone steps—those girls gave a bad image to the school. She thought of her father, how she felt she had failed him by not being bright at school. He did not mind, said he didn't. She knew that was true. But she still felt she had failed him. He was kind, considerate, but always firm and reserved. She was lively, giggly, and although she knew she was loved by him, at the same time she knew he often thought on and missed the son, Anthony, who died at birth. He only wanted her happiness. His health was not good—it had suffered from the years spent in the tropics. He now had glaucoma and severe stomach ulcers. William Riley had retired two years earlier and Meg knew that all they wanted to do now was move down to Weston-super-Mare, and live out the remainder of their lives in peace. As darkness fell, she walked slowly back, off the island, along the bank at the foot of Clark's Hill, treading softly tracks, pathways, fields she had known so well as a child, back to her parents. They were waiting patiently for her, hugging and receiving her as she returned.

Meg became determined to leave him, especially because of the way he had begun to hit her, knock her about. She had obtained a court order that he should be at the house at a specified time so she could get in to take away her clothes. But he failed to be there. Meg knew it was the influence of his father—old Jack did not want to see the marriage break up, partly because of his own standing in the local community, partly because Harry would need a woman in to cook and clean if he was going to get on with his work. Richards, the solicitors acting for Meg, wanted to pursue further, but Meg could see the effect all this was having on her parents.

Chapter Two, Town: People and Family

However, William and Renée were both of one mind: if it was right for her to leave him, then she must pursue the matter, but above all, it was for her to decide.

But how did Harry feel about all of this? Harry's view of life, marriage, and women had been coloured by the experience of his mother whilst a child. Jack had been, always was, a domineering sort of man. It was this in Harry's father that had enabled him to build up a business when most others had failed, and were failing around them. Harry had plenty of time to think over his situation alone, as he was, in the new house: his father was over the road, sleeping off the whisky in his chair. He stormed about, muttering and cursing, sorting out, or trying to sort out, meals for himself. It reminded him of the times when as a child he returned home from school to find his mother missing. When he and his father would muck in and sort out some supper. They knew she had gone by the fact that some of her clothes and a suitcase were missing. If these items were not there, then Harry knew he would have to search around the town to try to find her. Often May was to be found wandering around the crown meadows wailing and moaning. Young Harry found her; he coaxed her home, but he would face the embarrassment of other schoolboys seeing him. She would often be taken off to Powick Sanatorium—the Worcester County Pauper and Lunatic Asylum—only to return as if nothing had happened. It was assumed that her brain had been damaged by the peritonitis, which had flooded her body with poison. Harry and Jack became self-sufficient.

Harry thought on the bachelor days when they would take the train down to London. They would see a show, stop in a hotel for the night, and then return in the morning. Market Gardeners did not take holidays—these two or three trips in the year sufficed. Could Meg offer him the security and stability that he wanted? But even courting was a tumultuous affair. Meg was often dissatisfied with his dress or manners, or the state of the car, and at times she would storm off out of the car, raging and shouting, and complaining. Harry, despite advice from men friends that he should just drive off and leave her, stayed. He was beginning to fall in love with her. By the time they married, after courting for nearly five years, he was prepared and committed to the undertaking. Harry was genuinely in love with her. But was this love reciprocated? There was always a nagging doubt at the back of his mind as to whether she really loved him. And was there any truth in the rumour that she was only marrying him because there was no one else around and she wanted a home to look after? And what of those darker rumours about her and Susan? Meg leaving like this, after only a few months, seemed like a cruel re-run of the difficulties of his parents' marriage. His mother had left his father to return to her parents, now Meg had done the same.

Three days passed. On the morning of the third day a car—a taxi—drew up outside of the Riley's house. Meg in her summer dress walked down the path towards the car. Renée was with her. Meg handed the suitcase to the driver, who placed it in the boot. She said her farewells to her mother, then quietly got into the back seat. The car drove off. Meg returned to the marriage house, the Broadley small holding. Harry's love for her would never be the same; he could forgive her, but never trust her again.

For a short while Meg and Harry were happy and peaceful together. It was something of a second honeymoon—or the first real honeymoon. But as the summer drew on the rows started. He would come over from his father's, storming in, grumbling at what she did not do—that was, what she did not do on the land. Other wives of market gardeners would help with hoeing, tying onions, help out generally; all she could do was keep house. Admittedly, she kept a very good house, but it was the tradition of gardening families in the vale that the wife mucked in on the land.

Meg would simply walk out—go for a walk around the crown meadows, by the river, on the inside of the loop of the Avon; Hampton held too many memories, good memories, happy memories. Should she leave him again—really leave him for good this time? He said how sick of her he was. But then he could be so nice. Maybe they were just not suited—a mismatched couple. As the days passed and she contemplated seriously the thought of leaving him for good, a new thought crossed her mind. She was not sure. She checked the calendar, checked with her mother, visited the doctor. She was with child. That changed everything. As the weeks and months passed, she thought on the possibility that a child would bring them together. But the relationship was stormy—he spending his time with his father; she having to defend herself from his verbal and physical onslaught, though Meg was becoming a master of the verbal onslaught herself: the side swipe, the cutting, denigrating remark, the belittling body blow of a twisted half-truth. So she began to give as good as she was given. Soon, in exasperation, he would hit her. As the winter drew to spring, William and Renée moved to Weston. Later that spring in early May, Meg was delivered of a daughter, to be baptized Christine.

Four

With the arrival of a child matters seemed stable in the Broadley household: a calm settled in this their second summer. Christine grew steadily; Meg cared for her, cooked, washed and scrubbed the house, shopped, and chatted with friends, while Harry worked the land, drove to market, and took goods to the

Chapter Two, Town: People and Family

railway yard on the Old Worcester Road. Meg's parents now settled in Weston-super-Mare wrote often to her. Harry, however, was still tied to his father's apron strings—so Meg argued. Although he did the lion's share of the work, he was kept, effectively, on an apprentice's wages when he was a man of thirty-four with a wife and family to keep. Harry and Meg were not so much getting on better with each other; it was more that a troubled peace, an amnesty between the couple, unwritten, was in place. Harry was, as ever, worried about money, and would often rise at five o'clock in the morning to rattle the fire with a poker, mutter, mumble—and curse his luck. This would wake the baby, bring down Meg, and a row would ensue, usually cut short by Harry donning his cap, pulled, as ever, tightly down on his head, back first, then the peak pulled down firmly so as to distort the shape once the cap was no more than a few weeks old. Out he would storm with shirtsleeves rolled up, across the road to his father's, to sort out the work for the day. It was on one such day, a still July morning, when the heat was already building up, that Meg settled Christine in the garden in her cot, shaded with a parasol her mother had given her. She heard a click, turned to the garden gate, which led from the rutted and pitted drive that served the smallholding, and stood, frozen and transfixed.

"Hello Meg, hello. My, it is good to see you."

Meg did not move, did not speak.

"I, I just had to call to say hello" Tony continued, "I called at Mount Pleasant, greeted Mrs. Braband, but she seemed to know nothing of you. She seemed not to know you were still here in Evesham."

He gestured across the Charity towards Childswickham.

"Well, you see, it's the same old me," he gesticulated with his arms now touching his shoulders. "I have not changed much: a little older, a little greyer. But of you, how are you? I called at your parent's house in Hampton, but the new people told me they had moved, retired—of course, how foolish; your father now, must be, as you say, in his sixties."

Meg did not move, she looked, just looked, and felt as she had done in those days, harvesting in the war, she looked at Tony.

"You have not changed, no, it seems yes, er," regaining her composure, "how did you find me? How did you come here?"

"I'm here visiting on business, I thought I would call and see if anyone was still around, you know for, as you say, old time's sake."

"Your wife, your children . . . they were killed weren't they . . ."

"Yes. Yes," replied Tony, "I returned, as you most probably know, in 1946, I returned to Italy half hoping if my family were still alive, you know, . . . but I found they were not. The Germans had bombed them, bombed the whole village,

33

shelled it. Once our army had surrendered, the Germans destroyed . . . they did not want your allies to have it. But ah! Enough."

He moved forward to Meg; she stepped back,

"No, I . . ."

"Ahh, the baby, your little bambino! Ah, a boy?"

"No, a girl, Christine, Christine Margaret."

Tony crouched close to the cot.

"She is very beautiful, very beautiful, but then," he looked up to Meg.

Meg turned her head,

"You must go, you really must go, calling like this, my husband could have been here."

"Ah, yes, you are right. But it is only a courtesy call, looking up old friends, old times."

"Yes, it . . . , it's good to see you, but I think it's time you went, please."

"I go, yes, I'll say farewell. I'm glad I have seen you; I am glad you are well, you are happy, you have a good husband. I am doing well; my brother and I, we have a business, we now grow olives on our family land. We are the only two left—no one else, our family, gone! All gone. I, well, I have our business to keep me busy. Still, I am happy for you. I will leave you now, bye. Bye."

With that he turned and retraced his steps through the gate and along the drive. Meg heard the sound of a car door, the engine starting, and the muffled noise as the car drove away. She busied herself with the baby, with the kitchen, with some washing, preparing the dinner, trying not to think on things, pretending the day had been uneventful, nothing had happened, nothing could happen now, not now! Why did he come? Why did he come now? Now, of all times. That night she lay awake, fighting off the tears, as Harry lay snoring, trying not to think on how things could have been. She thought on her mother's words: the war, the war had changed all things, everything. Life would have been so different but for the war.

Matters did not improve between Meg and Harry. His father taunted him as to why she was not helping out on the land, pea picking. After all, they had taken on twelve woman from round the Fairfield to do the job; if Meg did her share they would have only needed eleven—or ten. With the plums coming in season, Harry was working fifteen, sixteen, eighteen hours a day: there was a bumper crop of Purple and Victoria plums in the Broadley orchard down Corn Mill Road. With the pressure of work, the cool amnesty between Meg and Harry was breaking down. They rowed longer in the morning, exchanged more venomous remarks, the heat of their relationship only cooling with the heat of the summer fading into autumn. One fine September morning Meg was bathing Christine. She carefully turned her over, to dry her back, when her knees caught her eye.

Chapter Two, Town: People and Family

Or at least the crease at the back of the knee caught her eye. She picked her up, carried her through to the hall, and carefully placed the baby down on the carpet, placing her as flat and level as she could—on her stomach. She looked carefully. The creases on her legs, behind the knees, were not in line; at least that's how it seemed. Still it must be nothing she thought. But then she placed one hand on the soles of her feet. Yes, indeed, one leg seemed as if it was shorter than the other. But it couldn't be, no, it couldn't! Please God, no, it couldn't be. There must not be something wrong! A visit to the doctor, several visits to the local hospital, and little Christine, just four months old, was referred to the Birmingham Children's Hospital. She had been born with a congenital hip disorder. The hip joint had not been formed properly in the womb, rendering her with a dislocated hip at birth—at least a hip that regularly slipped in and out of joint. By four months old the left leg was pronounceably shorter, by about a quarter of an inch, due to the malformed socket in the child's pelvis. On a rain-sodden October day the couple drove back from the Birmingham Children's Hospital, with Christine encased in plaster from the waist down, her legs splayed apart as far as they would go. With more weight in plaster, than in flesh and bone, the little fair-haired child would have to remain so for many months.

Christine needed constant care for the fifteen months she was in plaster. Bathing was difficult, likewise keeping the poor child occupied, not to mention catering for her toilet needs! But far from drawing Harry and Meg together, if anything, they grew further apart. To keep the peace he would keep out of Meg's way as much as possible. Indeed, he wished she would let him get up in the morning, sort out the fire, and then leave for work. But no. If he was having one of his usual moans to himself in the kitchen, she would come down to complain. As the winter drew on Meg got more and more used to the routine. Both greeted their second anniversary with muted respect, but not celebration. He spent most evenings over the road at his parents. This was for two reasons. He felt it was better to keep out of the way, it was clear they were not to get on, she did not want him around, so he would keep from under her feet; in addition, both his parents needed looking after—his father with his war injured leg and heart condition, and his mother who now could not look after herself let alone Jack. So, he would spend most of the evenings "over the road," but would return to lie in her bed. They both submitted to sex readily enough.

By the time the May blossom was beginning to fade, Meg was checking the calendar, seeing the doctor. Yes, she was pregnant again—it had to be his fault! He should have taken more care. But she had been willing. Harry was convinced they could not afford a second child. The markets were stagnant, the weather bad, they had enough of a struggle to keep the roof over their head and the business

35

together. The child growing in Meg's womb was not regarded as human—merely something happening to them that must be avoided at all costs. Harry spoke in hushed tones to the local chemist, after work. Money was surreptitiously exchanged, a brown paper bag secretly pushed into a pocket. The medicine would kill the child, force a miscarriage. Problem solved. A few weeks later Harry met the chemist again; it had not worked. He tried to pick a row with him, but simply bought some more of the medicine—it was stronger. This time Meg bled and Harry was convinced it had worked, but as the weeks passed it was clear the child had not been killed but was still growing and thereby creating an economic threat to their well-being. Was this bleeding a twin? Was it part of the placenta? Did the child growing suffer damage, or escape wholly unscathed?

The child survived this onslaught to be reminded by his parents on several occasions through his childhood that they had attempted to destroy him; further, that good money had been wasted on the medicines! Though this embryo of a few weeks gestation may seem insignificant, it held the complete life and loves, strengths and weaknesses, of the child, and the adult it was to become—in potential. The question "Should I have never been?" would haunt him through his childhood. Meg complained of these poisons, bought for her to take to terminate the pregnancy; but she readily took them.

Five

By late October the onion crop was finished and Jim and Doris saw the winter of 1953 slowly turn into one of the hardest for many years. Jim worked sprouts—about half an acre he had planted in the spring. After Christmas there was not much moving in the Vale; Jim was laid off for the first three weeks in January, so relied on the small plot of sprouts and a half acre of leeks which were nearly ready for pulling. He tended his leeks with the loving care a city dweller lavished on a car. Jim's care was not wasted, for the leeks fetched him a good price in the top—Smithfield—market. Towards the end of January, when the weather turned milder, Jim started pulling the leeks. He had just finished tying the leeks down in the ten boats he had pulled, when the lorry from Smithfield Market backed down the lane from Gypsies' Corner to take them away ready for the morning market. Jim declined a lift from the driver, as he had a couple of small tidying up jobs to do. By now it was dusk, and after tidying up in the Red Barn, cleaning off his boots, he slowly started to walk the crushed limestone of the lane, up to Gypsies' Corner, walking the well-trodden route along the Cheltenham Road.

He was not passed by one car or lorry for the entire fifteen minutes it took for him to reach the Broadley smallholding. He had thought of calling in to see if old

Chapter Two, Town: People and Family

Jack or Harry had any casual work. He knew they had about two acres of leeks on the sand ground. He stood by the driveway looking down past the hawthorn hedge, towards the house, and the land. He stood thinking of the last time he had looked down the drive—back in the summer when young Meg stood by the back gate with blood running down her head, holding on to young Christine, in her plaster. He looked and thought on. He thought better of it and continued his walk. He was short of work, but they were a strange lot the Broadleys. At least, the Groves, and the Broadleys in Badsey were likeable enough, but this side of the family, they were a rum lot, a strange lot.

"Aye", he said, turning, "she must be near 'er time soon, with that second 'un she's having."

He walked on, reaching home by his usual well-worn route. Jim and Doris settled down to their tea, for they needed to be up early the next morning. After tea Jim sat down at the table to read the local newspaper while Doris quietly closed the door behind her and stepped out onto the path that ran outside the terrace and walked, wrapping her coat tightly round her as she went. She passed three children, all with bare feet playing on the dirt between their small terrace and Bewdley Street. She walked to where the path split, simply a trodden dirt path with patches of grass and bare ground on either side, she took the left hand fork and went through a low gate in the wall, then entered through the back door into Bewdley Mission, settling herself down in a chair ready for choir practice. It was now nearly the end of January, and the grey wet drizzle that had dominated the Vale since Christmas was beginning to break. However, with clear skies, folk talked of frost. Frost froze crops into the ground. Jim looked out of the parlour window. He was due to be working for J. G. Taylor for the next three days, which pleased him.

"Shouldn't be surprised if we had some frost."

And with time-honoured stealth, he laconically pushed his chair back from the table, cleared the dishes, stacked them, and took them through to the kitchen.

The next morning was indeed a frost, a hard frost. People in the South East or in cities think of two degrees of frost as hard. Although the vale was sheltered by the surrounding hills, icy winds could still tear through. That night the wind changed from the prevailing southwesterlies to a biting wind from the northeast. The frost cut hard. Jim was at work at Taylor's by 6:30am only to find he was needed just for three mornings, leaving him little time in the afternoon that was of use, as it was dark early. The lorries started to arrive having collected nets of sprouts from the big estates on the Lenches, and from the North Cotswolds. Men and women tightly wrapped up in woollens and overcoats unloaded, sorted, sifted, and re-netted the sprouts. Jim kept a close count of the sacks unloaded, the sorting, and the growing piles of nets ready to be sent to the railway. As the days passed the weather became bitter and all were predicting snow. If snow came they would be laid off again, for there would not be enough picked on the hills, or moved down to the Vale to warrant this number of workers. On the Friday it came. About ten in the morning, from a greyish-peach sky, leaden, still, and bitter, it came: a fine, even, fall of snow. By two o'clock the last of the nets of sprouts went off to the railway yard, the lorry slipping and catching the old brick arch that gave access to Taylor's yard from the High Street. With a low moan from the axles the lorry turned left, moving slowly through the snow—heading up to the station. Jim sorted out the dockets in his tiny office, closed and locked the door.

Stooping to quickly clear the snow from the foot of the large doors, Jim then swung them closed and dropped the bolts on the inside, thus closing the yard, probably till the middle of the next week at least. Shaking the snow from his shoulders as he clambered through the small door within the main doors, he closed the latch, and walked down the high street, along Avon Street, cutting through the backstreets to the Bewdley Mission to meet his wife. The next day, Saturday morning, the last in January, early, the snow lay about three inches deep, compacted by people walking, and made treacherous by the overnight frost. Jim was off to his holding to pull, or more likely cut, leeks from the ground.

Six

Meg Broadley was up early that morning. She knew her time was near, but also Harry needed to be off. Harry was up early, rattling the fire in the kitchen, grumbling to himself—money worries, cursing the weather. Soon he had finished the breakfast that Meg had cooked and he was in the large shed scrapping ice of the headlamps and the windscreen of the Ford Pilot, throwing sprout nets in the boot, and driving off to collect three men from the Fairfield Estate to take them up to Holcomb Nap on Bredon Hill above Ashton under Hill. He knew the journey would be fruitless; they would not be able to drive up the narrow track into the field above Holcomb Nap, let alone pick sprouts. Harry pulled the Pilot up at the junction of Battleton Road and Fairfield Road to collect the men. It was still a few minutes to seven, so he decided to wait. Presently through the sleet of a slow, muted dawn, one of them came round the corner. Harry wound down the window.

"It's no use, is it?" said the man, about forty, clutching his jacket tight around his neck with gnarled hands, "it's no good, gitting um in this, is it?"

Pulling leeks, cutting cabbage, or picking sprouts was referred to animatedly

Chapter Two, Town: People and Family

as somehow "getting them"—a bit like the old rural tradition of getting a crop in. This had carried over to the market gardeners from the days in the eighteenth century when most of the land around the town had been farmland. Ron pulled his jacket collar higher up around his neck. He stood visibly shivering in shirt, jacket, and trousers—tied below the knee with string to keep them from catching his shoes.

"You're right" said Harry, "looks like we mayn't have any more today, but we'll not get to Ashton, let alone you blokes getting up the hill. What about the others?"

"They're with me. I was the poor bugger who had to come and tell 'ee! I take it you'll be in touch when things have cleared over a bit and we can get up there?"

"Aye, we'll be in touch" Harry replied.

With that Ron trudged back round the corner, along Battleton Road, and after a few yards disappeared into one of the houses.

Harry turned the car round and drove back. The sleet stopped and as the sun came up, the grey leaden weight of the sky began to break up. The morning was turning out quite good. Despite the snow, which hampered traction, a handful of pick-ups, small lorries, and market gardeners' cars were out on the roads. Most men were laid off from their jobs for the day and were making for the Charity to survey the scene, even though not much could be done.

Harry arrived back to find Meg complaining of labour pains. Meg still went shopping in the afternoon, once she had finished making some biscuits. When he collected her from outside Woolworths he could only just manage to get her into the car. He drove her straight round to Avonside Hospital. Normally the second child would be delivered at home, but after the problems with Christine it was thought wiser that she should be in hospital. The labour was over within two hours, but Meg was in too bad a state to take notice of the little red-haired boy who came into the world that evening. As the night drew on fresh snow fell, lending a crisp white carpet of greeting to the child's arrival. Meg was in agony— the after-birth would not come away. It was infected, compacted; they drugged her with painkillers. Harry was called. He phoned her parents in Weston. They were warned to expect the worst. She had been delivered, he said, of the boy, but carrying the weight of Christine's plaster against her abdomen had led to the difficulties, so Meg and Harry believed—or leastwise that was Meg and Harry's story, their explanation. They had to give some explanation to their parents, their relatives, friends. But was this potentially fatal complication caused by the medicine, the poison, taken early in the pregnancy to kill the boy? Perhaps the boy had nearly died, in the womb. Meg now nearly died. Was there a balancing of the scales of justice in this? Meg and Harry sought to deny any connection between what was happening now and the attempted abortion. Her difficult delivery, the impacted afterbirth, her near death encounter, this was blamed on Christine's plaster. The boy appeared fine and healthy. But Meg was slipping away. Harry spent the night by her side. She was delirious. He watched as the snow secretly spread across the ground, across bushes, across trees; how not a sound in the cold night air could penetrate. He thought on, cursed his luck, thought how he had lost his mother—oh she was alive, but she had left him. She was at home with his father, but was distant. Now he was to lose his wife. Silently the snow continued to fall.

By morning the worst was over. The fever had stabilized. There was hope. By the Sunday evening she was clear of the afterbirth, forced out with medication and surgery. By the Monday evening Meg was sufficiently conscious for the nurse to bring the baby in. In no uncertain terms she deposited the child on the bed, for Meg to pick up:

"Here, take him. Here's the little red-headed bugger who's caused all the trouble!"

Chapter Three
Beginnings: Infancy and Quietude

> ~ *"O Lord, for You formed my inward parts;*
> *You covered me in my mother's womb.*
> *I will praise You, for I am fearfully and wonderfully made.*
> *Marvellous are Your works, and that my soul knows very well.*
> *My frame was not hidden from You, when I was made in secret,*
> *and skilfully created."*
>
> PSALM 139:13–15

One

This is the story of a child; a child in this world—alone, yet amongst many. Amongst others, but estranged. He enters on a cold, snow-ridden January evening in this small town. The child arrives on this scene that winter evening in early 1954. He is sleeping wrapped in a cot in front of a fire, placed on the large settee in the living room. His mother is still ill, anaemic, worn from the delivery. His father, earlier that morning, has driven the Ford Pilot up to the North Cotswold escarpment to pick sprouts. Picking sprouts as the frost cut into his hands, and his breath froze on his grey overcoat. The light had come, grey, sullen, thin, reluctant to give of itself to the bleak headland that February morning. The snow lay compacted on the ground, on the stone walls, drifted into the corner of the field near the headland. The day was an apology for a day—not much happened, not much moved, save the thin wisps of smoke from the cottages in Saintbury and Willersley below the field.

The Broadleys had bought the sprouts "on the piece"; that is, another grower, the land owner, had sown the crop and raised it, then sold it on the piece once it was nearly ready. Jack and Harry had a gang of ten men picking the sprouts through December and January, but there were still a few sprouts left that had been passed over earlier as small or immature. Now they were ready, but there were too few for a land worker to pick them on piece-rate, so Harry was spending the day gleaning what was left. This second crop was reckoned to be sweeter—those who knew the vale, knew its land, what it could grow, these people reckoned that the sweetest sprouts came after the hardest frost. That day the frost did not relent. Harry left off picking about half past three as the light—already failing, having given of its thin powers—filtered through the steel haze of a February day. He loaded the four and a half nets of sprouts into the boot, tying the lid part shut with a short piece of rope. If the business did well that summer, they would buy a lorry, a three-ton Austin.

Meg finished ringing out the washing, hung it on the bleached wooden rails above the stove to dry, lifted the lid, racked the embers before emptying some more coal from the scuttle into the stove. She turned to the kitchen sink, washed her hands, dried them, then stood, looking out of the window, down the garden, past the bushes, gazing into the field of leeks. She was thinking of her parents in Weston, wishing they were here—or she with them. She turned as if annoyed with herself, left the kitchen hurriedly to raise Christine out of the pen in the living room. By now she was used to the weight of plaster, the weight of the splint, bracing the young child's legs apart. She laid her down on a clean towel, drew out the cotton wool, which acted as a nappy in the plaster openings, cleaned the child, replaced with new cotton wool, and hugged her. And hugged her.

Paul slept the sleep of angels. He was a good baby. The delivery may have been difficult, but he did not cry; he slept at night and ate well during the day. In the day his eyes were looking, always looking around—or sleeping.

Meg returned to the kitchen to prepare the tea as the clock in the front room struck four. She looked out of the window, over the leek field that was their land, towards the thin grey blue of the North Cotswolds on the horizon. There was a gentle tap at the door. Meg ceased her reverie with a sudden swift movement; she walked through the hall to the front door, returning the bread to the scullery as she did so. She unbolted the door, turned the key (for only rarely was the front door used—the side door or back door being the commonest thoroughfare amongst gardening families), and opened it. Looking out towards the hawthorn hedge and the Cheltenham Road—it was the Reverend Herbert.

He was shown into the front room and the best tea set was brought out.

"But do you love him?"

Meg poured another cup of tea, and passed it to him.

"I cook for him, I wash, I keep his house, I answer the telephone, but he gets so annoyed if I get messages wrong. He's so impatient, so crude at times; you

Chapter Three, Beginnings: Infancy and Quietude

know . . . you know, some of the things he says . . ."

"But do you love him? Remember your wedding vows."

"Mother was asking after you in her letter the other day, let me see if I can find it."

Meg went over to the sideboard in the living room and searched through the letter case in the bottom drawer.

"Yes, here it is."

She handed the letter to him.

"I see your father's no better. Can't they operate for the glaucoma? They can do wonderful things now."

"No, he's too old; it's just a case of managing, managing . . ."

At this Meg looked away into the fire. Reverend Herbert got up, and walked across to the French windows, and looked out into the garden. So how is young Paul—it is Paul you've decided to call him is it not?"

"Yes, oh yes, he's fine"

"And Harry, what does Harry think—after all, he's got two fine young children now?" said the vicar, turning and looking at Meg.

"Let me get you another cup, I'll just put the kettle on."

"No, no really, I must be going; I've got some people to see about a baptism, and with the weather and all, I must get quite a few things sorted out. Remember what I said about Christine; there is help if you need it. I know one young woman who would be delighted to help."

After exchanging a few parting pleasantries Meg saw him off, locking and bolting the front door behind her. She then settled back into sorting out the tea things. But she could not get her mind to focus on the job in hand.

Harry Broadley drove slowly off the sprout field; it was getting dusk, the frost which had barely loosened its grip on the land during the day, was now re-colonizing the mud, the crumpled snow, the ruts, in earnest—slowly freezing over the puddles in the track, slowly almost imperceptibly as the wheels of the car pulled out of the field onto the road. The frost was returning as the Vale battened down for the night. As the church bells struck four in Saintbury Church tower, Harry drove slowly over the frosty road towards Evesham. He thought on his daughter: tomorrow they would drive up to Birmingham, on poor roads, with winter conditions, to the Birmingham Children's Hospital—to see doctors yet again. He felt something was wrong; they weren't telling all, telling it straight. Had something gone wrong? She seemed fine when she was born, but the hip was dislocated—why the complications? He tormented himself with these thoughts. He turned left onto the Oxford Road, then after a short distance he turned right down a short but steep bank, checking the car as it rolled, with periodic squeals of its brakes. The sprout nets shifted. He stopped at the foot of the hill to sort out the nets of sprouts. He pulled the rope tight, even tighter, as if by tightening he could solve the problems in his mind.

"Why! why? Why do things have to go wrong!"

There was no one else around to hear his cry.

The snow deadened his shout. The mist and frost swallowed his words as they had man upon man, woman upon woman, child upon child for centuries. It could have been a Saxon farmer cutting kindling in the woods around the tiny settlement of Eoves-Holme, or Eofesham, in the eight century, near to where Evesham Abbey would soon be founded, a Saxon farmer cursing his bad luck, cursing the mists. The mists swallowed all. The Valley was damp, and on nights like this the mists swirled and set from the river, the frost glistening on the road. Harry leant against the car, pulling on the rope, screwing up his eyes, trying not to think of Christine—but the image of the plaster kept coming back,

"Why?" he murmured under his breath. "Why? You tell me that, why? Come on God, why?"

Because he was blanketed and enveloped by the freezing fog he believed no one else was around or could hear him

He straightened himself up, tied the rope, and got back inside the car. Harry drove on, following the road round through Childswickam and on through Mount Pleasant to Hinton Green, then up the Cheltenham Road to his small holding, home to Meg, Christine, and little Paul. He was thankful that his son was fine, alright, a healthy baby boy; indeed he was bringing himself up. He rarely cried, ate well, was no trouble at all. As the months passed he crawled, looked, marvelled, absorbed all around him from the small world of his cot. Soon he would be walking along the sideboard in the living room—he needed little attention, he was bringing himself up.

Two

So the babe grew; it chuckled and cried, ate and looked. It gazed from its deep azure blue eyes. It gazed in wonder at all. And the infant walked; and the sun rose and harvests were gathered, and crops were gleaned, and frosts bit, and seed was sown, and women did hoe, while men argued long hours in the market. And old folk died. Summers drew to autumn, and the mists rolled into frost, and winter winds bit hard as the year turned into spring. And the babe grew as the Vale brought forth its bounty. And the infant became a child. Little that was of the world outside impinged on this land. Mildew on young leeks was of more importance than the Suez Crisis; the passing of an old singer, with the loss of the

Chapter Three, Beginnings: Infancy and Quietude

"old songs," of more significance to some than the death of a famous movie star. And the child grew—and giggled with his sister. Harry proudly drove his new, second-hand lorry, while Meg cooked and swept. And they rowed; they fought, they disagreed about everything. Rare was the day that passed without tension, disagreement, or cross words. And the days when rows descended into violence increased.

The child grew, and explored. He explored the house, the stairs, furniture, the garden—he was inquisitive. He would sit amongst the long flower border once his sister had gone to school, making mud pies, then to present them to his mother in the kitchen. Or would sit amongst the flowers, tracing the patterns of an anemone with his finger: the landscape of the mind, of small-world play. Little Paul was thrilled, captivated—at night he would dream of this world, of exploring, of the house, and the depth and scale of the back garden. The lilac bush provided his first great sadness: he sat on the lawn and watched as it was dug up, heard the tearing of its roots. Reason had nought to do with his reaction—he watched and felt. He would take his mother a daisy chain, his father also. They were never together, or so it seemed. The raspberry bushes at the bottom of the garden were the limit of this world. He had been told so. So he did not go through. Or, at least, he would crawl in amongst them, and creep as far as he could to the far side of this, the boundary along the bottom of the garden, then he could watch. After the journey across the lawn, staggering widely on his short dumpy legs, he would sit, gaze, and rest. He had discovered this by following the old cat one afternoon. There he would sit. Sometimes giant legs would come quite close. Sometimes a gruff voice would call across:

" 'Ow do, young Paul; 'ow bist thee?"

But he didn't answer. He did not know what a question was. But it was more than that. It was only when people were close to him that he heard the words they said. He was used to people moving their mouth and seeming to make a noise. Eventually he realized that this mouth movement and noise was the same as when people were close to him and spoke and he was required to answer, to speak as well. For his hearing was not good. More pertinently there was his friend, his companion—that was the way he thought of it. This companion was a sound that was with him all the time, a continuous high-pitched sound. A two-and-a-half-year-old child does not have the conceptual ability or the language, let alone the vocabulary, to rationalize what is happening. In reality he had tinnitus which he could hear all the time, though it rarely caused any disturbance in him at this stage. However, it did mask and cause confusion when people spoke to him. Often he did not realize people were talking to him unless they were close up to him. Often when his mother tucked him in at night she was crying. His mother would always kiss him good night, but she would never answer his pleas enquiring what was wrong. His questions were never answered. So he took this as normal. Coupled with this hearing problem he began to grow quite happily in relative isolation.

The child grew—and in his mind the world grew. He would sit on the grass while his sister was at school, gaze at the buttercups, such was the mild kiss the air bestowed on the land as the spring drew on. At other times this scene was a forest of green floppy leaves; at yet others, small tightly crinkled bright yellow-green plants laid out evenly in rows. He was puzzled yet fascinated by these changes. Yet he was equally puzzled, but not fascinated, by why he never saw his parents together. On wet days Paul and Christine would sit and play in the living room: Christine played with her doll; he busied himself with scissors and a piece of fern-green cloth, making a set of clothes for his panda (a soft toy given to him for his second birthday by Meg's parents instead of a teddy bear). Soon his mother would come in with his medicine, cough syrup for his rasping cough. He was in many ways a delicate child, prone to throat infections, chestiness, wheezing. He was often at the doctors.

When he was well enough he would be out exploring the sheds. Beyond the raspberry bushes was now a world he could enter—officially. After struggling through them, pausing in the summer to pluck the fruit, he would cross the gravel drive, steering well clear of the big lorry, then descend into the main shed. It was a dark labyrinth! Tools, machines, string, boxes, and baskets of various sizes, and deep mud ruts; and along the right hand side, near the back, a window. Paul would climb onto the workbench and gaze through the window. The branches of an old apple tree would tap and tap on the window, so he would rub a small circular patch in the layer of dirt and condensation on the glass and look. Beyond was a wide expanse of land peopled with crops and starlings, or bare earth and frost, or men and women pulling onions, some sitting on up-turned crates. He would go out and play with their children. But he got dirty, and that was not to be! His mother chided him; she had enough to do already without this! Though secretly she did not want him to play with those children—they were labourers' children, and worse still some were gypsies!

So he would explore the sheds: beyond the workbench and window lay a wooden annexe, this was a whole new world of small doors, leading to a room specially made for him (or so he thought—it was really a disused chicken house). Leading out of the back of this little shed was a small trap door that slid up. This was to be his secret door to the world beyond: first he would descend into the darkness of the shed, passing through its wide open entrance, wide enough for the lorry to drive in and out; then past tools, machines, and an assortment of market gardening clutter, and so to the workbench, treading over a dirt floor and

Chapter Three, Beginnings: Infancy and Quietude

up a small concrete step into the wooden annexe, then to the right and through the small doorway into the chicken shed, then after checking that no one had followed, through the secret hatch into the world beyond! To a four year old this really was like entering another world—compounded by the fact that the weather had sometimes changed if he had loitered in the shed for some time. Beyond was a wide field, the same field he had looked at through the side window in the main shed, but this rear view was much more expansive—now the boundaries were different.

His world now quadrupled in size. In front and to each side was the land with its succession of crops and bare earth, bordered by a large ancient hedgerow: deep hedgerows, grassy banks with clumps and thickets of old black thorn, hawthorn, and occasionally pollard willows. The latter two were used less and less as habits changed: rarely now was the hawthorn cut for May Day celebrations, and chips made from thin wooden strips with pressed tin handles were now replacing the willow baskets, or pots as they were known. The hedgerow was wide, up to fifteen feet in places, and peopled by voles, vetches, cranesbill, mice, bird nests, and harebells, all surmounted by tall cow parsley. Occasionally the clumps of thorn were allowed to grow to full height and formed small coppices of three or four trees. In amongst these Paul and Christine would make a den! Often he would lie amongst the hedgerows gazing upwards, surrounded by the tracery of the grasses and wild flowers. He would turn over and from this vantage point on the ridge of the hedgerow he could look across the Charity to Longdon Hill with, rising behind it in a blue haze, the North Cotswold escarpment.

Longdon Hill fascinated him. He could see it from his bedroom. He could see the cars climb up it in the evening; he watched as their headlights bent in the night sky. He looked at its shape, the gentle rise on the left, covered as it was with orchards, then the steep line formed by its southwestern flank. He loved the shape of that hill, he knew it from different viewpoints, knew every curve from an early age. He loved that hill. His father laughed at his insistence that it was Longman's Hill; he had misheard or muddled the name in his mind. Hence the land between the house and the hill was named after it: Longman's Charity. He knew the lands were called the Charity, even if he knew not why, or was too young to comprehend. But these lands and the hill belonged together in his mind. The hill watched over them, protected them, gave water from its slopes, provided shelter from biting north-easterlies in the winter, yet was such a beautiful gentle hill. It was only small, was dwarfed by the North Cotswold escarpment behind it, but to Paul it was magical, protective. He knew it in all its guises, in all weathers, in all seasons, and so the hill gave the name to this childhood world: Longman's Charity.

Three

One afternoon Paul busied himself in the rear of the shed, sheltering from the rain. He could hear it as it ricocheted off the corrugated tin roof and watched as it swept through the apple trees, which frantically tapped on the windows as if to seek shelter from the storm. The wind made the rain seem worse than it was, likewise the tin cladding on the shed amplified the impression. Sat on the workbench he watched as a man and a woman continued to cut cabbage in the rain. The man was bent double cutting the cabbage with a knife he had used for years, which boasted a cutting edge worn to no more than one half of an inch in places; the man's thick tweed coat standing out stiffly from his legs in the rain, his head dripping with water. He rose to give his cap an occasional tug and shake the mud from his hands and to check on his wife, how she was doing. She sat on an up-turned crate, surrounded by a dozen or so cabbages. She methodically trimmed off any dead or yellowed leaves, rubbed off the dirt, which soon turned to mud in the rain, and generally cleaned them. Every now and then, she would wipe her hand on the apron she wore over her coat, then draw it across her brow.

The couple continued to work, for they needed the money. It was Jim and Doris Beason; for once Jim had swallowed his pride and taken work from "them Broadleys." Jim and Doris were always together, they had friends and commitments—Doris singing in the Bewdley Mission, Jim with his bike, which he still dismantled and maintained despite the aches and pains of rheumatism, which now he was in his late fifties prevented him cycling. The irony was he had bought the bike as a young man from the bike shop originally started by Harry Broadley's grandfather on the corner of Littleworth Street. The couple continued to cut cabbage through the day, Doris taking over when Jim's back got too bad. Both exchanged glances that betrayed the love that was still as strong as when they had courted together in the depression of the 1920s. By four in the afternoon they had cut nearly two dozen crates of cabbage, all neatly trimmed and clean, and were now stacked, covered with a tarpaulin at the edge of the field. Both were then ready for the walk back along the Cheltenham Road, home to a warm fire and tea.

Paul busied himself folding and cutting a cardboard cover (emblazoned with "J. H. BROADLEY & SON" in bold letters) used to cover produce in a tray or chip. He was trying to make a ship, but was having only limited success. He stopped cutting, raising his head to listen to voices. Two travelling workmen were standing just inside the entrance to the shed, sheltering from the rain. The taller of the two wore a cap pushed well back on his head, a cap worn threadbare at the edges and faded to a blend of grey-olive and earth-brown. His face was deeply riven with richly tanned skin; two clear blue eyes, heavily watered but sparkling, lay

Chapter Three, Beginnings: Infancy and Quietude

beneath sallow lids. His nose was pronounced as with all Romany noses, his upper lip covered by a thickly curling moustache. Despite being clean-shaven, his jaw protruded sharply, with faint bristles of grey hair amongst finely sculptured folds of olive coloured skin around his neck. His face had the weathered glow of fifty or more seasons spent on the road, travelling through Ireland, Somerset, the market gardens of Kent, and of the Vale of Evesham. He wore a close fitting sports jacket, tightly buttoned up—a jacket well worn, and almost moulded to his shape. His neck was contained by a bright yellow and brown woollen scarf, neatly tied and spread so as to cover the whole area between the jacket lapels and his neck. His trousers were of a black cloth, most probably worsted in their early years but were now polished smooth particularly below the knees and in the rear, the pebble-shiny smoothness contrasted with the frayed bottoms and widely stretched and likewise threadbare pockets. The trousers were tied just below the knee with string to prevent them catching on the black, polished hobnail boots. His companion was similarly dressed, though he was five to six inches shorter, his head surmounted by a neat trilby hat, matching his partner's cap in seasoning. This man was younger, in his mid-thirties, but with similar features. They were almost certainly related—if not brothers then part of the same large extended family. He wore a rough workmen's raincoat over his clothes, but with a pair of tight-fitting black trousers, white socks, and a pair of pointed patent leather shoes. Despite the contrast in dress, his face belied his gypsy roots and the winters and summers spent on the road. Paul by now had stepped quietly, slowly, creeping through the darkness till, partly hiding behind a heavy labourer's coat hanging at the side of the shed, he stood only about three yards from them. Both men stood, just within the entrance to the shed, sheltering from the steady unrelenting rain. He watched and listened to the drip, drip of rain that had managed to creep in under the corrugated sheets, some now forming small pools in the dirt ruts at his feet.

Both men continued to look out towards the gravel drive. Both stood patiently waiting. The younger man shuffled round, digging the point of his left shoe into the gravel, then cursing himself, lifting the foot up so he could clean off the dirt, quickly pulling out a handkerchief, spitting on it and then polishing the point, as he balanced and wobbled on one leg. The older man had stood still. Still as a hawk, his eyes fixed on the sky, watching for the slightest change in the sheet of mute grey cloud: watching and waiting like an owl, patiently waiting till the moment was right to grasp its prey.

At the young man's movements he stilled his observation. Then removing one hand from his trouser pocket he reached inside the jacket to pull out a mouth organ. He ran the instrument through his mouth, wetted his lips, blowing faintly, then removed it, polished the top on his cuff, then with speed and dexterity flew into playing a jig. Paul woke with a start—for he had fallen asleep on a pile of old sprout nets. He crawled onto his knees and watched, and listened with amazement. The iron ran to and fro across the man's lips, his back arched as he bent into the instrument. He blew and played, the jigs speeding as he warmed to his task. The sound flew round the shed. The young man, forgetting his new shoes span into form: stepping out to the sound, spinning and dancing a solo jig. The sound was higher than a melodeon and somehow freer—or was it this man's skill? His companion's dance flew from wild jig, to fifties jive, to popular swing style dancing, and, as the elder's pace slowed, it took the form of Cotswold Morris, then the young man would shuffle back into a jive, looking for all the world like he was on a town hall dance floor dancing to the latest craze. The music and the dance stopped abruptly as a lorry came into sight. It was as though the music and dance were not for ordinary mortals to hear, or at least not for non-travellers to witness—those of a different caste. This was not exclusivity; it held more with the fear of exposing the culture and values once held dear by all in the land, but now only rarely found: this was certainly true of the songs, music, and traditions of gypsies.

By the 1950s only a handful had not rejected the old songs and the old ways: scepticism took root as people left the land. The elder of the two was an accomplished musician—unlettered, in both words and music, but with a store of jigs, polkas, reels, and country-dance tunes in his head that he could play to order. By and large, gypsies were not welcome on the North Cotswolds, indeed between the sheep and cereals there was little work for them. The vale with its seasonal crops offered campsites and employment. The elder, the harmonica player, often played at dances, and for a number of different Morris teams in North Cotswold villages, but had to disguise himself. But then his appearance was seasonal, transitory, and he was equally at home accompanying in Cork or Limerick. He had no roots—had been born on the road, the memory of precisely where had long since been lost—but he always held a special fondness for the form and grace of Cotswold Morris.

The lorry drew up sharply. Harry jumped out of the cab, pushing his cap back on his forehead in the process,

"Whure the 'eck 'ave 'ou bin?"

Then turning round to indicate with a wide sweep of the arm to Sam to get some more crates he continued,

". . . you were s'pose to be up there ages ago!"

"If ee'll forgive us, and I'm sure thure be no cause for trouble, but we never got that message. All we knew was that we'as to come and see 'ee, seeing 'ow we'as looking for a bit of casual."

Chapter Three, Beginnings: Infancy and Quietude

It was the elder who spoke, touching the peak of his cap as he did so. There was a pause.

"All we knew is 'ou needed some extra 'ands a'cutting the cabbage. So 'ere we is to see if thure be any work."

"Yes, well, I had said otherwise—your friend, he took the message right enough, anyway, that's as maybe, but what I want to know is how am I going to get the stuff cut now?"

"Well if 'ee will allow us, we can get two or three hours in now—that is not counting the time we stand talking 'bout it," continued the elder.

The younger man just stood gazing down at his new shoes, looking at the scratches on the toes, caused through his wild dance! The elder's reconciliation was working. He was well experienced at sorting out differences amongst the hot-headed youth in his tribe—irate market gardeners were easy by comparison.

"Yes, well, come on then, jump into the cab round there now." Harry gesticulated towards the nearside door. Sam had finished loading the empty crates on the back, so all climbed into the cab. Sam's roots were in travelling, though he had settled in the Vale—a cottage in Cropthorne, for a peppercorn rent—since before the war. He said little, but thought much. Maybe the two labourers had received the message, maybe not. Maybe they had used the time to get the younger man his new shoes—after all, he had his working boots discreetly wrapped in a paper bag, tucked inside his raincoat. Sam looked at the younger man sat next to him.

"So," said Sam, "goin' cabbage cutting?" nodding down at the shiny new shoes as he commented.

The younger man shuffled uneasily.

Paul sat and watched as the lorry turned and drove back up the drive. No one had seen him in the shadows. The rain continued to fall. Soon his mother came looking for him—to bring him in, wash him, smarten him up: Eileen and Sylvia were calling for tea, calling to see the proud family. He sat, obediently while tea was served, while polite conversation sounded to the chink of teacups: he was learning to inhabit two contrasting worlds, emphasized by what he had seen this day. Miss Blunt, who lived next door, was an example. She had objected vociferously to the placing of the sheds—they were in line with the bottom of her garden. They ruined her view, a view that she loved, of the Cotswold escarpment. Some of the houses sporadically placed along Cheltenham Road were suburban ribbon development. Others, like the Broadley residence, set back from the road, were agricultural. Herein lay a contradiction—or in reality, a conflict. Miss Blunt's idea of the countryside was different to that held by market gardeners. Likewise she objected to the smell from the onion-washing tank. But what she failed to see was that the land looked the way it did through its use: this was as true in the Vale as it was on the North Cotswolds. But conflict there was. She complained long and hard, she even tried to involve the council on more than one occasion. But the land was agricultural—had been for generations, and all that the Broadleys had done was in keeping with its use. To many the sheds did look ramshackled, but they held a beauty of their own, a functional beauty: wooden posts, corrugated tin sheets, timber weather boarding, the worn homogeneous mixture of implements, crates, containers, tools, and so forth. Meg objected to the sheds—but this was more from snobbery: she didn't think they were good enough—she expected brick sheds, with neatly painted doors, along with potted geraniums outside. But those big estates that had such premises were in a different economic league to the Broadleys, father and son: a father and son who were doing well. They had a well-established group of customers up north, three pieces of land (two freehold, one rented from Christchurch Charity); and both were respected, after a fashion, in the daily markets.

Paul sat on his bed, his hands under his chin. He looked out of the window. The rain was unrelenting, so he watched as Harry and Sam worked on the new shed: it was now nearing completion. This shed was the same size as the other, and was being built alongside the former—effectively doubling the storage and parking. Harry and Sam were putting the last of the sheets of corrugated tin on the roof. The whole structure was made from redundant telegraph poles, cut into sections then clad in the tin. This new shed was for the lorry to live in, plus storage for produce at the back: large, cavenous to a child, open-fronted, and with electric lights! This time Meg objected—for this shed interrupted her view! But such concerns were way above the child's head. He was blissfully unaware of such developments. He sat there looking. Watching, as the rain poured down, felt a special sense of grace, of preciousness to the moment. He wanted to hold it in his hand, to keep it like it was forever. But already he knew the anger, the fear, the hatred that lived in his world, alongside that which seemed good and precious.

At times this small four-year-old had been found outside the front gate, next to the main road, screaming: screaming, rolling about kicking—holding his head, his ears, always holding his ears and screaming to drown out the noise. For it was at times like these that the sound in his head—the tinnitus—merged with the anger, the shouts, the cursing, the fights, the violence of his parents as they fought and rowed. And he could not cope. It seemed to the neighbours who gently picked up this child as if he was fighting imaginary phantoms, demons. They tried to still him, quieten him, reassure him, took him back through the gate, at least tried to take him back down the path, but the screaming and kicking got worse. It was as if the cause of this behaviour was in the house, taking the boy back was like threatening to throw him into the pit of hell. Often a neighbour, or even a passer-

Chapter Three, Beginnings: Infancy and Quietude

by would leave the child, unable to get him back down the path, so they would go into the passageway, but as they reached the back door they witnessed a man and a woman in the full throes of a fight, a pretty bloody and nasty fight. Neither seemed aware of the little boy's absence—crouched as he was under the hawthorn hedge, screaming, crying, trying to escape the demons. Neither had realized his absence. That was until the neighbour informed them. Then Meg would run up the path get him and bring him back. Oh the disgrace! Oh the shame! How could he do such a thing! The boy was roundly chastised and sent off to his room. Even in the quiet after the storm it was pressed home on the boy how he must not do this sort of thing, go near the road, he was scolded for bringing shame on his parents, bringing the neighbours—or even strangers—into their affairs. He was even taken to the doctors: such behaviour was not normal (neither was that of the parents—though the subtlety of this latter point was lost on them). The doctor feared autism; after all, he was a strange little wisp of a child.

Four

A door opened. Meg and Harry came out, his mother holding Christine's hand. Despite his age, Paul could sense the foreboding and the anger in his mother and father. They looked as they did when they were about to fight and shout at each other. Not only could he read this on their faces, but he could sense it, almost as if it was in the space between them, in the waiting area with them. He also knew that the shouting would not start here—not in the hospital—not with all these people and their children around. No, it would be kept for the journey home. For other couples, Christine's condition, her growing disability, would have brought them together, but this was not true with Harry and Meg. Meg taunted Harry that Christine's problem came from his side of the family (a great Aunt somewhere back in times past had been born with a dislocated hip). But that was only half of the story—yes, Christine had been born with a dislocated hip, which went unnoticed until she was a few months old, but the months encased from her waist down in plaster seem to have done little to solve the problem. The problem now was that the hip joint was not developing properly; indeed the socket was actually crumbling. There was talk (overheard by Harry between the doctors) that possibly an artery had become blocked or strangled, its flow being restricted, thus depriving the joint in these crucial formative months.

Meg and Harry could not completely dismiss the thought that there was a curse on their marriage. Superstition was still only just below the surface of the brave new modern world of post-war Britain. Or did this belie a deeper problem: that they were never meant to marry, that their marriage was certainly not made in heaven. Both Meg and Harry had regularly been to church as children and teenagers. Both had been confirmed in the Church of England—though in Harry's case this was more through pressure from his father; scepticism and atheism grew as he became a young man. Meg by contrast took her faith seriously, yet despite the doubts—severe doubts—she had pursued marrying Harry. But if there was superstition there was no justice in Meg's comment to Harry, no sense of searching for God's truth, only recrimination. She felt an overwhelming sense of guilt and pain for Christine; she felt a mother's anguish at seeing what was happening to her baby. All this could have been made easier if she had had her husband's love—if she would have, could have, allowed her husband to love her, or if she could have allowed herself to love him. There was no justice in her remarks, only bitterness and hatred. Christine's disability caused them to spend more time together, but it did not bring them closer; it was a cause for further division. There were added pressures: of watching Christine, making sure she did not dislocate the malformed joint, coping with getting a shoe built up an extra inch for her left leg; the journeys on bad roads, often in winter weather; dealing with doctors in faraway hospitals, trying to get the truth out of them when a veil of well-educated professionalism descended.

All this led to the growing sense of frustration and inevitably of anger. Paul heard it, observed it, felt it. Of course, this was not the only cause for division and rows between them; no, this was only one of a long line of causes. But what of Christine? Christine just seemed to take it all in her stride, for she was a bright, cheerful, and gregarious child. She was now settled at school, playing with other girls, involved in everything. Meg's mother complained that she was growing into a proper little tomboy! Apart from visits to the hospital she took no time off school. Of course, she was not allowed to do PE for fear of dislocating the leg; one teacher claimed it would be alright, that she believed there was no risk (despite the advice of doctors) so Harry went in to school to give her a piece of his mind.

As the years passed the left leg became relatively shorter, prompting remarks of "peg-leg" from the boys, but Christine could look after herself! As she got older treatment followed treatment, one doctor followed another, one operation followed on from other operations. Attempts were made to slow down the growth of the good leg with an operation; then it was found arthritis had set into the problematic left hip in her late teens. After two operations on the left socket, then a hip replacement and a revision many, many, years later, matters were finally resolved. By the time Christine was forty, they could build up the malformed socket with bone grafts, finally righting what had been at the root of the problem all along.

Chapter Three, Beginnings: Infancy and Quietude

Five

The main building was Edwardian, solid red brick with a pitched tile roof, tall, white window frames, numerous small panes of glass, dark brown polished floors, and doors leading to rooms full of children with wooden desks. As Paul entered through the hall with his mother, overhead were the curved timbers inside the pitched roof structure with lights hanging from the ceiling. They turned down a corridor at the far end of the hall. He noticing the curved glazed bricks on the corner, then pulling on his mother's arm as he stopped to touch them. They continued down this short dark corridor, suddenly it opened up into light, around them were windows, everywhere windows, and at the end of the corridor were two doors. They followed the other mothers and children through the door to the right and were welcomed by the teacher. The room was bright and airy, like the corridor with windows everywhere! Paul ran over to the far side of the room and pulled himself up so he could see out. All the mothers were sitting talking, or more accurately, listening to the lady in the middle, while the children busied themselves exploring. Soon the visit was over. These two rooms had been added in the early 1950s, with a metal and glass corridor linking them to the main school building—Evesham Council Infant School. They walked through the main school, past classrooms and out through the main door in the side of the hall, out into Chapel Street. They walked the few yards up the road till it joined Swann Lane where Harry was waiting with the lorry.

"Couldn't you have brought the car!" chided Meg as she clambered in, "there are other people around: look there are the Smiths!"

The child looked out of the window back at the school. Over to his left he could see the small building he had just left—the roof was funny. It first rose in a low pitch from the wall, then changing and rising steeply, with a chimney in the middle. Over to the far side was the small extension they had visited, all metal, with a shallow pitched roof covered in tin sheets. Over to the right was a much bigger building—it looked like the building they had just left—red brick, white wooden windows, pitched tiled roof, but it was big!

"Two rooms up," he commented, "look mum, two rooms up."

Harry and Meg stopped their fierce discussion and turned to the boy. He just continued looking out of the cab window, his eyes now fixed on the tall black railings surrounding the playground.

"Is that a bomb house, like Mrs. Sharp has got in her garden?" he said pointing at the large rectangular structure in the playground—likewise made from red brick, but with a flat roof and no windows.

"Yes," said Harry, momentarily ignoring Meg, and smiling at the boy's comment: it was indeed a bomb shelter, built during the war.

"Oh I see, take more notice of Paul than me, when I asked you, told you how much it meant to me that you brought the car this morning!"

Harry muttered some obscenity under his breath and with a snort, threw the lorry into gear and drove off. Paul looked round as they passed the whole of the large building—Evesham Council Junior School—following the black railings round till they ended, encircling a small green garden with a willow tree in the centre. The road then turned sharply to the left and descended a short hill, then to the right. The lorry passed a meat factory, finally joining Bridge Street. Harry drove past the Methodist Church, then up and over the Workman Bridge. Once the traffic had cleared they turned right into Waterside. The lorry drew up sharply. All this time the couple had been rowing.

" 'ou can get out and walk if it's not good enough for 'ee, go on make your mind up!" shouted Harry.

Paul had been dreaming of the building he had seen, the playground, the willow tree he had caught a glimpse of in the little green garden at the end of the big building—it must be part of the school as the railings carried on round it. He watched the swans on the river as they waited on the Workman Bridge. He was aware of the row his parents were having but drifted off in his mind. He came too with a jerk—for he fell forward off the seat as his father jammed the brakes on.

"Look what you've done to him; oh you're so cruel," said Meg, changing her tune. "If you've hurt him, I'll kill you I will, Harry Broadley; I'll swing for you; see if I won't! And I won't have you use that language in front of him!"

Harry looked, he watched as his son climbed back up on the seat, then in silence drove on. The rest of the journey was completed in silence—a silence loaded with enmity.

A few days, or was it weeks later, Paul stood on a bright, cold morning, holding his mother's hand, waiting outside the door to the Infants' School. There was little room between the door, the side of the building, and the railings, set in the low purplebrick and redbrick wall next to Chapel Street. Both schools had been built many years earlier, before the First World War. The infants and juniors were purpose-built premises in their own land; the plot was not large, but sufficient. Tarmac surrounded both buildings, divided to the rear by a brick wall to form an infant playground and a junior playground. Both schools had separate outside toilet blocks, the infant one being reached along a pathway that snaked its way under a lean-to along the perimeter wall; the juniors had to brave the elements. Despite being in the centre of a rural market town, the schools, the playgrounds, the Edwardian style of architecture used, the railings, the tarmac, the factory next door, all looked in keeping with schools in larger towns and cities further north in the Midlands: red brick, purple brick, dressed stone, purple grey tarmac, black

Chapter Three, Beginnings: Infancy and Quietude

railings, white window frames, and the sounds and cries of generation upon generation of children. Silence and order, alternating with screams and chaos, as the children erupted from within.

His mother did not come in with him; none of the parents did. The children entered the building, being shepherded through the hall by the teacher. Welling up behind them like a tidal wave were the rest of the children, ready to enter. Paul entered the metal and glass prefabricated structure of his classroom—it was still new, having been built to cope with the increase in numbers, the post-war baby boom! He glued himself to the sand tray, once they were sent off to their tasks, staying there for the whole morning. He rushed to his mother when he saw her as she came to collect him for dinner. There was no nursery education in the school, so the rising-fives came for mornings only for about half a term before starting in the term in which they turned five. He was not sure about school at the end of the first morning, but as Christmas approached, he began to take it in his stride. Gradually the idea sank in with him that after Christmas he would be starting full time—stopping all day as it had been explained to him! This was possibly a bit much. He had enjoyed going in the mornings, coming home for dinner, having a nap, and then playing in the house, or the garden, or down in the sheds.

Six

At Christmas when they visited his maternal grandparents in Weston-super-Mare, it seemed as though he talked non-stop to Meg's father, William Riley, about his time at school. His parents commented that it was as if no one else had ever been! But William listened, and loved him. Possibly William found in Paul the son he had never had, or even the one, Anthony, William and Renée's first child, who had been stillborn all those years earlier. He loved his grandson and shared with him, gave him his time, and his grandson felt the same; William was becoming more to the little child than his own parents. Paul would recount all, talk about what he had done, talk from pictures in books that William directed him to get out of the bookcase to share with him. This frail, elderly, nearly blind man had been ill for a long time—stomach ulcers for more than twenty years, kidney problems, glaucoma and creeping blindness. He wore dark glasses all the time, had been blind in one eye for most of Paul's short life, and now the other eye had lost the ability to discern form: only light and colour registered. William walked with a stick all the time now: the child would guide him, walk with him. The family would always walk on the promenade, the seafront, in the afternoon. However, William became breathless quickly and often and needed to stop to recover—Paul would dance around him, pulling his jacket.

"Panty, Panty, come on, please!"

The name stuck because William moved slowly and panted to catch his breath when they were out walking. The thought that this condition was permanent was beyond the conceptual abilities of this small child. Likewise, the very idea that he might be terminally ill was utterly alien to Paul—William would get better, they would continue as friends forever. Because, however difficult walking was, talking, exploring books, the two were inseparable. When William slept in his armchair after the seafront walk, Paul would sit on the floor at Williams's feet, quietly content.

Paul started full time in the January; later that month saw his fifth birthday. He enjoyed being at school, working in the class, reciting rhymes about the alphabet and the sound of letters. He began to make friends, but he did not like dinner times, sitting in the hall with all the older children, it was all a bit much. Already, even amongst these five- to seven-year-old children there was a pecking order, threats and intimidation. Most children at the council school were from poor families, from the council estate, and those who either did not live in the small suburbs of Greenhill or Bengeworth, or lacked the influence to get their children into a nicer primary school. For example, the Church of England schools in Merstow Green or in Bengeworth—or the private school in Greenhill. Most children at Swann Lane (a name used to refer to both the infants' and junior schools) were looked down on. The comment as often spoken with a sneer: you only go to Swann Lane!

Paul stood against the classroom wall. It was mid-morning play and he leant against the cold metal panels on the outside of his classroom. The frost had not relented, it had not released its grip; even the roof of the junior school was covered with a thin white dusting. The sun was bright, but failed in its strength that February morning, as he stood in his little camel-coloured duffle coat, a scarf tightly wrapped around his neck, his hands thrust firmly in his pockets. The buildings seemed almost dark against the brightness of the sky. Sheets of ice covered the playground, most of the children were queuing up to have a go sliding on the ice. Many juniors had come through from their playground to slide as well, so had his sister, determined to have a slide. School mistress after school master would warn her not to run, to be careful when it was frosty. They would cry, "Beware, you will dislocate the hip!" Her little brother watched her: that smile, the guts, the mop of blonde hair. He loved her, wished he could be as brave as her. Neither teacher nor junior bully stopped her having her slide! He would often stand in the shadow, under the corrugated tin roof of the lean-to, praying that nobody would notice him, nobody would pick on him. Then when she had finished playing, instead of going off with the rest of her gang, she would take the hand of this shy and scared little boy, and support him.

Chapter Three, Beginnings: Infancy and Quietude

Seven

As spring turned to summer Paul's health improved only a little. He was now in a proper classroom in the main infant building, with windows looking directly on to the back of Wilmott's factory. He continued to be troubled by illness: throats and colds, chest infections, recurring tonsillitis. It was beginning to affect his schooling. As the autumn drew in he was away from school a lot. Meg was embarrassed at having to write notes all the time, so she pressed this on Dr. Appely. Yes, he would need his tonsils removed, but the doctor countered that the boy could not jump the waiting list, and besides he was young: he was not yet six years old! However, the woman at the surgery phoned the next morning to say that Matron would be writing to inform them when the child could go in—he would only have to wait a week or two.

The day came when his father drove him with his mother into Briar Close, the cottage hospital, not far from the railway. Paul settled himself in and waited. The sights, the smells, nurses, and bright lights, it was all new, so different. In the morning a doctor visited him, before the operation. He was dressed in a gown and they put a mask over his mouth—he breathed in, and the noise (the tinnitus) in his head got worse, much worse. Paul tried to fight off the sleep, then gave in, and sank away. Many hours later, much later, he lay still in his bed. Gradually he came round. The sound in his head was back to being his friend. Slowly he looked and took in, then slept; began to rouse himself again, then slept. Finally he woke—it was night time. He lay, hurting, stiff, and feeling very leaden, but his mind was bright, alert, aware. It was dark, but there was a faint glow of light (from the sister's office). The ward was quiet and still; all were sleeping. He felt loved for the first time in his life. He felt so loved and cared for, and he felt wanted. He felt a sense of preciousness welling up inside him. More than that, he felt smothered in love. There was no way he could articulate his feelings, being not yet six, but he was overwhelmed by a sense of grace, of *grace*, of muted joy. He desperately wanted to hang on to the moment, to the sense of joy, of inner warmth. For a long time he lay there. He began to become aware of a nurse asking him if he was alright, offering him a drink. He felt so loved—he just could not cope with it. He stayed in the hospital for a week, by which time he was ready and raring to be out and back to school, though he had a deep seated sense of foreboding about going home, but he ignored it and pushed those feelings away. The sense of love, of grace, almost of holiness, that he had felt on the night after the operation stayed with him, stayed with him like a comforter.

Returning to school, he settled in like any other child; but his progress was not good, nothing out of the ordinary, he was just a slow learner. He soon began to feel at home in the infants: painting at his easel in the hall; singing, or opening his mouth wide and pretending to sing; meeting up with Christine at play time and dinner time now that she was in the junior school, but being very afraid of the other children, particularly the rough and ready jungle warfare that went on in the playground. Despite his workload, Harry came to collect them mid-afternoon at the end of school; he was often rushing to get there having delivered goods to the railway. Christine would collect her little brother from his class and then run out to the front of the playground to the car or lorry waiting in the road. Christine was boisterous, lively, and lovable. She had lots of friends and was always in the forefront of whatever was going on; whatever was happening she knew about it or was involved in it—good or bad! So there were inevitably times when Harry would be waiting to pick the two children up, and he would be summoned in to see her class teacher, or the headmaster.

"Them teachers, what do they know?" Harry would mutter under his breath as he walked through the playground, Paul and Christine in tow.

When confronting them he would pull his cap off, stand there with his hands on his hips and talk back in very loud animated tones, complain that Christine was being picked on, and what about the others! Paul did not want to see these confrontations, he did not like seeing the anger—so he slipped away, he slipped outside. He did not understand what was going on between grown-ups in this grown-up world. So he would walk out, across the small playground in front of the Infant School and then out through the side gate, the infant entrance. Here in Chapel Street, which led down from Swann Lane, there was an embankment made of smooth red bricks about six feet in height, sloping from the wall of Wilmott's factory, sloping at a forty-five degree angle to the road. He felt safe and secure here—he was hidden from the school, hidden from these grown-ups. Nobody really noticed him there, or at least, nobody approached him. Likewise when he stood with his parents or near a teacher, no one really noticed him: he was learning invisibility. This had its advantages—he could miss out on nasty jobs, he could listen in and hear what grown-ups were saying, he could easily slip away without being noticed; but it was also like when he asked questions and no one answered him, he had learnt this early on. Paul would sit on this embankment, throw stones into the gutter, or slide down it, or just sit holding his head in his hands asking the noise—the tinnitus—in his head to be friendly or be quiet. Sometimes the noise would suddenly become louder in one ear then travel, fly over his head, to the other ear: he giggled to himself when this happened. Other times he felt a pressure in one ear as though something was blowing up inside his head. This he did not like.

Although his tonsils had been removed the previous winter, Paul was still

Chapter Three, Beginnings: Infancy and Quietude

prone to chest infections, sore throats, and now an assortment of childhood illnesses: recurring mumps, measles, and so forth. His attendance in middle infants was sporadic. However, whilst off school that summer he went one June evening with his parents to Wickhamford to get a kitten, the owner's cat having produced a large litter. The Broadleys had two cats before—both had been tough strays that had at separate times simply walked into and taken over the territory of the sheds as a most desirable residence, being well stocked with mice and voles, and boasting warm dry corners to curl up in during the day. Timmy, the new kitten was really for the whole family but eventually all acknowledged he was Paul's—besides Timmy had laid claim to the boy. The cat and boy adored each other from the start. With recurring illness Paul got to know the cat intimately. Timmy slept on his bed, Paul brushed him, played with him, fed him, loved him. The feeling was mutual. On long summer evenings they would lie together in the bushes spying the territory, looking for birds, or other cats, and watching people coming and going down the lanes.

Because of his sporadic attendance at school the child was not learning to read and write like the others. By the time he was in the top infants he was sitting firmly in the back three rows of the class. All children were sitting in specified desks—the brightest and cleverest in the front, the slow learners and illiterates at the rear; already children were being talent spotted and groomed for the few grammar school places that would be available. Paul had mastered a handful of words and could read a few books, which were borrowed from the class for five-year-old children, books that were kept in the cupboard, not kept on show. He was not alone; there were probably about ten or twelve at a similar level. He was a slow learner; in addition his progress at school was limited by his illness.

Paul had just returned from a particularly bad and long and troublesome bout—he had been experiencing great difficulty with his breathing, and had been away for three weeks. (It was not until he was an adult that it was spotted by a hospital that he was in fact asthmatic, had been born so.) At playtime they were all standing between the bomb shelter and the main junior school building, about fifteen or eighteen from his class. They were all talking about when they would be going up to the juniors, it would be soon—when they came back from the summer holidays. He tried to join the conversation.

"You don't know what we're on about. You don't belong to our class, you're never 'ere" was the response.

It was true—he didn't feel part of the class, he had been away so much. The others moved away, ignoring him, most distancing themselves from him.

Chapter Four
Love: Sickness and Death

> ~ *"The little hills rejoice on every side.*
> *The pastures are clothed with flocks;*
> *the valleys also are covered with grain.*
> *They shout for joy! They sing!"*
> PSALM 65:12b–13

One

The clouds were piling up from the southwest: patches of clear blue sky were soon obscured by the voluminous white, ever changing, never holding shape for more than a fraction of a second. The great banks of white and grey clouds rose, reformed, spread, grew, mushroomed, broke up, and reformed—but all slowly, ever so slowly, so that most people did not notice, simply took the sky as static, never changing. The breeze wafted across the track, creating spiralling little eddies of dust. The track or lane sloped down towards the brook. Beyond the brook the land rose gently, then sharply into the orchard-covered slopes of Longdon Hill. A horse, harrow, and man were barely discernible on the southern tip of the low hill, which from this angle looked like a triangle of patchwork tagged onto the orchards.

The wind buffeted and blew, with the clouds piling across. To the north of the lane, bent over long-handled hoes, two women and a man stood, their clothes flapping wildly in the breeze, thin wisps of hair dancing from the sides of the headscarves worn by the women. They worked in a line with the man ahead of the two women each to a furrow rhythmically chopping at the soil and weeds

Chapter Four, Love: Sickness and Death

between the rows of tiny cabbage plants. The man stopped, raised his head, and arched his back, stretching up as he did so, and placed a hand at the base of his spine. His eyes lighted directly in front of him onto the backs of some houses, about four hundred yards away, which formed the edge of the newly built council estate. Over to the man's left was the new lane, dusty now from the dry weather. He placed the wooden staff of the hoe in the crook of his arm, took out tobacco paper, and rolled a cigarette, rolled with dexterity in less than a minute, unaffected by the blustery breeze. He lit-up, bent back over his hoe, and proceeded to continue with his day's task. Rising in the distance, beyond the brook was the blue-green haze of the North Cotswold escarpment. Over behind them, with a smooth wide curve, was Bredon Hill. The three continued hoeing rhythmically; the two women by now had overtaken the man, who had stopped again to relight his cigarette.

Later in the day, after noon, the weather began to change; the clouds continued to pile up from the direction of the Vale of Gloucester and the Severn estuary, pushed on by westerly winds, channelling past Bredon, and into the funnel that was the Vale of Evesham. However, the wind had dropped, and as the breeze fell the clouds darkened. Bredon Hill became obscured, covered in a heavy grey mist of low cloud—as the old saying ran "when Bredon Hill puts on its hat, men of the Vale beware of that." The rain was not long in coming. First came the cool slap on the skin of damp air. The rain came in sheets, each washing across the land, the small cabbage plants waving madly as the rain pinned them to the ground. The three labourers hoeing simply carried on. The air still smelt dry: they were right, just as soon as the sky had darkened it began to clear, initially as small patches of grey-blue began to break in amongst the blanket of cloud. But then the grey began to give way to a peachy, silver-grey and white as the rain eased and the shower began to abate. The sky remained overcast, but with a high cloud layer, and a few patches of muted blue to reassure that it was still summertime. The breeze picked up a little, lifting some of the newly fallen rain from leaves, blades of grass, and crops, sending it tumbling over the ground like dancing dew.

Scrambling through the hedgerow onto the lane came two children. Both about the same height, the girl holding the boy's hand and leading the way. The girl had shoulder-length fair, wavy hair lifting in the breeze. She looked all around her. The boy had short red hair. He looked to the ground, kicked over some stones, then stopping, pulling on his sister's arm, to crouch by the grass and wild flowers growing by the side of the lane to look at some small happening. The girl pulled her hand free and ran ahead.

"Race you to the brook" she called back.

The boy stilled his reverie, got up, and with a wobbling gait that belied his six years of age, ran after the girl. She, with longer legs, stayed ahead of him. Besides, she was twenty or so months older than him. However, she ran with a pronounced limp—as if the left leg was not as confident as the right. Breathless, the girl ran past the three land workers, blithely continuing their hoeing. She ran on to where the lane gradually sloped towards a patch of darker growth: a meandering line of thick grass, cow parsley, clumps of May flower, green bushes, the occasional stunted willow or yew, and the ubiquitous hawthorn and blackthorn so characteristic of the Charity. The girl skidded past the curve of the lane where it turned sharply right, headed straight on for a few yards, past a smallholding planted up with rows of runner beans and young parsley plants, over a slight rise in the lane marking a small bridge over the brook, to disappear into the thicket. The boy ran, then walked, then trotted, then walked trying to catch up with her. He paused for a moment to watch the land workers hoeing then he gazed around him and then he slowly shuffled down to where his sister had disappeared into the thicket. She was sitting on the bottom of four wooden steps that were set into the bank of the brook. From where she was sitting she could see the lane in front of her and watched the slow progress of her brother down the lane.

This point in the brook was one of many where gardeners had set a small number of steps into the bank, the purpose of which was to give access to the waters: with care, a man or woman could step down and place a crate of onions, or a boat of leeks, into the brook, leave them soaking, then return to wash them. The bank on the opposite side had been artificially widened to create a smallholding pond, with a length of iron railing thrust into the sides and bed of the brook to prevent the crates floating off downstream. Paul and Christine sat on the bottom step, surrounded by the thicket, gazing into the brook, there were no crates floating there at this moment. They played idly with a stick in the water.

"Do you think there's any tadpoles?"

"No", said Paul, "no, they be all gone now. They'll be grow'd up!"

"Can't we look?"

"Yes, why not!" and before he'd finished this answer, he was up to his knees in the cold brown water, flicking water towards his sister as he did so.

The search was, of course, in vain. Early in the spring they had proudly returned from the brook with jars of tadpoles. For days Paul would watch them. Only to find one morning they had disappeared with no explanation. Now, of course, in the brook, they would be lucky to find any frogs, let alone tadpoles: most would have migrated upstream. The children were screened in on all sides: the steps were set in a thicket, while on the other side of the bank there stood a line of tall mature cow parsley, with its stems and branches ordered like some

Chapter Four, Love: Sickness and Death

giant engineering project with, surmounted on the ends of the slenderest stems, hundreds of the tiniest white flowers, forming greenish white triangular cups. All was still and damp from the rain, and now that the afternoon was drawing in, the dampness rose, and hung as a thin mist around the brook.

The two children slowly made their way back up the lane, moving at such a slow pace for fear that the day would end. They passed the three workers, still chopping at the dirt and weeds between the rows. The clouds were now patches of warm grey, almost brown-grey, set amidst a heavy deep mauve-grey sky, while the breeze brought ever more clouds piling up from the southwest. The boy stood in the shadow of a cloud and within seconds found he was in the gentle brightness again, then the shade returned, such was the scurrying of the wind-born clouds. He giggled, and looked at his sister. He loved her and felt safe with her. They laughed and giggled as they explored around some of the sheds bordering the lane, peering in to see an assortment of wooden boxes, crates, tools, string, and muddle. Sometimes they even saw a wearily sleeping, worker. They both looked skyward. The cloudbank was becoming thicker: Bredon was again covered. The wind became sharper, slapping their faces with a new dampness.

"It's going to rain Christine. Christine, it's going to, it is, I know it," the boy said so proudly.

That night, it was to rain continuously till early morn.

Two

These two children lived on the land, grew up on the land. The boy was quiet, observant, and reflective. He was the sort of child who would stand aside rather than join in; observe and listen rather than talk. From an early age he explored imaginary worlds within the geography of his mind. He soon learned that these worlds were safer and often righter than the world outside. Not that he disliked the real world. The rest of his family would often find him either in the corner of the front parlour room, or his bedroom, snuggled up, talking to his cat, Timmy. Or they would find him in some corner of a ramshackle shed fabricating models of ships and airplanes from card, or sat amongst the flowers and bushes drawing worlds amongst the dirt—imagining roads, hills, rivers, and woods. As he became a little older, they would find him sat squat, or lying amongst the hedgerows surrounding the smallholding, gazing up at the tall architecture of dew-laden cow parsley. In the house these imaginary worlds would be fuelled by books. He could not read, but would find pictures to look at, imagine himself in that world, imagine what was happening, and drift off. Books were extremely rare.

Neither of his parents was educated in the sense of being bookish. His father firmly believed they were a total waste of money. Meg was too busy running the home and looking after his sister to worry about books. Both parents would have been only too glad and proud to show their small collection of books to any visitor. But the books lived in a small glass-fronted bookcase in the front room—a room only used for a few days at Christmas; the rest of the year it was kept immaculate, smelling always of polish. The room and its furnishing were presented as a showpiece, a representation of happy domesticity. If the vicar called—he was sat in this room, not in the back room, the general living room, as a rare break in protocol! Paul would often get these books out and gaze through them, but was often chided for moving them, or for causing more dusting. However, different rules applied when they visited Meg's parents in Weston-super-Mare: then he shared books with William. William sat there quietly with dignity and grace. William, would talk gently of things he had done, places he had been, and Paul would listen intently. William would get his grandson to bring out the atlas. He would talk of places in Africa he had worked. The boy could figure out the shape of the countries from what William said.

Once, the whole family went out to the back garden of this neat little Edwardian house to stand beneath the trellis, and pose for a photograph. Meg and Harry loitered in the kitchen while William gently held the boy's hand, talking to him about the garden to try to disguise the dark whispers coming from the kitchen. Then when the couple came out, all stood with smiles while Harry readied himself with the camera. Paul just stood, looking down at the ground, sulking, despondent, puzzled at what was going on. He did not feel right about what was happening. Here they were, all stood smiling; but that was not how his mum and dad were. Didn't Panty—William—know that? The boy sulked, did not want to be part of the photograph. Harry proceeded with the snap: and there they were, all smiling, as right as rain, except for William, stood stiffly with his dark glasses covering his nearly blind eyes, and his hands on the boy's shoulders. The picture was of a happy family, the pretence of happiness, except Paul stood in the front, head bent low, his face to the ground.

Paul and Christine were as different as chalk and cheese—copper and brass the Reverend Herbert would call them: she with fair yellow hair, the other with a shock of red hair. He was so different from his sister, they were like two halves of a whole: that which she lacked in her character, he had. That which he was lacking in, she would provide. They often made little homes in amongst this world: deep in a tall thick hedgerow, deep amongst the hawthorn and blackthorn around the Charity, moving in with bits of old material, a tin mug, spying out for people passing, planning how they would eat, cook, clean, sleep, then returning home

Chapter Four, Love: Sickness and Death

in time for tea. Across the lane from their father's smallholding was a crop of mature asparagus—often called 'gras, or even "asparagrass". The plants grew out of evenly banked ridges. Each ridge was about a foot high, eighteen inches wide, and was complemented by a similarly proportioned furrow. In the spring, men and women were up before dawn to gently cover the newly emerged asparagus tips with soil to protect them from birds—hence the ever growing ridge over the roots and emerging stem; this also ensured a tender bud and white stem to the asparagus. Each morning for about two or three weeks in the spring, Paul, if he was awake, would look out of his window and see men walk down the lane: he would listen to the sound of muted chatter, the sound of their hobnails on the stone track, their breath mistily drifting on the air, intermingled with the smoke from a Woodbine. He would watch them, bent double, gently heaping the soil up from the furrow, to cover the newly emerged 'gras tip. Then after about two to three weeks it was ready for cutting. But not all: some shoots had to be left to grow and mature during the summer, to provide strength for the rootstock. Those shoots left to grow would reach a height of three to four feet, forming a bushy plant of rich green feathery fronds; beautiful, silky, and soft to touch.

Where the tops of the plants spread out they met over the middle of the furrow, forming a continuous vault—a vault some three-and-a-half to five feet in height if the growing season had been good. The woody stems from which these fronds grew, and the thin lattice tracery of green, looked for all intents and purposes like the vault of a cathedral. In mid to late summer Paul and Christine would crawl along the furrow, beneath this lattice tracery, or they would run along on all fours, in parallel furrows, racing each other. Then he would flop over onto his back, lie along the length of the furrow, gazing up at the vault of green latticed tracery, shooting up and over from the white and brown woody stems, flowing in a perfect curve, with stems and fronds progressively getting smaller and thinner till they met, touched tips, and intermingled over the depth of the furrow, the rich deep green of the lower fronds giving over to bright greens nearer the top of the plant. The boy lay for what seemed an eternity, watching as the tracery of the vault gently wafted in the breeze, the intermingled fronds twisting, parting, and re-joining to form new patterns. He would raise his hand, gently brush the fronds, unable to believe the softness and delicacy of this tracery. He would lie, happy, surrounded by this green organic vault, feeling safe, not secluded, for he could see the sky, hear voices. He would hear a scurrying, then appearing over the top of the ridge to the left of his head was a tiny vole. He lay so still, so quiet that the tiny creature descended the ridge, puzzled by this enormous blockage across its route, sniffed the air, sniffed at the blockage, probably smelled a trace of cat on Paul, and shot off down the furrow at the fastest pace it could muster. By now he would have got his breath back, so he lay still, silent, watching, smelling, feeling the gentle breeze on his cheek, cooling his cheek exactly in time with the moving vaulted tracery above him. His reverie was broken by a voice:

"Paul, Paul! Where are you?"

It was his sister calling. He pulled himself up and round on all fours, and proceeded back down the furrow, allowing the lower fronds to brush over his face and arms as he worked his way back along to the lane. Together they would potter slowly along the lane, or along the narrow grass ridges which separated one holding from another, past the brook, the tadpoling steps as they called them, till the afternoon gave way to evening, and it was time to then proceed aimlessly back along the dusty lane, scramble over the hedgerow, and down onto their father's land—home territory.

The evening was drawing on. Christine went on ahead; he loitered around the sheds, watched as a vole scurried out from amongst the crates stacked against the side, wondered if it knew the vole that had come and sniffed him back in the asparagus fern. Walking slowly across the deep, dried ruts in front of the shed, pushing his way through the raspberry bushes that separated the land from the back garden, Paul felt reluctant to go home, make the final journey across the lawn and up the passageway into the kitchen. It was as if something was holding him back; he had sensed happiness, joy, but did not want to leave it. This small, thin, shy, and immature boy could not rationalize these feelings but somewhere deep in him he did not associate home, inside this house, with the feelings of joy and happiness he had just felt lying amongst the asparagus fern, or the feelings he had when he sat at the feet of William Riley. He reluctantly walked across the lawn, turned and looked back at the raspberry bushes, then up to the sky. He threw out his arms and twirled round and round, and round again, spinning with his arms outspread, till his legs gave way and crumpled beneath him in this giddy, delirious, giggling stupor. He lay on the grass on this cool, damp, almost magical summer's evening, looking at the heavens. The sky was clear, perfectly and completely clear. The child lay, looking up at the deep blue firmament, the thin veil between him and the tiny twinkling stars beyond. Slowly he rolled his head over and let his eyes follow the sky down, through the deep ultramarine blue, through perfect graduations to the rich azure blue near the horizon. The dampness, now soaking through his shirt, brought him back to earth.

He got up, crossed the remainder of the lawn, like the Rubicon between two worlds, then he entered the deep passage, walked past the outhouses on his right and to the kitchen door on the left. Pushing gently, and stepping up over the deep stone step, he crossed the terracotta quarry tiles to sit on the floor between the larder and hallway doors. Paul sat transfixed. He had returned home full of

Chapter Four, Love: Sickness and Death

intense joyous feelings, pregnant with the pureness and vibrancy of the natural world of God's glorious creation; but he was now confronted with the sight of rage: his parents' rage—his mother screaming and shouting, his father's roaring anger smashing and breaking anything in reach. He tried to hang on to these feelings of joy; he was bursting to tell what he felt.

The little boy listened; he had no choice as retort followed retort between these two people. He found it hard to think of them as his parents during such rows. As always, the row was not over a particular difference of opinion or aim. The row was not over whether they should go out, or what colour tablecloth they should buy. No: the root was much deeper. It was as if their whole life together was one long row. It was as if they continued on from where they were last rowing, interjection followed interjection, rebuff followed rebuff, spite matched spite, hateful sneer mounted on hateful sneer, always about what the other was supposed to have said, or what was implied in the subtlety of how something quite incongruous had been said. Each partner dredged the depths to find the smallest, tiniest little detail or imperfection in the other to then drag to the surface, sharpen with one's wits into a weapon, and then spit out as a gibe to try to loosen the sureness of the other. Ultimately the aim was to hurt, to destroy, to ridicule and reduce the other to a sour humility, a false humility. The aim of these exchanges was to win over the other—win petty little points; nothing, absolutely nothing in the life of the other was out-of-bounds. Absolutely nothing: the smallest detail of sexual relations, sexual prowess, family background, weaknesses of character, friends, failings within the home. Then there were the children: they were the ultimate weapon, playing each other off on who cared the most for the children, who really wanted them! There were no deterrents in this home; no weapon to hold back and threaten with, all was fair play: the dirtiest, meanest, most underhand remarks were all used equally. Indeed, as this store of weaponry was used up, each descended lower and lower in the depths of what was unspeakable: and spoke it. Inflection was all-important; both were becoming masters of the sneer, the jibe of hate.

There was nothing creative in these exchanges, nothing of letting off steam. Both parties were incompatible; this is why the rows seemed rounds in one long row. It was as if they were rowing about their very incompatibility—trying to prove how they should never have married by slagging each other off. Harry was the stronger in these arguments: he was taller, more powerful. He could out-shout Meg, but she was becoming the dominant partner in the underhand jibe. However, she was wedded to the idea that all she was saying was the truth, that he was innately inferior, so was his family: she could not see that her sense of superiority, coupled with the use of any remark denigrating him and his family, was in reality no more than lower middle class snobbery parading itself as self-righteousness. They argued over the housework, delegation of duties—he claiming she should get involved in his work, help out when they were short of hands, tying onions, picking beans; she responding that there were plenty of women round Fairfield to do that sort of thing! She would counter with how he spent most of his evenings across the road at his father's, and consequently how he was neglecting the children. This was possibly the lowest point reached. She had more contact with the children simply through looking after them; after all she was their mother. As a result they would start to look on him as the ogre in all this. But Paul could never quite believe in this simplification: that it was his father that was wrong, and that she was right, and that any means was justified by his mother to counter what he said and did. The child could not marshal this feeling into thoughts, or words: but there was a deep-seated underlying sense of the truth and of justice in him that in some ways caused him to withdraw. Also, as his childhood drew on, this caused much righteous indignation and anger in him.

When the row reached this point, unless the couple had already come to blows and the row had ended prematurely with Harry storming out of the house, sitting or standing transfixed in the kitchen, only a few paces from the rowing couple, Paul felt himself slowly, smoothly being sucked into himself. Gradually he lost the sense of meaning in the words; he could still hear the violent ripostes, but it was as though a wall of glass slowly appeared around him: an immunity screen. He would see the blow—nearly always by Harry to his mother—see the blood, smell the blood, feel the revulsion in him, sense his nose and mouth curl up, fight the creeping tide of nausea, as the couple gripped and struggled with each other, feel a dizziness, a dark, grating numbness. Sometimes Paul would fall against them shouting "Stop it! Stop it! Stop it!"; other times he would fall in a heap on the floor, huddle against the kitchen grate and in muted sobs, convulse with his head tucked against his knees, arms locked around his legs—locked in the foetal position, the muted sobs disguising the battle within, against a dizzy, suffocating, rasping darkness, fighting desperately to keep hold of himself, not to fizzle out, or disappear. He crouched there, wishing his ears could stop hearing, but then there was the constant sound in his head, the tinnitus, which at these times raged and screamed in his mind and merged with the pain so that the noise (of the tinnitus) was the sound that a severe headache would make if it could make a sound; and the pain in his brain was what the noise would be like if it felt. The vertigo would intensify—that is, the world around him started spinning. He would close his eyes but he still sensed himself spinning, spinning, growing thinner and thinner, like he was being sucked down. He wished it would all stop—the noise in his

Chapter Four, Love: Sickness and Death

head, the grating rasping dizziness and being sucked down, spinning. He wished he was not there, wished he had never been born: not suicidal thoughts—no, wishing, even praying that he had never been born, never even started on this life, fed by the remarks made by his father that good money had been wasted on trying to get rid of him before he was born. . . .

Then he would find his mother pulling him up, trying to comfort him, trying to unravel the tightly knotted arms and legs, calming, soothing,

"It's all right, he's gone, it's alright he's gone . . . come now, you can stop crying now, come he's gone . . ."

Paul withdrew.

Not physically, but inwardly. Yes he had gone, the row had stopped, but he did not feel right about it. He felt dirty; dirty and unclean; soiled; not the same. He accepted his mother's soothing, nigh smothering. He began to associate the loss of rows, the lack of conflict, with his father's absence. But something did not feel right when his mother said, "he's gone, it's all over," as if "he" was the sole cause of these rows. A small boy of six could not judge between the two warring parties and decide whether everything each party had said was permissible, or whether the good was compromised for the sake of a retort. He just withdrew—passively accepted his mother's cuddles, but withdrew, not trusting this world, this life. Earlier in his life he had run out of the kitchen, up the front garden path, screaming, crying, bellowing. By the time his seventh birthday approached, he just stayed put, suffered the sights . . . and withdrew.

Three

Night time was when many of the sights and sounds he had witnessed returned and preyed on him: the sight and smell of injury. The violence of nature around him did not worry him, but, the violence at home did. It threatened his security, left him puzzled—puzzled by his love for his parents, his need for security, stability, and peace. One dream kept returning. He was with his parents and sister walking down a shopping street in nearby Cheltenham. Although he started off holding his mother's hand, somehow they became parted. Then he would look ahead and see his mother, father, and Christine walking about a few yards ahead. He was following them but the space between them grew. Try as hard as he could, he could not keep up, the gap widened. He started to walk faster, almost run, but the gap widened, widened; he called out but they could not hear, people filled up the gap between them; he was slowly, inexorably being left behind. No one could hear him. He would wake, feeling so sad, so empty, so cold, almost as though he was going to disappear, be sucked in on himself. He would call for his mother, but she was busy downstairs in the kitchen. The muted sounds of a row would drift up from the kitchen. Paul would lie, trying to find something to think on, or to look at. He would look at the narrow strip of plaster at the top of the window, the rebate that linked the window frame to the wall, and focus his eyes on it. But it would go blurred, almost as if it was moving, then the silky smooth cream of the plaster and paint changed into a python, slowly slithering along. He turned over and buried his head in the pillow. Timmy would come up, the door creaking gently as the cat pushed its way in. He would become aware of the cat's rasping tongue, gently licking his face, so he rolled over and hugged the cat close to his chest, and the two would drift off to sleep. Often the dreams would be so vivid as to wake the small child. Sometimes there he would be with his sister, walking across their father's land, with wild flowers growing where a crop had been harvested, their colour so vibrant and clear he wanted to stretch out and touch the brilliant red poppies, or velvety blue-mauve of a harebell, but as he stretched out, he woke. He lay there desperately wanting to get back to the dream.

On one Saturday morning, after Harry had gone out slamming the door, and the noise of rowing had ceased, Paul slowly got out of bed, wiped the frozen condensation from the inside of the pane of glass, placed his eye to the window and looked. Looked and gazed at the wonder of the icy green-white colour of trees, the ice-covered back garden, the whitish-brown that fringed the lawn, and further off, the steel grey of the sheds and blue-green of the patch of leeks growing beyond the raspberry bushes. He slowly, almost invisibly, slipped through the gap between the door and its frame, descending the stairs to see his sister just ahead of him walking through the hall. Their mother was trying to hold back the tears, trying to stifle the sobs, the feeling of desperation. Hugging and kissing the children, she pulled up two chairs from the kitchen table, placing them close to the kitchen grate. Paul put his toes against the grey enamelled side of this tall, hot, grate, watching as his mother lifted the lid, after first putting the curled end of the handle into the squared depression. She poked the coals, raising sparks that jumped, flitted, sparkled through the opening, up against the tall, round, smooth pipe that took the smoke away through the wall into the chimney-breast. He looked on the smoothness of the pipe, felt a sense of thinness coming over him, creeping, suffocating, then he shook his head, looked at his sister, and giggled as their toes touched and tickled. His mother, rushed to the larder, returning with a small packet of fizzlers. Upon discovering they were a bit soft and stale, she placed them onto of the kitchen grate, giving them time to warm, and freshen. This small boy felt an almost precious holiness to the moment, sitting there against the grate on this cold February morning. The fizzlers were duly declared freshened up and eaten lovingly one by one.

Chapter Four, Love: Sickness and Death

Once, as if to apportion time with the children to each other as a you're-not-spending-enough-time-with-her-or-him, Paul found himself bundled into the cab of the ochre-brown Austin lorry. Peering over the top of the door, with J. H. BROADLEY & SON MARKET GARDENER & MERCHANT EVESHAM painted in cream flowing letters on the door panel, he could just see the passing landscape through the window. Progressing slowly, they drove on through roads and lanes, and thence down a bumpy track to a farm in Wormington, with a small round hill just over to the other side of the lorry, Dumbleton Hill. Fascinated with this new world, and then finding himself inside the box on the cab roof, he could view the trees, hedgerows, fields, the hill, and the cows in the fields. His eyes turned sharply to the smell assaulting his nostrils from the rear. Thump, another shovelful landed; thump, another. Sticking out of the piles of brown manure were little straws, falling or poking this way and that. Fascinated with the sweet, acrid smell, once his brain got used to it, he watched, as the steam rose from the growing heap on the bed of the lorry, wispily circulating and spiralling into ever new patterns, blending with the breath, exhaled with a grunt from the farm labourers, piling the manure onto the tail of the lorry with long curled pitchforks. Once the loading was complete the lorry slowly lurched back down the lane swaying on its springs, the acrid smell wafting away behind it. Soon the lorry had returned to the main Cheltenham Road, and proceeded past Bredon Hill and back up to Hinton Green, then along to Gypsies' Corner. Shortly after, the lorry slowed to walking pace, then lurched left and down across the hardcore-filled ditch and through the grey weathered gate posts, and onto the "top ground."

This ground was rented by the Broadleys from Christchurch College, Oxford. The ground was considered amongst the best arable land surrounding the town, because of its good fertility. One part near the main road suffered from bad drainage (the Cheltenham Road cut through the watershed, for this land actually drained into the Charity Brook). The Broadleys hired a large dredger to dig through the top soil, to place drainage pipes in the flooded gravel that provided a continuous bed, about ten feet deep beneath the entire ground. Paul watched, fascinated by the machine, only then to be horror struck as he saw his father, down in the excavated hole, treading and sinking into the waterlogged gravel. Harry had gone in to move a broken pipe, but was being sucked down, and down, into the gravel: he was going to drown. The realization struck Paul like being hit by a train—his feelings about his parents were confused and contradictory, but like any young child he saw his parents as the ultimate security. A rope was thrown to Harry; a second one thrown around his head and shoulders. Thankfully he was pulled out to safety. But the image of this scene, the fear it generated, kept him awake at night. When he spoke of it to his mother she only commented that it was a pity Harry had not drowned.

The lorry drove up onto the ground. The sun was drawing down on the horizon, over towards the ridge of Haselor Hill. The summer's evening was still, pregnant with expectation. Over to the southwest was Bredon Hill, in full view. The light caught the gentle undulations of the hill, highlighting woods, moorland pasture, dry stone walls, all bathed in a golden evening light. The lorry proceeded at walking pace, the differential and axles wailing and moaning at the slow pace. The lorry rolled from side to side as two men rhythmically pitchforked the manure off the back of the lorry onto the ground. Following at the same pace were two more men who spread the manure around with the timeless measure of men scything wheat. As the lorry reached the ridge, the watershed leading to the River Isbourne, the whole procedure started again, this time returning towards the Cheltenham Road. Paul watched from afar. He had crawled out of the cab on the initial run up the ground, to stand afar and gaze on at the sight. Paul watched transfixed with a sense of preciousness, holiness, desperately welling up inside him: he wanted to grasp the moment and keep it. He looked to the sky, saw the thin wisps of cloud high up, he wanted to reach up and touch them; he could see occasional stars peeping through the deep ultramarine of the heavens. He lowered his eyes to the horizon, to Bredon Hill, then lower still to the lorry moving along the ground, keeping rhythm with the men working. Steam rose from the piles of manure spread over the ground. He saw steam like smoke rising from impish little flames, dancing gaily up and across from the piles. He desperately wanted to hang on to the moment, to a sense of joy, of inner warmth. It was like a sense of grace pervading the moment.

Paul stood by Sam, an old hand who had worked for the Broadleys for years. Samuel Tobias Isaiah Cooper was tall, thin, but very muscular, gaunt, but genial, affable, and always trying to make peace between people. Like the Old Testament priests and prophets of his namesakes, he held to God's law, carried the Bible in his head, from which he would quote readily in any situation—the "good book" held life's answers. He dressed in the old clothes—collarless, striped, twill shirt, heavy corduroy trousers, held by braces, tweed jacket, always with one button done up, a jacket now shapeless from the years of wear, years of rain, of sun, of labour, and of toil. His face was tanned, rugged, bristling with a poorly shaven shadow, and like all gardeners around the vale he wore a cap—now pulled into all sorts of shapes and contortions by years of use, yet even in high summer, if he was working in his shirt sleeves, he would have his cap on. Paul looked up at him, at his height, his strength, and felt he belonged: belonged to the scene, to the land, to the rhythm. In a timeless, measureless rhythm, the action continued before him—like it had for thousands years (with the exception of a motorized lorry in the place of a horse-drawn cart), the scene was almost Biblical as men

Chapter Four, Love: Sickness and Death

pitch-forked the straw and manure onto the land, while the other men spread the goodness around: the vale and the land laughed and sang of the fecundity and bounty of God's good creation.

Four

The journeys to Birmingham Children's Hospital continued, Paul's mother and father looking distraught, puzzled, worried after each visit. There were other journeys; much longer ones. The family would go to visit Meg's parents in Weston-super-Mare, usually on a Saturday or a Sunday. All would pile into the old Ford Pilot, duly loaded with gifts of fruit and vegetables, then they would set off down the Cheltenham Road, Harry stopping by the top ground just to see it was all alright, or to confirm some point verbally with a casual worker employed to tend the crops. Then the real journey would start: down alongside the Cotswold escarpment, the hills ever on their left, down through Hinton Green, Sedgeberrow, the Tibble Stone at Teddington Cross, through Bishop's Cleeve, Cheltenham, and Gloucester. The first break was here in Gloucester. Harry would pull the car up near the docks, Meg would get the flask and biscuits from the boot, and all would sit in the car, still wrapped up in overcoats, hats, scarves, or caps—their Sunday best. Or sometimes this first break would be in the car park to the side of Gloucester Cathedral, the view being an important part of these breaks. They proceeded down through the Vale of Berkeley on the old A38, still with the Cotswold escarpment on their left, but now Paul could catch glimpses of the River Severn on their right: tantalizing glimpses of the dark brown river, with occasional silver white flashes as the sun caught the water, surrounded by low green meadows. The journey proceeded, with occasional rows and disagreements between Harry and Meg, and with stops for the children to relieve themselves. The countryside passed at a regular, ordered pace—fifty miles per hour, no more, no less, providing conditions would allow. On they would go, over the River Frome, on through Woodford, Thornbury, Almondsbury. Sometimes the car would stop suddenly, then reverse, and Harry would get out looking at a roadside fruit and vegetable stall, stand there, push his cap back with one hand and scratch his head, then return muttering about how on earth anyone could sell produce for that sort of money. Bristol was the next stop, when more biscuits, or sandwiches, and another flask were consumed. Then a toilet stop by the Clifton Suspension Bridge—walking over the bridge and gazing down over the side to the tiny cars and boats below, while Harry drove the car over for them to meet him on the other side.

Longman's Charity

They travelled on down into Somerset. Paul could not wait to see William and to be with him. It didn't matter about dinner, or what they were to do in the afternoon—just to be with him was enough. They would all go for a walk on the promenade, William in his Cream Panama and white jacket, with Meg on his arm to help guide him; or they might walk along the old pier to Birnbeck Island. Here the boy would see a steam paddle ship, and pull on Panty's arm, asking if they could go on it—go away to sea on it. Maybe they would see the lifeboat launched down its slipway from the pier and island. Then they would walk slowly back along the pier, Paul holding onto William's hand as he walked; they stopped for him to recover, then walked again. But soon it was time for tea. William would treat them all to tea in some nice hotel, maybe the Grand Atlantic. But all too soon it was time for home. Time to give William and Renée a farewell hug—then off, back up the A370, through Worle, Congresbury, Flax Broughton, and back to Bristol. Here, Harry would stop and get two large cabbage crates out of the boot and place them in the rear footwells; Meg would spread blankets over them once Harry had finished and before they had left the city, Paul and Christine were snuggled up on the makeshift bed, fast asleep. Dreams of the day, dreams of steam paddle ships, dreams of donkeys on the sand . . . dreams of William.

Paul would look forward for days, weeks, before these trips: he looked forward to seeing William, he looked forward to pouring over books with him, even though neither could read them. William could talk him through them, the red-headed grandchild would follow the frail elderly man's instructions and talk to him about what he had discovered; he looked forward to walking in the fresh sea air on the promenade with him. This child quite honestly preferred to be in the company of William Riley than in that of his own parents. William was a quiet, thoughtful gentleman, calm and tender; had always been—leastwise in the time he knew him. He responded to this like iron to a magnet. Meg often referred to Paul as being so like her father it was unbelievable, others who had known William Riley in Evesham commented on the similarity—Paul was his maternal grandfather's son more than his parent's son.

One day, when the journey was completed, he was shocked, horrified to find William in bed: in bed in the rear downstairs' room. Paul stood just inside the door in the darkened room, the curtains drawn: fearing to approach, not believing this was the same man. Renée came in and placed her hands on Paul's shoulders,

"You must not stop long; he sleeps most of the time now."

Paul approached slowly and took the frail elderly man's hand; it felt so thin and cold. The sun was bright beyond the curtains; it was a hot summer's day, yet William's hand was like ice. William's breathing was very shallow and irregular.

Chapter Four, Love: Sickness and Death

Paul whispered "Panty" quietly, convinced he had brought this state onto William because he had given him the nickname. William fought to catch his breath, and then rested, breathing ever so shallow breaths.

"Come Paul, we must let him rest."

Renée shepherded the boy out of the room.

To this puzzled child, William had always been frail, delicate of health, blind—he was sixty-eight years of age when Paul was born, so that Paul took his state of health as normal. He had not stopped to think about whether he had always been like this, he simply expected everything to go on as it was, except he had this deeply rooted belief that the number of visits would increase, even that William would come and live with them or they with him. He went back into the front room with the others. After half-an-hour, whilst they were talking animatedly, he took his chance and stole quietly out, went back into the next door room and sat with his back against the wall, sitting as still as possible so as not to disturb William. After an indeterminate period of time—probably more than an hour—he felt a hand on his shoulder.

"You can stop for a moment, but he is really too unwell," came the reassuring words from his mother as she put her hand on the boy's shoulder.

Paul pleaded: "But I won't worry him, I'll just sit here, just for a moment, please, please!"

There was something holy, something precious, something still and beyond time as the grandson simply sat waiting on William, attending though unable to do anything to help the frail elderly gentleman. His mother forgot the time; Paul did not notice the time, just sat on the floor, his legs curled up under him in the darkened room while William rested, dozed, slipped in and out of consciousness. All Paul wanted to do was stay there, attending, waiting . . .

The next visit, a few weeks later William was not there. After dinner they went to visit him in Axbridge Hospital. His parents talked in hushed tones about a second stroke. Paul stood at the foot of the bed, holding onto the tubular steel bed frame with both hands, just looking, saying nothing, not moving . . . just watching. Two nurses tried unsuccessfully to give the frail old man some strawberries and cream. He could not take or swallow them. Then Paul found he was ushered out onto the veranda. It was a gloriously hot summer's day. The very earth sang, hummed with the heat. He hated the sun, hated the summer. Why should everyone be so happy when his Panty was not well! If only he could get close enough to hug him. Hug him just once more, but the nurses would not let him near. All he wanted to do was climb up onto the bed, hug him, and curl up with him.

Five

Paul sat on the grass, his back leaning against the sheds. It was a hot sultry day in early June. The boy looked longingly at Longdon Hill. He was thinking about William. He wanted to be with him. He wanted him to be better: desperately. There was so much he wanted to do and say to him. He now often ran through little conversations in his mind with him. Imagined how he could help him, where they could go, what they could see—or what Paul could see for him. He knew William was ill; knew his mother and father, and Renée, looked sad and grave when the subject came up. But Paul knew it would be alright; he knew Panty would get better. He really believed he would. How could it be otherwise? As he sat looking on the scene before his eyes, with the whole earth so full of re-birth, as new life both wild and contained (as in the crops) vibrated with joy, how could it be otherwise? He felt the miraculous wonder of the land, of creation; he was reassured by it. William would be alright. He talked to God about it. He had prayed to God that he would get better. He felt convinced William would be alright. It was just too unbelievable that he would not get better. He sat there. His classmates were all playing out and about together, but he stayed alone, thinking on William, convinced that because he was thinking on him, he would recover, he would get better.

There came a time when the phone was being used more and more in the evening. Usually it was used only for occasional local calls, but its main purpose was as a business phone (communicating with wholesalers in northern cities— Leeds, Newcastle, Gateshead, Manchester, or further afield to Glasgow), the phone being used in the early morning to check the safe arrival of goods and discuss the price obtained. Sometimes these calls were punctuated by a brusque exchange of words about not getting enough money or the quality of the goods not being up to standard, but telephones were too expensive a way of having a row. Harry would take the order for the next night's delivery by rail then end of call: no time for idle chat—it was essential to keep the calls to a minimum. Using the phone in the evening was new. Also his mother was using it. Often it would be someone ringing in. Paul grew suspicious; he found out from his mother it was Renée. His suspicions increased, particularly at the still quietness in his mother after these phone calls. Then on mid-summer's day, the phone rang, about half past seven in the evening. Paul stood near the living room door, so as to be near his mother. Between the words, quietly spoken there were small muted tears: his mother was crying. He knew. Paul knew; a dull cold emptiness crept over him. He heard the click from the phone, then his mother walking through the living room door.

Chapter Four, Love: Sickness and Death

"Mummy"

"Yes"

"Is William all right, please mummy, is Panty alright?"

"Oh yes, oh yes, he'll be fine now. He's gone to a better place, he's . . . yes, he's not in pain now. He's not suffering."

She lifted her hand, gently touching her eyes with her finger, then brushing her nose lightly.

"Yes Paul, he died, he's dead, only about an hour ago; Renée's gone home from the hospital. . . ."

The little child let go of his mother's hand, let it slip gently. Then giving her a big hug, pulling her head down to his level.

"Mummy I love you, I love you."

Then suddenly:

"Mummy, can I go see him, can I go with him, can I die too?"

"Oh, Paul, Paul, it's not that simple, you see, you see. . . . It's not as simple as that."

She looked at the child, frail, short; apart from his shock of red hair, she could see her father in his face. She could see quite vividly the resemblance, the similarity between their features, and realized how much of him there was in the boy.

Six

Paul and Christine knelt on the large upholstered stool, peering out of the front room window of Renée's house at the lawn. It was covered with flowers: wreaths, bouquets, and in the centre a floral cross. Smooth and silent, a large black hearse drew up. Quietly, one at a time, the mourners walked down the garden path, first Renée, then his mother and father, other friends, mourners. Soon a neighbour was tapping on his shoulder,

"Come now. It's time to come with us."

"But why can't I go, why . . . I want to go see him too, can I go with them?"

"Come, Paul, come with Christine, we're going next door, just for a little while, just till they come back."

His mother had decided he was too young to go to the funeral, ignoring his pleas that he could go one last time and say goodbye, give William one last hug. She believed, mistakenly, that a seven-year-old could not fully understand what was happening. Despite his immaturity, William's grandson had a depth of understanding and empathy with his grandfather, and understood in his heart what had happened, and knew he had the rest of his life to get through, somehow.

Quietly, with gentle acquiescence, he stepped down, his hand held, and went round through the hall and out across the back garden to the neighbours' house.

In the days to come, Paul stayed in his room, or huddled in a corner in the garden, sat in his den in the hedgerow, spoke little, ate little. He chatted and played with Christine, but his heart was not in the games. A cold, grey stillness came over the child. He brooded. He thought. He pondered, watched; thought of William, loved the memories, and feared what was to come. Most in his class at school were looking forward to going up to the juniors after the summer holiday, now only a few weeks away. But he wanted to run to William; he desperately wanted to run to him. Paul grieved. He grieved in the only way a seven-year-old child, immature for his years, can. He grieved in puzzlement: puzzled by these feelings, puzzled by those around him. Not wanting to believe what had happened, wishing he could change the event by shutting it out. But overall, wanting desperately to just be with him!

The sadness, the loss, stayed with him. Not just for a few weeks. Not just for a few months. The loss of William, of something unfulfilled—for he had only known William from the visits to Weston, then Axbridge Hospital—this loss stayed with Paul for most of his childhood. Often he would wake in the night to the noise in his head, the sense of the world spinning and the conviction he was being sucked down. Waking early in the morning, often feeling dreadfully lonely from the dreams, which had worried and preyed on him, he would lie watching the ceiling, exploring, imagining the cracks as a world, like the pictures of rivers and the land where it met the sea, like in the pictures he had looked at in books. There were memories he explored, and feelings he held. But there were images he could not get rid of: of his mother's blooded face, or the hurt he could see in his father's face because of something his mother had said: an expression soon to be transformed into anger. There was the memory of the sights and smells of breaking cups, food flung across the kitchen, or the chairs hurled across the living room. But above all, the sweet acrid smell of blood when one of them injured the other: whether it was his mother's broken nose; or the gash he saw, with blood streaming from it, along the deep forehead of his father's balding head.

His sister, Christine, escaped through school friends, but Paul bottled this up, he was perplexed, and dwelt on these feelings: he was a still, quiet, reflective child. "Still waters," as the Reverend Herbert called him, "still waters run deep." This small boy could not cope with or reconcile these conflicting feelings: feelings of both love and revulsion for his mother and his father. There were the feelings he had of delight, of gladness, of oneness, of the simple joy of being alive, and the newness of exploring the world. He was trying in his simple child-like way to balance these feelings with the darker sights: the noise, the smell, and the anger of violence.

Chapter Four, Love: Sickness and Death

As he lay awake, still and quiet, the sounds would start. First the quiet shuffle on the landing, then the creak of the stairs. Then, if it was his father, the rattle of the poker in the kitchen grate, tapping the poker on the side, the replacing of the lid, then the raking out of the fire box. Then his mother would descend the stairs. There would be muffled sounds from the kitchen, directly below his bedroom. A few muted exchanges, words, indiscernible, but the tone of the voices said all; sshhh sounds, probably about waking the children, then, as if neither could restrain themselves, the row would be under way. The boy knew what came next: fear—fear welling up in him, as if from the stomach, creating a sickly tight feeling in his throat. The fear of waiting. Will it break, yes: the hatred exploded, the wailing tone of pure hate in a voice; the cold antagonism of it. Maybe he would descend the stairs to see his mother crying. If he pleaded with them, with his father to stop, then he was for it. If he stayed in bed, then the cold sweat of fear remained, the dry suffocating hand creeping through him, in him. He sank into the pillows to escape: to inner worlds—hugged his panda tight, hugged the already tear-stained and threadbare little bear.

There he lay. He would think of William, feel sad, and cry: the tears were for William, albeit reflecting his sadness and loss—but they were not for his parents. Sometimes Christine would come in from her bedroom and comfort him, but she was a deep sleeper, and often did not wake. But there was Timmy. In a row, Timmy either headed to the great outdoors, or retreated to Paul's bedroom and the two would lie with the bedclothes covering them as a first and only line of defence against the world; the boy sobbing his little heart out into Timmy's fur, while the cat purred and licked his face as if to dry his tears. Another day had started.

Chapter Five
Summer: Vibrancy and Joy

～ *"You visit the earth and water it, You greatly enrich it. . . .*
You water its ridges abundantly, You settle its furrows;
You soften the earth with showers, You bless its growth.
You crown the year with Your goodness,
and our paths are full with Your abundance."
PSALM 65: 9a & 10–11

One

The line of lorries stretched back along the Old Worcester Road in the direction of Greenhill. There was a gap in the traffic at the junction with Briar Close Lane, the approach to Black Bridges, but the queue then continued in front of the row of Victorian cottages along the side of the railway station. Sometimes, and now was such a time, the queue of lorries would stretch back to the junction with Greenhill. Lorries would form a patient line extending north up the centre of the main road in Greenhill, straddling the white line so as to allow normal traffic to pass by on each side of the queue, leaving neat gaps at each road junction; likewise they formed an orderly line, only close into the kerb this time, heading down along the High Street into the centre of the town. All these lorries, pick-ups, even (though rare now) a horse-drawn cart, were loaded with fruit and vegetables. A glut, an overabundance (the gathering in of runner beans in addition to the plum harvest), caused this mass of vehicles with their single destination. They waited patiently for the lines of traffic to move. The two lines—one running down the centre of Greenhill, the other coming up from the

Chapter Five, Summer: Vibrancy and Joy

High Street, would, with courtesy and good manners, filter alternatively into the Old Worcester Road. The object of all the drivers' attention was the railway—the goods yard. Harry had arrived early, having loaded the lorry by ten in the morning, intentionally missing the sale at both the top market and the central market, and reached the end of the queue whilst it was still in the Old Worcester Road.

It was a blisteringly hot day in August. Paul and Christine were by now sitting in the wooden box unit mounted on the top of the cab. The lorry moved very slowly, so the risk of any injury was negligible. Harry sat in the cab, the windows wound down, his shirt sleeves rolled up as far as they would go, his cap pushed back on his head. His right hand spread, resting on this deep forehead. The hotness from the engine was insufferable; the heat from the sun excruciating. Behind him, behind the cab, stacked neatly, were over five hundred chips of plums—Victoria, Purple, and Egg plums. Each chip was covered by white card with red printed lettering stating, J. H. BROADLEY & SON, FRUIT & VEGETABLE GROWER & MERCHANT TEL. 5849 TELEGRAMS: BROADLEY, AVONDALE, EVESHAM. Each chip was brand new—made of creamy white, thin wafers of wood, woven into shape. Each had attached in its centre a pressed tin handle, with small side clips (cut into the pressing) for folding down onto the chip to prevent the handle from closing once opened. Each chip held its consignment of plums, protected from the torrid sun by the cover, held in place by two rubber bands. The tin handles were made from recycled metal. Paul would peer inside the handle, bending and squinting sufficiently to read the writing: "peaches in syr . . . ," but the rest was indecipherable. Early in the morning he had helped load the lorry—well, he had managed to carry the occasional chip of plums over to the lorry, in the cool dewy early light. Sam would interrupt his fast rhythmical loading to take the chip from the little boy, who was struggling to hold it, doffing his cap as he did. The boy helped by proudly counting the chips as they went on to the lorry, but then lost his count, only to see Sam blithely counting away. As the morning drew on, the heat became intense, by midday it was insufferable.

The lorry made slow progress. Very slow progress. Once it had left the main road and entered the rough surface of the goods yard Harry banged on the inside of the cab roof to signal to the two children that they could climb down. They knew the signal and carefully clambered over the side of the box into Harry's arms—Harry having got out of the cab after giving the signal. The yard was large, yet even by the standards of the Vale of Evesham it was woefully inadequate at this time of year. While Harry and Sam made their way slowly toward the goods wagons—Glasgow being scrawled in large chalk letters on the guard's van at the tail end of one of the trains—the two children walked over to the right, Christine carefully holding her brother's hand. They walked past the buffers at the end of each pair of sidings—each with a guard's van, inches from the large round steel plates that formed the buffers. Paul paused to look inside the vans, but Christine pulled on his hand, gently reminding him that their father had expressly forbad them from going in any of the goods wagons. Their progress was slow. Their little feet stumbled over the clinker and stone hardcore that formed the foundations of the sidings.

Once they had cleared the sidings—eight in all—they sat on the edge of the grass embankment. The embankment—about forty feet high, heaped up to form a plateau on which the tracks had been laid—gave a commanding view of the river. They sat together at the top of the bank watching the scene. Before them the Avon carved its way gently, slowly, through the rich soils of the vale; it lay at the foot of the embankment, separated from them by a flood plain. The flood plain was planted with an orchard—plum trees, young, each no more than a yard and a half high. The children sat at an obtuse angle to the lines of trees so that the grid was viewed irregularly: rows stretched out in one direction to the left, and in the other direction to the right.

Straddling the river was a large metal railway bridge, linking two tall embankments, and beyond all, Clark's Hill rose, marking the edge of Hampton village. By this point the river meandered wide and was relatively calm, though still waters were deep and in parts treacherous. The river level was low: not much rain had fallen over recent weeks, thus the banks lay exposed: open, pale brown, steep, dry, and crumbling. The river flowed slowly between the banks, the surface white and gleaming in the sun. Trees on the far bank cast their dark reflection on the water's surface. The scene was tranquil and pregnant with a fecund beauty that vibrated as if it would continue so forever. They sat, or lay, watched, or dozed, for an eternity: the river flowing on. A myriad of flying insects danced in the air around and in the long grasses on the embankment below their feet. A train, belching out white to grey smoke, strained as it came into sight over to their left. Slowly it made its way across the horizon, no more than three hundred yards away. Its progress was slow: Paul watched as unhurriedly, but strenuously, it made its way along the lines. The wheels and the track rattled and echoed inside the steel walls of the bridge as it began to cross the river. As the engine cleared the bridge Paul got a better view of it: 2-4-2—he counted the wheels beneath the gleaming black and red tank. His eyes then rested onto the rest of the train. He counted the wagons. First there were ten double-length goods wagons, each resting on double bogies, then came the single wagons. He counted: thirteen, fourteen, fifteen . . . thirty-seven, thirty-eight, thirty-nine. Christine spoke:

"What are you doing?"

Chapter Five, Summer: Vibrancy and Joy

"Shhh! I'm counting!" he replied. "Forty-one, forty-two, forty-three, and finally the guard's van! That makes forty-three wagons, and the ten doubles and the guard's van, that's fifty-four—what a train, just wait till I tell dad! Come on, let's find him."

He gave his sister a friendly prod as the guard's van rolled and rattled through the bridge, the engine now out of sight. They rose, legs stiff from sitting so long in the grass and wobbled back up to the top of the embankment. The boy ran ahead.

Christine called after him. "Stop! Paul come back!"

He stopped.

He remembered his father's advice to them: the goods yard was full of lorries, pick-ups, and vans. Christine caught up with him and they walked together to the siding parallel to the edge of the embankment. So he stepped up onto the guard's van, holding onto the thin metal rail that ran down with the two steps from the rear platform.

"Paul!" his sister said in a commanding voice.

"I'm just looking—it'll be safe, there's no engine at the front—come on!"

He climbed the steps and stood on the platform holding on to the rail, with the two lamps mounted on it. He turned and looked at the van: it was built of a steel framework, with walls made from wooden planks, each about a hand's width. They ran vertically, and smelled of fresh creosote. He peered into the interior. His eyes could see nothing; they took time to adjust from the bright sunlight.

"What's in there?" said his sister, who now stood behind him.

But before he could answer, indeed before their eyes could clear, they heard footsteps and voices. Quickly they ran down the other side of the guard's van and thereby found themselves in-between the train they had just left and the next siding—which likewise had a train with an identical guard's van. Both trains were made up of single goods wagons. Each body was constructed (like the guard's van) from a steel framework with wooden planks, but was simpler, more boxlike in shape than the complex structure of the guard's van. Each wagon stood on single bogies that were black with grease and dirt—except for the face of each wheel, which contacted the rail: this inner face was gleaming, bright, pure, spotless metal. Each wagon had a large, wide, sliding door on each side—stretching from the floor to the roof. As the sidings were arranged in pairs, and as they were now in between a pair of tracks, the doors were closed—only the outward-facing doors were open for loading. It was actually quite cool and quiet there between the wagons. As if in the distance, they could hear the muffled voices and shouts, the engines running, the thump, thump as crates were manhandled into the wagons, as chips were stacked, goods loaded. The two rows of wagons protected them from the noise—it seemed as though they were hundreds of yards away from it. Likewise, here in the shade they felt more refreshed. The two children walked carefully, cautiously, gingerly, between the wagons. Both trains were long and when half way down, Paul noticed that the door to the wagon on his left was open—just slightly, about one hand width. He put his arm up and pulled on the metal rail at the base of the door. It slid open. He pulled himself up, struggling with his legs to find purchase on the wheel, or any other part of the chassis.

"No! No! Paul, don't—it might be dangerous!"

By now he had pulled his body onto the floor of the wagon and only his legs could be seen flailing wildly like a fish out of water as he wriggled about. He twisted and turned while the sound of voices and feet walking on the hard core beneath the rails, grew louder.

"Paul! Paul! Quick, someone's coming—quick—get down—they're coming now!"

Paul turned round having finally got himself in through the door. He looked out through the gap but could see his sister nowhere—she had obviously run on ahead. He looked both ways but could not see her—only the two men walking along from the rear end of the train, the direction they had come in. He dived inside the wagon, behind the door as the two men walked past. The boy could not see them, but could hear their conversation—something about the number of wagons, the time the guard would be coming on duty. However, what struck him more was the smell of cigarette smoke that drifted in from the men. It mingled with the creosote, with the smell of the greased metal: his head began to spin. The noise in his head started to get intense, the vertigo started. He closed his eyes and fought it; he lent back against the door, sat down and put his hands over his ears. With all his concentration he tried to fight the spinning sensation, the grating, rasping, and the cacophonous noise in his head, but as so often happened in these attacks he seemed to pass out, disappear into a thin white nothingness . . . and sleep.

Christine had run ahead a short distance as she could see there was a gap in the train; a gap of about two yards where the wagons were not coupled. She clambered through, over the rails and immediately found herself in amongst a throng of people shouting—and lorries, and all sorts of containers, packed with fruit or vegetables being loaded onto the wagons. She stood blinking in the sunlight, trying to take in the cacophony of sight and sound. She tried to thread her way past the lorries and count back to where her brother might be. Then she realized she had no idea which wagon he was in. The line of lorries ended. Beyond them the remainder of the train, the rear dozen or so wagons had their doors closed and sealed: they had already been loaded. Some had a cardboard cover with the name and details of the grower printed on, just like the covers on

Chapter Five, Summer: Vibrancy and Joy

her father's chips of plums, these covers were folded and jammed into the handles on the door: many growers or merchants would buy the space of a whole wagon. Christine did not know what to do. She walked back to the gap through which she had come. She waited for Paul to appear through the gap. There was no sign of him. She tried to look through the gap, holding onto the buffer of one of the wagons.

"Oi! Get away kid, what are you doing?"

"That's right Bill, you tell 'er, what bist thee doin' 'ere kid? Get on back with thee!"

Christine looked up. The two men had paused, stood as they were on the flat bed of a small lorry. A railwayman looked out from the open door of the goods wagon and added his contribution:

"Go'n—off with 'ee!"

Christine turned. She walked back up to the rear of the train and round the back of the guard's van. She looked down between the two trains. By now she was shaking with fear and fright and was near to tears.

"Ahh, there 'ou be!"

She turned and saw Sam coming over to her. He had walked along the back of the sidings towards the edge of the embankment where both he and Harry knew they would be. She turned and told her tale. Sam comforted her, then proceeded to walk down between the two trains, as he did so, he called back to her:

"'ou stay there my maid, right there, I'ul 'ave a look down 'ere."

Sam tested all the doors to see if any were loose—on both trains—but none were. He paused at the gap where Christine had told him she had clambered through, turned and walked back, again trying all the doors. By the time he had returned to the two guard's vans, Christine was in tears.

"Come on now, my girl, don't 'ee go frettin' your pretty little face, come on now, we'ul find 'im. None of these trains is movin' 'fore six o'clock, so don't 'ee go worryin' your pretty little 'ead."

Upon which he picked her up and held her in his left arm. She placed her arms on his shoulder to steady herself, whilst he proceeded to walk along the rear of the sidings, back towards the Glasgow train, and Harry Broadley's lorry. Harry stood, his legs apart, one hand on his hip, the other pushing up his cap scratching his head. He looked around, his eyes flitting everywhere, yet not stopping on any one thing. Lorries were trying to manoeuvre their way out from the line of stationary vehicles having finished their loading, men shouted and engines revved, tempers frayed in proportion to the insufferable heat. By now it was two o'clock in the afternoon.

Harry saw them and called over: "There you are—where've you been!"

"I'm sorry Mr. Broadley." Sam always referred to his employer like this, despite Harry's insistence on them both being on first name terms, "but we can no find the little 'un anywhere!"

Sam proceeded to tell Harry what had happened whilst Christine was put in the cab—with strict orders to stay there!

"Come on, get a move on, there still a hundred lorries waiting to come in" called one railway man to Harry and Sam as they walked away from the lorry and started their search. Sam walked back to explain what had happened while Harry started the search.

"Kids! What on earth are they doing here on a day like this?—God Almighty!" came the reply. However, just then his son dawdled into sight, from the direction of the front of the trains. Sam called after Harry, who turned and ran back.

"Thank God you're all right! You had me so worried, now get in that cab, now, quick!"

The boy clambered in—obediently—and sat next to his sister. Sam got onto the back of the lorry and stood behind the cab holding onto the wooden rails that extended up beyond the cab like a fence. Harry got in and started the engine. It would not start. Cursing and swearing he got out of the cab and went round to the front of the lorry and started to crank the engine furiously. The sweat was pouring off him now as he cranked and cranked.

Sam advised: "Steady, steady, please Mr. Broadley, slowly, you'll never get 'e goin' like that!"

Harry stopped and stood up, stretched his back, pushed his cap back and scratched his head, then started again to crank the engine. This time following Sam's advice, the engine fired up on the first turn. Harry got back in the cab having first pushed the cranking handle behind the seat. He manoeuvred the lorry cautiously out from the line of stationary vehicles and in front of the line of trucks waiting to take his place.

"Oi! wait a moment! Gi'us a cover, you ain't put un' in the door" called Sam. The lorry juddered to a halt. Sam jumped down and took the cover from Harry.

"I'ull meet 'ee at the Central," he said, and then turned and ran back to the wagon, rolling the card, he then pushed it firmly between the handle and the door. Harry meanwhile drove down to the front end of the wagons to join the queue of lorries waiting to leave the yard. The sky was cloudless, the heat searing: the day was now advanced, but there were still many gardeners and merchants full to the brim with frustration, frayed tempers, angry with overloaded or badly loaded wagons, held up by lorries with boiling radiators, as they fought desperately to get their produce onto the wagons by the deadline.

Chapter Five, Summer: Vibrancy and Joy

Two

So what had happened? Paul had woken with a start: the noise from outside the wagon had woken him—men banging and shouting, engines revving. He shook his head and rubbed his eyes; it took him a moment to get his bearings. He looked around him: stacked in both ends of the wagon were chips of plums, with a bar-like structure—no, it was more like a gate—holding each section or stack in place. He looked up at the roof—the inside of the roof of the wagon—there was a glint of daylight through the ventilators. It was cool, remarkably cool, inside the wagon. Then he remembered what had happened, remembered Christine. Quickly he turned round and pushed his head out through the gap in the door. No one was around so he jumped down out of the wagon and pulled the sliding door to. He gave it a good hard shove so that this time the catch engaged. Then, after looking around him, he ran down between the two lines of wagons—missing the gap through which his sister had gone only five minutes earlier. He ran, trying desperately to catch his breath, he ran till he reached the front of the train. None of them had engines, but over in front of him he could see several locomotives, just like the 2-4-2 he had seen earlier. They were being prepared over by the engine sheds, ready for the night's journey. He wanted to stop and look at them, look at what the men were doing to prepare them, but he thought better of it. He made his way carefully over the rails and around the front of the wagons, back towards the Glasgow train. Here he met up with Harry, with Sam, and quickly got back in the lorry.

The queue to leave the yard was almost as bad as the line waiting to get in. Once Harry had reached the Old Worcester Road, he could then proceed eastwards—but in a parallel traffic jam, in the opposite direction, to the one still feeding into the railway yard. He waited patiently for his turn to cross into Briar Close Lane, then to drive over Black Bridges, over the Great Western Railway, then over the London Midland and Southern Railway. The traffic was bad, but not as bad as on the Old Worcester Road. The lorry stood, the traffic was not moving and the heat burned down onto the cab roof. Paul looked over to the right, past his father. He stood up on the seat to get a better look.

"Dad, look, its Sam!"

Paul was right. Over and down to their right, walking across the wooden boards that made a crossing for railway workers, the boy could see Sam. He walked slowly, constantly looking to his left and right in case a train was coming—he crossed the spurs leading into the sidings, crossed the Great Western, crossed the London Midland and Southern, crossed a further set of sidings, then after climbing the shallow bank, disappeared behind a pub—The Oddfellows Arms.

He would be at the Central Market before them! Harry smiled—he also watched Sam, and knew that he would have time for a swift half in the pub before continuing on past Briar Close Hospital to the market. (Sam only ever drank halves—half pints—for most this was all they could afford, for Sam it was a way of controlling what he called the demon drink.) The traffic moved steadily, a few yards at a time. Half an hour after leaving the railway yard, they were drawing into the Central Market (one half of a mile distance from the railway yard). Sam was standing blithely passing the time of day, waiting, languidly. He had almost certainly had at least two half pints, and what was more, had enjoyed the walk from the sidings to the market.

"What kept 'ee?" he said with a smile.

"What do you think!" Harry replied, as he got out of the lorry, slamming the door closed with frustration at the traffic and the weather. "Phew, this heat is something else."

"I've checked out: Mr. Broadley senior"—the name by which he always referred to Jack—" 'ee bought them 'uns over thur'!"

Harry walked over to the stack of wooden trays containing spring onions. He looked at them and exclaimed:

"What . . . ," crying out profanities, "what on earth has 'ee been playing at!"

Harry pushed his hand into the trays of onions, separating the bunches, then taking one out to smell them.

"But these are rubbish, I can't send them these!"

Longworth's in Gateshead, a wholesaler, had requested twenty trays of onions to go with the four hundred chips of plums due to be sent the next day. Because he would be tied up getting this day's five hundred chips of plums to the railway, Jack was to go to the Central Market to buy the twenty trays. It was late in the season for spring onions, and old Jack Broadley had never excelled at buying in the pressure and speed of an auction sale, but even so, he should have done better than this.

"It's no good, Sam, you're goin' to have to go through these, strip them down, wash them, and re-pack them—take the yellow leaves off. I can't send them like this!"

"That's alright, I'll do 'um for 'ee, it'll keep me out of mischief, and any road it'll be a bit cooler down in them sheds than out 'ere." Sam was pleased with the possibility of a bit more overtime.

"You get 'um loaded up while I get the labels and covers."

Harry turned and walked out from under the large canopy of the market and over towards the main gates. To one side stood a red brick Victorian building: tall and narrow, with a large painted board above the windows: C. SHARP—PRINTER.

Chapter Five, Summer: Vibrancy and Joy

Paul was already stood outside the door, waiting for his father; he stood, thrilled at the opportunity. In they went. As always, he climbed up on the counter, to watch the machines—a giant guillotine, two large printing presses, the sight of trays of metal type, the smell of turpentine and ink. While Paul looked on transfixed, Harry waited while the assistant fetched the covers for him, and the box of clips. The woman handed the packages to Harry:

"I'm sorry but we've only been able to do three quarters of your order, it's the same for everyone, we're only doing three quarters of all orders at the moment, there is just too much demand."

Harry nodded understandingly, thanked the woman, and then, helping his son down, walked out through the door, down the three stone steps, and across to the lorry. Jack had grumbled at him for laying-in a store of covers, clips, and rubber bands, but he had been proved right. This consignment was simply to keep up their stocks. If he had followed Jack's advice they would have run out by now. It was typical, just typical, he thought. Here he was trying to do his best and all his father could do was moan! And what was more, he could not even buy decent onions when the market would have been deserted on such a day as this. Harry continued to moan in his mind as they got back into the lorry and drove out into Avon Street. Harry drove over High Street and into Swann Lane. The traffic was lighter but still it was stop/start all the way. Paul and Christine were quiet—they could see their father was absorbed, they could tell by the way he was gripping the steering wheel. Sam had stayed on the back of the lorry with the onions; he could also see that Harry was in a foul mood. However, he was not surprised, considering the quality of the onions. He knew that Jack had probably spent too long drinking in The Cross Keys in the morning to get to the sale in time to get the good onions. He knew Harry knew; but he kept quiet. Finally, after a long, humid and sultry, airless and stifling day, they were back. They were all hot, sticky, and tired. Christine was asleep. Harry came round to open the door and carry her into the sheds and across the garden into the house. Paul followed, while Sam looked on from his perch on the back of the lorry: that man's goin' to blow a fuse in his brain one day if he doesn't slow up a bit, he thought to himself. He shuffled, where he sat, stretched out his legs and muttered quietly:

". . . 'baint he just? Harry Broadley—'ou bist goin' to have to slow down a bit, my son, certain on a day like this 'un, and it ain't over yet!"

He turned and proceeded to unload the trays of onions. Once done, he started to unpack them, strip off the yellow leaves, and wash them down thoroughly with the hosepipe.

Three

It was still only early evening. Paul ran out of the house once tea was finished, disappearing through the raspberry bushes at the bottom of the garden. He walked slowly past Sam who had broken-off repacking the onions to finish the tea Harry had brought him from the local store—a large pork pie, tomatoes and bread, and a bottle of beer—he would work till late, and, like so many gardeners and field labourers during the busy season, he would sleep over night in the shed on some old sacks. Sam smiled, Paul smiled back; then walked round to the back of the sheds. He then navigated carefully between the rows of young sprout plants so as not to damage them.

When he reached the end of the row, he walked to his left, till, reaching the corner of the field, he disappeared into a large thicket: a group of trees, making an oval, encompassed a depression three to four feet deep. The trees were all hawthorn. The boy settled into the hollow, looking over its rim, through the undergrowth and towards the brook: rising beyond it was Longdon Hill. He settled back, looking up through the canopy: it was August and the foliage was a deep rich green. Bird nests were now abandoned, all the young birds having flown.

On the branches, the unripe haws were beginning to swell. A hallmark of the Charity was the thorn: mainly hawthorn (often called may or mayblossom, maythorn, sometimes quickthorn, though rarely whitethorn . . .), but also with some blackthorn. Much of the original thorn was to be found around the brook. These were examples from the earliest scrub (including heavily pollarded willow, ash, and hazel), which predated the original enclosure of the land in the eighteenth century. These clumps were tall, thick, mature, and impenetrable to all but small mammals—including children! Then there was the thorn planted as small hedgerows dividing the fields, which were subsequently laid to orchards in the nineteenth century. These orchards were then felled after the First World War to provide the acre o'land for each man in the parish returning from the war. Fresh hawthorn had been planted along new pathways, tracks, or ridges—some quite ancient—which divided the plots. In early spring, say the first couple of weeks in March, the hawthorn stood, trimmed but sullen, its woody stems dark grey-brown, with thorns thrusting at all angles, themselves a slightly warmer, redder brown. The tight intricate twists and convulsions of this rugged, defensive tree, would then give rise to tiny shoots of the most intense vivid, lime green: only for a few days each spring. It was one of the first trees to sprout new growth. It was as if it had developed this capacity after centuries of containment into hedges and field boundary markers, only occasionally being allowed to grow to its full

Chapter Five, Summer: Vibrancy and Joy

size. The new leaves were perfectly formed miniatures of the full-sized leaves; clean, pure and unsullied, intensely green, set off against the rugged grey-brown knotted stems and twigs of thorn.

In May, once the leaves had opened, the flowers would appear: tiny white to pinkish-white flowers, the scent heavy on the air: the Midland Hawthorn often before the Common Hawthorn or Whitethorn. The scent became intoxicating, especially in the small copse or clumps down by the brook. The air was also full of insects—bees, wasps, flies—all trying to get their share of the thousands and thousands of tiny flowers. From a distance some trees appeared as ghostly apparitions such was their covering of white flowers. When the flowers faded, the leaves took on their full-grown mature appearance, boasting a rich sap green. Birds, from finches to sparrows, would nest in them.

As the months passed the green leaves would become darker, glossier, more grey and grubby: weather-worn, tired. By high summer, the green apparel would take on an appearance in keeping with the dark, dusty, convoluted stems and twigs, uniquely hawthorn. Then, in the autumn, the mature fruits turned through green-beige to brown, finally to red: rich red haws, bulging and bursting with the seed for new life. They were a feast for birds—blackbirds, robins, wood pigeons, thrushes, and to occasional visitors such as redwings, fieldfares, and hawfinches. By late September the noise from squabbling birds in the hedgerows could be heard a good distance away. Whilst sitting in amongst the deeper hedgerows, Paul witnessed mice, voles, and even squirrels pluck the haws: gently, nervously sniff them, then quickly nibble, turn the fruit, nibble again, look around to ensure no predator was threatening, nibble again, then discard the fruit and run off. The harvest was so great that even by Christmas, when the trees were bare of leaves, there were still bright red haws to be seen. But the most incredible sight the thorns could hold was in early spring. The boy was quite bursting with joy, with an intense fascination and wonder with life, when the first signs of a brilliant green dusting appeared on the hawthorn. Then, upon closer inspection, he would observe, close up, the tiny leaves beginning to burst out: the joy was almost too much to bear. This sight, coupled with celandine around the brook, primrose at the foot of hazel or ash, was so joyful—the warmth in the air was gradually breathing life into plant, into animal, into bird, loosening the winter straitjacket, wakening, but with a mellow ease. The world was magical, and creation sang. . . .

Paul turned over, stretched out his legs where he lay, and looked up through the canopy of hawthorn, through the leaves and the twigs, and viewed the sky. The day was still hot, the sky clear, but the heat was more manageable. He gazed up through the leaves and thought about the day, the excitement of the railway, the people around the goods wagons, the engines, the temperature, the sun!

Longman's Charity

He gazed up at the sky. It was absolutely clear, not a bird or a cloud dared to break the continuity. The air was clear crystal-white with just a hint of blue, then as his head turned and his eyes took in the horizon, the air took on a luminosity; a thin magical veil of the gentlest blend of Prussian blue and cerulean blue hung over the whiteness, as if it was not part of the sky. He cherished the peace. He adored the quiet. He gazed around him from the seclusion of the hollow, bounded by the defence of the hawthorn, backed by his father's land: he surveyed the scene, the air, and loved the world. At moments like this he felt the least pain about William's death. The memories were good memories, but oh he missed him so much, so, so much. Meg also missed William—grieved—but could not talk about it. She remained closed up and silent. Her grief came out in the near daily rows with her husband. And her father's death had triggered other memories in her, recollections of her own childhood, which were beginning to impinge on her son at bed time. . . .

He could not move such was the heat that still soaked the day through and refused to let go—even now in the mid-evening. Drowsy and indolent, but he did not feel sleepy, simply weighed down by the heat. He turned over, returning to lie on his stomach. His chin rested on the dry earth—compacted as it was into a bulwark, hidden most of the time by greenery, but for those who stopped and looked closer, they would have seen a tell-tale sign that feet had pressed and compacted the earth on the bank within the hedgerow. Paul's eyes looked out through the leaves and grass, out onto the Charity: nothing moved. Nothing stirred. The day was far advanced, all was tired, a sultriness hung heavily. The earth breathed shallow and faint—it seemed as though the very trees had stopped living and all was petrified in the heat. The horizon looked thin, vague, indistinct; it was as if all life was fatigued, lethargic. Falling away from him in a slender curve, the land yielded to the heat and begged for rain. Before him young cabbage plants wilted, trapped by their roots. Further off still lay the brook: its level was now low, having drained almost every drop of moisture from the dry earth.

Slowly, imperceptibly at first, a dark figure began to move in and around the brook. Slowly, unhurriedly, a man appeared over the brow of the land. At first only his head could be seen. Then his shoulders, and the cap became clear on his head. He was bowed over, his hands pushing a bicycle, his body lost in a raincoat. He pushed the bike stoically, resigned to his labour, not with the spirit of joy, of sylvan pleasures, but plainly, unaffectedly, with toil and drudgery: there was simply no other way to earn a living, no other way of getting home—of surviving. As the man came into view, Paul could see clearly: tied to the cross bar was a hoe. As the man neared the end of the rise, he saw who it was. Yet he had half-recognized the man from having seen part of him in the distance. Chowskie, as he was known

Chapter Five, Summer: Vibrancy and Joy

by the other gardeners, was in his late-fifties, Czechoslovakian, having come to England during the war as a refugee. He had returned to the continent with the D-Day landings, by which time he considered himself as British as the men he fought alongside in his regiment. However, his English was poor—both spoken and written—therefore he said little. By now, over seventeen years since he had fought for the liberation of Europe, he was somewhat disillusioned with the British. He still had great difficulty in communicating—though he had command of a few rudimentary swear words that he used as simple common nouns or adjectives to describe the nature of a merchant who had cheated him by giving him a pitifully low price for his produce. He had taken on one of the Hampton Charity holdings after the war, and tended it with loving care: in some ways it was the neatest, cleanest, most well-kept holding in the Charity. He divided the plot into blocks and rows, grew a wide variety of vegetables—sprouts, leeks, and cabbage in the winter, onions in the spring, parsley, runner beans, French beans, and lettuce in the summer, and a few rows of potatoes, beetroot, carrots, and radishes for his own table.

Chowskie had managed to get hold of the metal-framed wooden body of a railway goods wagon, which he used as shed. This structure looked incongruous next to the lane, on the edge of his holding—a railway wagon, with its characteristic curved roof replaced, with sides patched-up, with diagonal metal struts running from the corners down to the central area of each side. He had tried to get on with the others around him, but he was not one of them—indeed it had become a point of contention with those born in the Vale, born in Evesham. Their attitude was one of uncompromising prejudice; they feared that which was different amongst them. Hence he withdrew. He only dealt with others if he had to, using his broken English.

Each evening Chowskie could be seen walking his bike along the lane from his holding, on the left hand side, and further down from Harry and Jack Broadley's land, towards the brook. He walked his bike all the way back to his tiny cottage in Childswickham, three miles away. He was now prematurely old—arthritis had set in years before, caused by the years of doubling over in all weathers to tend his crops. He still rode some mornings, along through Mount Pleasant, then joining the main Cheltenham Road, turning right to take him towards the Charity. But these mornings were becoming rare. Often he would walk the last mile, pushing his bike, with the hoe strapped to the cross bar and a faded grey-brown wooden apple box mounted against the handlebars over the front wheel, containing a long knife, a ball of string, and a tin box with his dinner inside.

That evening, it was even more difficult for him to push the bike over the rough white stone of the track. The weather was still hot, the evening sultry, humid and oppressive—sticky. Yet he pushed the bike as he always did, his arms held high on the handle bars, with his head bent low over the cross bar. He wore an old khaki raincoat that was threadbare at the elbows, tied at the waist with thick white-beige string. Beneath the coat was a red-and-blue-check thick wool shirt, while on his head he wore an equally threadbare cap that was at least two sizes too big for him. He wore a pair of grey Wellington boots, which were covered at the top by the raincoat. His face was worn—care worn: the flesh hung low from his cheeks, the tissue beneath his eyes puffy and swollen, his skin rough and tanned from the years exposed to wind and sun. Yet his eyes were bright, lively and glowing, despite their smallness. They were often watery, but their blueness reflected the depth of his soul, the depth of his feelings.

Chowskie was an intense man. He was a solitary man; a lonely man. No one had managed to pierce the protective screen he had built around himself. Some told stories that he had been married before the war, that his family had been lost, that he had been in the resistance after his family had been wiped out, but were these stories only rumours, gossip? No one really knew the truth. He seemed always to be carrying a burden, a burden he did not speak of. He was grateful, very grateful for the freedom to come and settle in England, to work the land— "like my own village," he would say. He never drank in the local pubs, shopped only at the Bluebird store, by Bates Garage, spoke little to people, though he could be seen occasionally in the Roman Catholic Church (on key church festivals) near the railway station. On one occasion when the two children were talking to him by his shed a metal icon of Christ fell out of the wooden box on his bike as he removed some sprout sacks. He dived for it, grabbed it before it fell on the ground: "Jesus, Jesus, he look after me! Save me!" And he crossed himself; whilst rubbing the icon between finger and thumb with his other hand. Christine laughed; Paul was puzzled.

Most local gardeners did not welcome him, they regarded him as a foreigner, as an alien; however, Harry would comment, when such remarks flew around, that if it wasn't for the likes of him, then they would not have the freedom to express their opinions—that Chowskie had done as much as they had against Hitler and his gang. Paul was puzzled, fascinated by Chowskie—where had the man come from? What had happened to his family? Why did he speak to nobody? Afraid to speak to him, to ask him these questions, Paul watched him as he slowly pushed the bike up the lane and past the thicket in which the boy was hidden, buried in the hawthorn.

But Chowskie was not alone amongst the more eccentric of the Charity holders. Ol' Grumpy dressed and appeared similar to Chowskie but was totally different in temperament. For all his introversion, Chowskie was polite,

Chapter Five, Summer: Vibrancy and Joy

considerate, well mannered, and kind; he simply did not mix: he was a loner. Ol' Grumpy was something different. Christine and Paul did not know his real name; indeed, for that matter, many of the other children growing up around the Cheltenham Road only knew him as Ol' Grumpy. He held land further on along the brook from where the two children still went tadpoling, and had thoroughly deserved the name he had been given. He always chased children off when they came near—not that there were that many, no more than a dozen children from around the Cheltenham Road or the Fairfield Estate went down the Charity. His rallying cry was that it was a place of work and that kids should not be around. The narrow neck of the lane between the willows and Ol' Grumpy's shed had to be approached with caution and with trepidation. He would bellow from where he was working on the land and wave whatever implement he was using threateningly. So they would race through to get further beyond. If they were unfortunate, and approached while he was working in or around his shed, then they were really in for trouble. He would grab them by the collar and drag them back along the lane to the point where it turned up away from the brook and fling them on to the grass verge, ordering them off.

Ol' Grumpy dressed in thick woollen tweed trousers, the old style shirt, white with blue stripes and no collar, and always a tweed jacket, brown, lovat greens, and greys in colour. He always seemed to wear several layers of clothes too many—he was stocky to start with, and the numerous layers of wool and tweed did not help his appearance, likewise his ruddy red complexion. Like Chowskie, he always wore a cap, indeed such headwear was the hallmark of Charity holders and market gardeners generally in the vale. He worked long hours, as did many holders, but unlike Chowskie he did not use a bike as his means of transport. He had a small Austin van, which when parked outside his shed would give a visual warning to the two children of his presence. But this was not always reliable. He lived on the Fairfield Estate, so often would save petrol by walking to his land. So the absence of his van did not always mean it was safe to pass. Even if he could be seen working some distance from the lane, his wife might be working near the shed, or washing produce in the brook. She would raise the alarm and he would come running. Old Grumpy's shed was the smartest down the Charity. It was a wooden structure with a concrete floor (as distinct from the more common compacted earth floor), with a side window made from a wooden window frame, with curtains hanging within the panes. The building was topped off by a pitched roof covered with boards and roofing felt. At the rear was a brick-built chimney-breast, with one single chimney pot on top. The whole building was approximately fourteen feet by ten, and set at right angles to the road. Stood behind this shed was a larger shed of much rougher construction that was used for storing trays, boats, crates, and in the summer season, produce ready to be sent to the market.

Ol' Grumpy would often sleep in the former, smaller shed—which was why it had the brick chimney and fireplace. In the right season it would be necessary to be up before dawn to start gathering in the produce, and likewise men and women would be seen working at their crops until the last glimmer of light was fading from the day. But it would not be fair to say that Ol' Grumpy was typical of the Charity holders. Most holders were affable, amiable, and liked having the two children around. They knew they were market gardening children, that they respected the land. Their father advised them to reply to any holders complaining about them by saying, first of all, who they were and, second, that they lived on this land. Throughout his childhood, adolescence, and early adult years Paul was a common sight amongst them—always being known as " 'arry Broadley's little 'un": even in his adult years when he had moved away from the area and was teaching in London, he would always walk the lane, when he returned of a weekend—still known as " 'arry Broadley's little 'un."

Going beyond Ol' Grumpy's holding, about three hundred yards further on, the lane veered away from the brook. At this point was an old holding pond, about thirty feet by ten, that had been cut at right angles to the brook, with a narrow neck of only three feet through which the waters swirled into the pond. There was an island in the middle—no more than three feet across, too small to clamber onto or stand on, but on it yellow flag, ragged robin, and other rare wildflowers grew, likewise around the margins of the pond. The pool had been created as a holding pond—like the one by the Red Barn, which Jim Beason used—but this one had not been used as such for years, hence its development into a miniature nature reserve. In spring it was teeming with tadpoles and frogspawn. Paul would often return and lie amongst the grass, the reeds, and the flowers surrounding it. He would watch as birds came to drink from its waters, or splash amongst the shallows. He would watch as dragonflies soared and hovered and hunted over its waters; he watched as the tadpoles grew legs, then later lost their tails and migrated out through the neck of the pond—off either upstream or downstream leaving only a handful of them to last out the summer. As the heat increased, the pond's level dropped and the island in the middle grew in size.

This part of the Charity was worked by Mr. Phipps, who always waved to them, watchfully kept an eye on them, always stopped whatever he was doing to pass the time of day. They often saw him hoeing, even if there were no weeds to dislodge: "Ahh, it do the soil good to be turned e'ry now and then," he would tell them. He was a tall, thin man. He stood holding the top end of his hoe in both hands, the blade sunk in the ground, the whole, vertical, so as to lean

Chapter Five, Summer: Vibrancy and Joy

with his weight resting on it. He always wore a wide-brimmed hat—straw in the summer, felt in winter. He dressed in the old style collar-less shirt, with a thick pair of leather braces holding his corduroy trousers up, the turn-ups breaking over his boots. He would stop what he was doing immediately to enquire how they were, how Mr. Broadley was, and his good lady, and of the health of their grandparents. Mr. Phipps was poor, but polite, respectful, and respectable: he was a churchwarden—it's that Jesus thing again thought young Paul. Mr. Phipps only stopped for a few minutes, then he would touch the corner of his hat and add that he really must be continuing with his work. The two children would then walk on either to the pond, or return to their father's land.

Mr. Phipps was aware of how scared they were of Old Grumpy, and showed them a safer way home. If they crossed the brook by the foot of his land, walking carefully across the narrow footbridge, which was made from two old railway sleepers bedded into the bank on each side, then they could walk along the narrow grass-covered earth bank, no more than two feet wide by one foot high, which ran up and away from the brook. The bank marked the boundary between two other holdings—Mr. Phipps was acquainted with both holders and knew they would not object to them walking along the bank. So they did. This route brought them to a narrow overgrown lane that bordered their father's land: it ran alongside the thick hawthorn hedgerow the boy was lying in. Therefore, they could walk not so much in a circle, but a square—the boundary of which was over a mile and a half.

Once Chowskie had passed Paul turned over onto his side; he was getting stiff. He looked up again through the leaves, through the twigs, through the hawthorn and breathed deeply, drank in the air. It had been a long day: a long hot day. There was now a dampness in the air, the light was failing, dusk was drawing in. Pulling himself back through the hawthorn and out onto his father's land, he stumbled at first, his legs were unsure, unsteady; likewise his eyes could not take in the dusk, the grey mists of darkness slowly creeping across the land, enveloping the sheds. So he walked and wobbled his way back across the field of young sprout plants. He walked along the side of the shed, resting his hand against the crates stacked at the side for support. As he cleared the side and came around the front of the shed, his eyes blinked from the light of the electric lamp in the shed and a voice disturbed his silence:

"'Ow bist?" said Sam, the stump of a woodbine stuck to his lower lip, "'Ow do, young Paul?"

The boy stopped and collected his thoughts:

"Hello Sam, I forgot you were still here."

"Aye well, I bist just finished, as 'ee can see."

Longman's Charity

He gestured over to the trays of onions standing, leaning against the side of the shed, gleaming from having been sorted and sifted, then washed with the hosepipe. He had done a brilliant job on them. The boy smiled a smile of surprise and pleasure at the sight. It was worth more to Sam than thanks from his employers: Paul's appreciation was genuine; Harry was usually too preoccupied to offer genuine thanks.

"Anyhow, I bist finished. 'Ou ought to be off afore they git frettin' about 'ee young Paul!"

So the child bid him farewell and ran out of the yellow semicircle formed by the electric light, and made his way across the gravel drive and onto the back lawn. As he walked, his pace slackened, his reluctance grew. From the kitchen he could hear sounds. Sounds he knew only too well. His parents were arguing: arguing and fighting. He took one sorrowful look back across his shoulders to the land, the hedgerows, the hawthorn, Longman's Charity, and to Sam, tidying up in the halo of yellow light before he settled down at the back of the shed for the night (to be up at five-o'clock to start the next day's work). Paul walked across the lawn to the passage. The noise from the kitchen was harsh, violent, uncompromising. He walked with foreboding.

Longman's Charity

Part Two
The Village Idiot

*"I am a reproach among all my adversaries,
but especially among my neighbours,
and am repulsive to my acquaintances;
those who see me outside flee from me."*
PSALM 31:11

Chapter Six
Abuse: Sanity and Dis-ease

> ~ *"In You, O Lord, I put my trust,*
> *let me never be put to shame.*
> *Deliver me in Your righteousness,*
> *and cause me to escape;*
> *incline Your ear to me,*
> *—and save me!"*
> PSALM 71:1-2

One

Paul sat bolt upright. It was the first Monday in September. It was the first day of the autumn term of the new school year. He sat behind his desk, his arms folded stiffly across his chest; he had a broad smile across his face, he was enthusiastic and pleased with his new teacher, his classroom, his first morning in the Juniors. He had been so worried, so fearful, but as it turned out everything was alright. They had lined up in the playground at 8:50am and then Mrs. Burridge came down with the other teachers to collect them. They formed rows of neatly dressed children, each line gradually getting taller—reflecting the varying ages of the children.

Walking proudly in through the school entrance, inside were cloakrooms on the right, and another set of wooden doors with glass windows just ahead of him. He walked through them, then on, through the hall and through further doors at the other end, and up a wide stone staircase. Turning back on themselves, they then crossed the upstairs hall, finally to enter the classroom door at the far end.

Longman's Charity

They were then assigned to their seats. Mrs. Burridge had taken the register and was now talking to them about the school and about the work they would be doing. Soon they were lining up for assembly and walking out into the hall.

Sounds of hushed silence greeted them, reverential silence, as a tall, thickset man—the Headmaster—entered. The silence in the hall as the Headmaster entered was solid, measurable, complete. It contrasted with the memory, still fresh and echoing in his mind from half-an-hour earlier, of clanging bells, the rasp of grit-strewn, pot-holed tarmac, the cacophony of screams and shouts and scuffling from scab-kneed boys and girls, the heirs—the sons and daughters— of market gardeners, that had bombarded his ears as he stood in the playground before the bell, waiting with his sister. He had tugged on his sister's arm as the swirling hoards dived and swerved and skidded, throwing grit up from the surface over his legs. With the bell, the screaming shouts of urgency had ceased and all froze to the spot. On the signal from a teacher who had just come out to ring the bell, they lined up. Now all the older children gently guided, directed, steered, and ushered any who looked lost and bewildered into line.

At first, lessons seemed straightforward enough, but as the days and weeks passed, his lack of skill in reading and writing began to show. It was decided that he would need some help. Therefore, one Monday morning he found himself being shepherded out of the class and into the hall with six other children, not all of them from his class. The teacher sat them in a circle and proceeded to give them each a copy of the same reading book. Once they had tried to go through reading the book, they were set some work and the teacher came around to help them individually. The boy was fascinated, but it didn't really make any more sense than when he attempted to read and write in class. He was also worried by the two boys sitting next to him. They were plotting and scheming about whom they would get at playtime, how they would go about it, and how they would get money. Paul was scared. The two boys—Alan, the ringleader, and Gary, who simply followed whatever the other said—were much older than he, and they kept looking at him with a suspicious gaze.

"'Ou wana be in wi' uz, eh?"

The little red-headed boy looked away, looked back to his book.

"'Ou be 'arry Broadley's kid baint, 'ou,? Alan repeated.

"Wot's a matter, cat got ee tongue, 'as ee?"

Alan stared at Paul through broken front teeth, a stare framed by a gaunt, scraggy, turkey-neck, a wild mop of unkempt yellow hair, and eyes that darted and strove to light on something that would give solace.

Paul didn't answer, merely looked at his book. Alan and Gerry continued to stare, their eyes burning into him: he feared to look up.

Chapter Six, Abuse: Sanity and Dis-ease

"And just what do you think you are doing Alan Smith?"

It was the teacher who had brought their malicious bent to a close. Worried sick for the next half hour, Paul could not get the encounter out of his mind. But by playtime they had forgotten all about him and were concentrating on the bullying, blackmail, and extortion they had planned—though it was small fry really; threepence here, an apple there. If they strayed too far, they found they had threatened one girl, who was considered part of another gang, then they were for it: after school they would get done over down in the Crown Meadows. Such skirmishes had the making of gang warfare, but then the injured parties forgot to turn up, or there were errands to run, and it was soon forgotten.

Three times per week Paul was taken out of class to join this small group to help him with his reading and writing. By Friday of the first week he was firmly resolved to learn as quickly as possible: he did not like being with this group, with these other boys. Whether this fear and revulsion added anything to his development is questionable; what was important was that the individual attention gave him the motivation to learn: reading and writing began to come together for him. A combination of this individual teaching, and his motivation to get back in the classroom away from this group succeeded. Within a few weeks he was told he did not need these extra lessons any longer. He left the hall that morning feeling a million miles high: I can read, I can, I really can, and I can write; well, not much, but better—at this point he looked at the other boys—better than you can, he thought. His look had been spotted by the others. They looked back, and sneered at him for being a creep. Thus, he was now beginning to catch up with the rest of his class—in literacy skills.

There was one other factor in the boy's learning and development that was resolved at this time: his eyesight. Nobody had noticed how he poured over a book. Even if they had noticed, no action had been taken: he was considered non-academic material, he was left to his own devices. There were three areas of work for children in and around the town: the land (market gardening), shops and a handful of tiny offices (secretarial or clerical work), or one of the small factories. Paul was only knee-high-to-a-grasshopper and not very strong in constitution. Although this counted against him in the stakes for being a land worker, his teachers, without a second thought, considered him marked out for market gardening: his father was a market gardener, likewise his grandfather afore him. Therefore his education—and thus the attention he would receive—would be governed by this conclusion. The sons of gardeners needed very little in the way of education: enough mathematics to count a stack of plums (multiplication helped speed this up), enough literacy to fill in the dockets having delivered the goods to the railway, or to read the instructions on a seed packet, and enough general knowledge to hold a conversation while in the public bar of the Railway Arms. Paul was slow learning to read and write and had not displayed much ability at anything beyond addition and subtraction: he was not bright—therefore he sat, not in the back row, but the row next to the rear. The bright children, those with the potential of going to Prince Henry's Grammar School, were seated at the front. Mrs. Burridge soon began to question the way the boy screwed his eyes up to see to the front of the class, and how he always worked with his head very close to the book. Mrs. Burridge wrote a letter to his mother about this. His mother took him to the opticians. He returned with a pair of spectacles—he was, as it turned out, short-sighted.

There were other primary schools in the town. Both Merstow Green and Bengeworth were Church of England Schools and took a different class of child. Then there was the Catholic school, which took Catholics and nothing else. So Evesham Council Junior School (Swann Lane for short) took all-comers of every shape and size and behaviour and background and parentage and religion and ability. After four years it handed a chosen few to Prince Henry's Grammar School, the remainder to Evesham County Secondary Modern School, or, if they travelled in from the villages to the east of the town, Blackminster Secondary Modern School. Most of Swann Lane's pupils lived in the town, or its immediate environs. Most of their parents worked the land or its related sub-industries, such as nurseries or seed merchants, or they worked in the factories. A handful cherished thoughts of the closed, almost secretive and unattainable crafts—working either in a garage or on the railway—but these trades took on few from this pool of labour. And this was the boys. At this time in the 1950s and early 1960s, the girls' highest ambition was to have children and run a home for their husband—the highest prize for their ambitions being to live in one of the new council houses on the Fairfield Estate. Most of the children in Paul's class came from the Fairfield Estate, or down-the-Bewdley.

Across the other side of the road from the juniors stood two further classrooms, recently built and similar to the huts in the infants school: grey aluminium, plate glass windows, cheap pink bricks, a low tin-covered pitched roof, set immediately behind the pavement, with a railing next to the road—lest any child came running out and into traffic. The huts had been built for expansion: the post-war baby boom. Indeed the school was really pushed for space: games were held half a mile away in the Crown Meadows next to the river, or a class could be seen walking—a neatly ordered line, in pairs—the opposite direction along Swann Lane to go to the Jubilee Hall for gym/P.E. Then the entire junior school walked to the Jubilee Hall in perfect silence, flanked by their teachers, as the clock approached midday, where rows of tables were put out for dinner. The

Chapter Six, Abuse: Sanity and Dis-ease

Jubilee Hall (an old Victorian building) was also used for the Christmas Concert and for special occasions such as prize giving.

That Christmas, Paul's year was predominant in the Christmas production, but he was scared stiff of taking part, of going on stage—he ended up as one of the shepherds, sitting atop of tables against the wall at the side of the hall with two other shepherds, ready to walk up and onto the stage at the appropriate moment. But his nerve went, he simply did not move, he stayed where he was while the other two went up. It was no loss to the production; with shepherds coming from other sides of the hall as well, and from behind the stage, there were too many to fit around the holy couple and a scuffle ensued!

Playtime was the time when Paul was least confident and most afraid. The playground seemed vast. He would often seek out his sister at playtime—to hold her hand and shelter behind her strength of character. He feared many of the other children and would purposely wander: he would walk around the playground according to a predefined route so as to pass the time away and avoid trouble. He would often walk around the infant playground, around the building, and back again, then risk crossing the junior playground, walk through the wide gap in the dividing wall and back into the infant playground. He then discovered there were other children doing this, trying to keep out of the way of the more strident elements of the playground society. Although Paul had children he could talk to, play with, chat with and walk with, at playtime, there was really no one friend whom he could really get to know. Whenever he asked anyone back to his house, or to play out, the answer usually came back as no, or the visit was deferred—most families wanted to avoid the Broadleys.

Two

The ballroom was alive with bright-light-partying squeals of enjoyment. Around the sides were tables with approximately five or six places at each. Food had been brought round for the children who were now either finishing their jelly and ice cream, or were dancing in the centre of the ballroom. It was mid-December and the annual League of Pity party in the Marine Ballroom. Children from all over the town and vale came for the afternoon's festivities. Although many of them were themselves deserving of charity, most spent the year collecting copper and silver coins in their League of Pity blue and yellow papier-mâché egg-shaped money boxes to present at this the annual party for the poor and needy. But there were well-heeled children there too, presenting their bulging money boxes, the boys bowing in their crisp black suits, the girls curtseying in their wide-splayed, many-layered party dresses, then to receive their blue and yellow badge in honour of their donation. Sitting at the table watching the others as they danced, Paul was too shy, too reluctant to get up with the others and dance. They had finished eating, so he sat watching. The music stopped, a voice announced the final dance and all were now urged to join in. All the children got up in their squeaky, awkwardly shaped best frocks and suits, some trying to rub out the gravy or jelly stain. The accordion started playing "Cock O' the North"; Christine and Elizabeth came over to persuade Paul to join in, but to no avail. He sat there, the only one not joining in—and hated himself for being so shy, so afraid.

The League of Pity (a branch of the NSPCC, founded in the late nineteenth century) held parties all over the country. These gatherings were essentially wealthy, philanthropic people having pity on poor little children. As such they were part of the outpouring of charity by the well-off. For many a sort of religious obligation lay behind such charitable ventures; for others it was more subtle—how could they face their God and claim to love their neighbour in Africa, in Asia, in South America when they so woefully neglected their brother and sister living next door to them. There was much charity in the Vale, much religion, much spirituality, some quite deep. Much that passed for religion in the town came as part and parcel of culture and roots. During the nineteenth century there had been a small influx of people from Northern cities. Why Evesham?—because they knew the name from the trays and boxes that ended up in the little corner shops from which they would buy their sustenance. They brought with them their religious traditions of the chapel and nonconformity, of hymns and the gospel, and the righteousness of hard labour and pity for the poor. They would sing the lines of the Victorian hymn writer:

> The rich man in his castle,
> the poor man at his gate,
> God made them high and lowly,
> and ordered their estate.

They met a well-ordered and age-old rural tradition—nigh on a thousand years old—with the parish church and its vicar at the centre. The commonly held belief was that religion was for the old, the sick, and the dying. If they partook it was at Harvest, Christmas, Easter, and Whitsuntide. This religious calendar was coupled with those activities that were a fusion of Pagan and Christian: wassailing and its offspring, carol singing, celebrations on Plough Monday, and so forth. These traditions best survived in the Cotswolds, and in the older Evesham (pronounced: Ayssum) families. But deep down there was an underlying thread, a sense of grace which meant they knew there was a definite moral order, that there was a God, a Creator, a reality beyond themselves and their humdrum existence—but a personal God? A self-sacrificed, dying, and resurrected living God?

Chapter Six, Abuse: Sanity and Dis-ease

Most would not have considered themselves poor, but had very little: just a few sticks of furniture, enough money, just enough for food and clothing, though "it were al'as a struggle to find cloth for the littul 'uns." They could always do with just that little bit more, but they managed to get by. And they gave thanks; the widow's mite being a just and profoundly true metaphor. The poor rural peasant/working class, proud and independent, gave freely, especially to a lone travelling land worker looking like he was on hard times. He would be taken in, fed and clothed from the scant subsistence level of their possessions, even though it then meant they would have to do without, for they knew that if such a man had tried to appeal to the more well-heeled he would have had the door slammed in his face. In the North Cotswolds the Methodist tradition had taken deep root alongside the Cotswold Morris, and ancient English Country Dances, which were a right and proper, and respectable ways to dance. Methodism reflected the absence of much of the traditional songs, but all the same, they were proud and independent people. In the Vale, older traditions persisted through the nineteenth century—then died very suddenly with the social upheaval caused by the First World War and the arrival of the motor car, whereas the Cotswold tradition, with its way of life stretching back a thousand years, hung on until the 1920s and 1930s: nonconformism held out to the bitter end, whilst the growing wealth amongst many freehold market gardeners led them into municipal pride, the boast of doing what was right for the church—that is, the Church of England.

Within the town of Evesham there were Saint Lawrence and All Saints, the main parish churches for the town: two separate churches in the grounds of what remained of Evesham Abbey—one for the ordinary townsfolk, the other attended by the more well-to-do. But this was the Church of England.

Up near the railway station was the Roman Catholic church and its school. The Church of England's school was set over the other side of Merstow Green four hundred yards away from its mother church. To many the Catholic church was still considered to be somewhat foreign and unhealthy. Then there were Anglican churches in the parishes of Bengeworth and Hampton, still to an extent separate villages. The Church of England's presence was completed by the church in the graveyard along Waterside (for funerals and committals) and the church, recently built on the Fairfield Estate, which belonged to, and was part of, Hampton parish. The nonconformist element, which was strong, was served by the Methodist church, standing by the river at the foot of the Workman Bridge, the Baptist church along Cowl Street, the Bewdley Mission, amongst other congregations. Between them their congregations believed in the rightness of their own brand of Christianity, used their religion for their own strength, and for their own thanksgiving and charity, but accepted the boundaries between the denominations as God-given. There were families who were noted as religious, those who went to church, supported the church, and supported the local community. Such churchgoers expected prestige, status, and deference as a result, believing they had a divine right to the best pews in church.

Many of these people also took a pride in sin: "well it don't really hurt any'un do et!" Wives of leading business market gardeners would regularly sleep around, then put their Sunday best on and parade off to church, considering themselves better than the poor and the lowly. These were women whose husbands would fire on the spot a casual workman who muttered the word "cuckold" under his breath, who would give the lowest possible price per bunch to onion tie-ers, beating down the cost of everything, then give handsomely to the church roof restoration fund—thereby showing concern for God's building but not for his people. Then there were those who were "a bit gone on this 'ere religion." It was reckoned, according to the average gardener at the market, that they did not think much to so-and-so's religion if it made them so standoffish; or they would note how "that 'un go saying 'is prayers en All Saints, with 'is thees and thous and 'I'm not worthy' but 'ee goes rampaging like a mad bull through the sayul, pushing in front of every'un else to get to them leeks!" Such views reflected a deep-held universal view of the hypocrisy that religious pride could breed. But many families who were thought of as religious would be considered good and honest, and "basically they be decent enough sort." Such families or individuals were looked up to as spiritual role models—not necessarily the clergy in the various churches in the town, but ordinary people. Such a position held with it responsibility.

And then there were the Broadleys: old Henry Broadley had come from the smoke-wreathed, emaciated pride of urban working-class Lancashire in the middle years of the nineteenth century. His son, Jack Broadley, had built up a business in market gardening. Jack considered he had a position to maintain in the local community, went to church at Saint Lawrence most Sundays, and was thankful for the grace that allowed him his success. His son attended the Church of England School on Merstow Green, which, when the time came, led Jack to arrange a place at the Grammar School—in keeping with his own perception of his local status. Harry sang in the choir at Saint Lawrence, and was confirmed in his teens, accepting what he was taught about the divine order. Then there was Meg. Her father, William Riley, born in 1887, had his roots in the frugality of the semi-Irish East End working class docker community. With the absence of male influence (a father who had disappeared), lovingly cherished by his twelve older sisters, he adopted a brand of low church Christianity, characterized by restraint, self-improvement, and abstinence from alcohol. He went to night school, ambitious for advancement, and moved out with his young family to Evesham to live an honest, upright, quiet life: measured, ordered, and godly. Renée, his wife, came from a similar background in Bristol. Meg went to church at Saint Andrew's, the parish church in Hampton village, where she was married to Harry Broadley. But there was another religion, a secret religion, that Jack Broadley and William Riley were adherents of, a secret society that accounted for the rise in status and their success as businessmen—freemasonry. At this point in its history freemasonry was quite happy to go along with Christianity, provided it was considered the superior of the two—the lodge's secret gnostic knowledge was seen to transcend the truths of the gospel, for many.

By the time Paul and Christine were at Swann Lane, the relationship between Meg and Harry was tense, brooding, and sullen at best; violent, destructive, and menacing at worst. Meg kept his home, had borne his children, scrubbed and cleaned and cooked, but did not love him. Harry by this time was an arrogant fire-breathing atheist, muttering violent criticisms about the church, condemning those who attended, including Meg and her parents. Meg gradually ceased to go to church. She held to her beliefs, but looked on and condemned Harry for his foul temper, rough breeding and manners, and his atheism: condemned him before God.

Meg decided that her two children should at least go to church for a while, they could then decide for themselves if such a habit was of value to them when they grew up. One fine Sunday morning the three of them walked around to Saint Richard's, the church hall on the Fairfield estate—although they lived within the Hampton parish, those living in the eastern half of the parish attended this new church, Saint Richard's. It had been designed so that chairs could be put out, facing the sanctuary with its neat trim altar, candles and all, set apart from the main hall. This had been done so that wooden doors forming a screen could be drawn across the sanctuary, sealing it off from the bulk of the interior, which could then be used for whist drives, bingo, jumble sales, and local meetings. The building had risen with the houses on the estate (the old parish church could not accommodate the number of people living on the estate who wanted to attend the Church of England). It was built of pink, utilitarian, post-war bricks, and was single story, with a low pitched roof surmounting tall thin metal-framed windows. There were no pews inside; the faithful sat and squeaked on tubular metal and plywood stackable chairs, reflecting the worst of cheap 1950's design. Marriages, baptisms, and confirmations took place here; interments were carried out in the main town graveyard along Waterside (not in the ancient graveyard around Hampton parish church).

So, Paul and Christine would walk round together to Saint Richard's each Sunday morning—along with their mother for the first year. Then Meg ceased to attend, leaving them to go themselves. Along with about a dozen other children from the estate, or from Cheltenham Road, they would sit in the front two rows whilst the proud and the humble from that part of the parish came in to give thanks, say their prayers, plead and bargain with each other, with the priest-in-charge, or with God. The service each Sunday, a sung communion, was very high church Anglo-Catholic, with the heady smell of swirling incense, intoned creeds and prayers, readings spoken clearly and projected even for the most hard of hearing. Fascinated and mystified by the ceremony—the distance, the enigma, the beauty—Paul sensed holiness amongst the people. After the service they stopped behind for Sunday school, to learn the service, the creed, the whys and wherefores: he was proud when he got a question right. There was his sister and five others. Christine started to help with the Sunday school for the younger children. Meg's mother wrote from Weston of her concern for what was happening. This was not concern over their church going, that was to be praised, but the *type* of church: high church. From her low-church scriptural-base Renée was critical of the mystical, and of Popish Romanism (she had become an Evangelical after William's death, distancing herself from his secret masonic religion; though to be fair, William had apparently sought to combine the truths of Christianity with the lodge). Meg took her comments, but did not act upon them.

The priest-in-charge was young and dynamic, and traditional and conservative in his churchmanship. Paul liked him and responded to his warmth, his friendship. In addition Paul's religious understanding had been fed by material from school, from hymns, from comments by those around him. When he was seven, around the time of William Riley's death, he had been found wandering around the suburb of Greenhill to the north of the town trying to find Jesus—at least that is what he said to the people who saw him, a couple who had known Meg's parents before they moved away. The couple knew the child would not normally be wandering around by himself—clearly puzzled and disorientated—at such a young age in the opposite part of town. From his replies to their questions, it became clear he knew, from school assemblies, the hymn "There is a green hill far away . . . where our dear Lord . . ." and had assumed that it referred to Greenhill, the suburb, and he was trying to find Jesus, to ask his help: his mother and father had been fighting again, his mother had a black eye, his father's head was bleeding, and he was scared, frightened by it all, and he felt funny—there was this noise in his head, and, and, something else was happening, but he was silent about that. . . .

Chapter Six, Abuse: Sanity and Dis-ease

So Paul and Christine started confirmation classes: he initially went along because his sister did, but he listened, thought, felt, and took in. The boy's approach was unorthodox, unfussy, and direct: if God existed and loved him, then *He* must help him, must do something about his rowing parents, about the noise in his head, about, about that which he would not think about, would not own to in his own mind, would not own what was happening to him. . . . If Christ had died for him then why was he suffering and hurting so much? There was too much escapism in this—he half expected a thunderbolt to rain down on his parents, to frighten them into changing their ways. When he was ten, despite concerns from his mother that he was too young, he went forward with his sister for confirmation, having already met the giant, ageing, and white-haired Bishop of Worcester walking in the cloisters of Worcester Cathedral with the other confirmation candidates.

Paul understood what he was doing, understood what was required in terms of a personal commitment to Christ, to the gospel, but perhaps there was too much escapism in his commitment, a hope that through such a vow everything would be right in his life. Many years later he would look at the little book that had been given to him in the confirmation classes—*The Sanctuary of God*—which asserted in one sentence that God would uphold, save, and help those in need, who committed themselves. He had underlined this sentence with such severity and ferocity with a ballpoint pen that he had gone right through the page, the ink damaging the page underneath, the imprinted groove from the pen, could be detectable ten pages further on. His understanding of the cross of Christ was, of course, that of a child and lacked the wisdom of maturity. Perhaps he was too much *in* the suffering to appreciate its value. Yet the confirmation commitment was two-way; Christ did preserve him over the coming years, even though those who should have cared for his welfare consigned him to hell! He was to go through fire and water and emerge relatively unscathed. By his late-teens he may have forgotten Christ—but Christ had not forgotten him.

So what was it that was troubling him so profoundly? Paul and Christine were confirmed in Saint Richard's, his maternal grandmother sending him a copy of the Book of Common Prayer as a present. Many in the rest of the congregation were a bit sceptical of the eagerness of these young children (aged between ten and twelve years). There was a strong element of snobbery, lower-middle-class snobbery, especially from key families, families who considered themselves important to the smooth running of the church, men and women who felt the church would collapse without them to open it up, clean and polish it, play the piano, welcome people, shake their hands briskly, and serve tea and coffee.

By the time he was confirmed Paul had developed a nervous habit of nodding his head, or laying it on his left shoulder. This was even more pronounced when he was sitting in church: the trauma of rows and violence at home, his tortuous shyness, the teasing and taunts of other children . . . but there was more, a white emptiness invaded him at night, when he had gone to bed, after, after. . . .

After the service other children in church would tease him about continuously nodding his head. Some, albeit a minority, of the more proud adults would comment that he should not be there, it was upsetting to see, or at least he should not be sitting in the front row with the other children. Paul's confidence was waning, he knew what people were saying, he was embarrassed.

Then the priest-in-charge who had been so inspirational moved on, eventually to become a chaplain in the Royal Navy, and Paul ceased going to church regularly. Christine continued, helping with the Sunday School, and Paul still went along occasionally, but gradually less and less until he ceased going altogether. He had not lost his faith, simply allowed it to go underground—a bit like Chowskie. By this time he was moving on to secondary school and there were many problems pressing in on his little life. The trouble for some of the congregation, though it was only some—a vocal minority—was that they were more concerned with doing things properly: putting on well-presented services, with everyone on their best behaviour, all problems neatly brushed under the carpet, ready to stand before the vicar, as if ready for a presentation photograph. The Broadley boy and his psychological problems upset this serene picture. If Jesus had walked in sweaty, dusty, exhausted from tramping the hot, dry roads of Palestine, in tattered robes and dishevelled hair, some would have promptly seen him out, or made him wait in the cloakrooms until a more convenient moment.

Three

"What d'you get?"
"I got some sherbert," Ian answered. "What you get then?—gi'us a look!"
He grabbed Anthony's bag and exclaimed,
"E'ur you got more than me, how come!"
"Because I got more money than you!"
(Anthony was well spoken . . .)
Ian gave the other kid a shove. They stood outside The Bluebird, the local store and Post Office run by Bates, next to their garage, on the Cheltenham Road. Opposite them was the entrance to Fairfield Road. The shop was a two-storey, detached building, Edwardian in style, the whole front of the ground floor composing of a shop front formed from wooden casement windows painted blue

Chapter Six, Abuse: Sanity and Dis-ease

and white. Paul and Christine were next to come out of the shop, followed by Noel and Dominic. They all looked busily in their paper bags to check they had not been done—fishing out black jacks, sherbert sticks, flying saucers.

"Here, look: a snake!" Noel dangled a wine gum in the shape of long thin green and yellow snake in front of Christine.

"Orr, leave off you!" she said.

Sucking the paper on the corner of the triangular shaped Calypso—a frozen drink—Paul started to suck the orange flavoured ice inside.

"Gi'us a suck!" shouted Ian, as he grabbed at Paul's arm.

Paul swerved round on his feet to avoid the grabbing arm, slipped, and dropped the Calypso on the tarmac forecourt.

"Look what you made me do!"

"Oh no, you're not gonna sulk now are you," Ian replied.

"Stop it you lot! Here, have one of my tip-tops, it's strawberry, is that alright?" Anthony handed him a long, thin, frozen tube. The boy thanked him.

"Stop arguing you lot and come on, let's get across the road," Christine added.

They walked to the crossing, stood by the Belisha beacon and waited for the traffic to stop. Once it did they crossed, keeping their eyes fixed on the road—traffic now was fast and dangerous, the road being ten times busier than it was just five years earlier. They crossed safely and stood leaning and swinging on the iron railing by the footpath leading from the rear of Fairfield Place, Paul found a threepenny bit in his pocket:

"Hey, I can get some more sherbert!"

He ran to the zebra crossing and waited for the cars to stop. Christine just caught up with the back of him. The car coming up the hill stopped. Paul started to cross, accelerating into a run. Christine ran at him, screaming for him to stop, and grabbing the back of his shirt as another car overtook the one that had stopped. The second car screeched past, juddering to a halt fifty yards past the crossing, having past within a hair's breadth of Paul. The others ran up. Ian shouted obscenities at the driver for not paying attention and nearly killing Paul, who was shaking, having collapsed on the road as his sister grabbed at his shirt. They walked along the road slowly, joking with each other, trying to make light of the incident.

In a moment Christine had saved Paul's life.

Together, loosely in fours, fives, sixes, any number up to about eight, they could be seen playing around the area: Careless' Field over the other side of the road; down the drive (a mud and stone lane linking the Cheltenham Road, alongside the Bluebird, with Hampton); down the Charity; round Fairfield; or out along the Cheltenham Road. They all lived along the Cheltenham Road. Ian's father worked in market gardening; so did Anthony's. Noel came from a family of seven children, a Catholic family living a few doors up from the Broadleys. David was a different kettle of fish entirely. His parents were very, very middle class: Daddy worked in an office away in somewhere-or-other. David wanted to go to a private school when he was eleven—Mummy had told him he did. He did not play with the others for long, once his mother overheard them singing a rude children's song, and objected to the company he was keeping. Anthony was quiet, level headed, mature, and sensible, a born leader; he kept things in order, and stopped squabbles getting out of hand. Noel was the youngest, and was regarded as the baby in the gang. Ian was a bruiser—happy to take on anyone, well, not really, but he was thin and wiry, and looked as if he could take on the world and defend his corner. The two Broadley children completed the gang. Paul was a quiet eight-year-old becoming more and more withdrawn, inhabiting the fringes of this group. Sometimes Martin, Noel's brother, would join; sometimes one or two of Christine's friends from Hampton or Fairfield would join them. Christine, now ten years old, would often spend more time with older girl friends, often going off with them after school, indulging in pop music and boys. . . .

They continued as a group out along the Cheltenham road, walking slowly, scuffing up the grass, kicking twigs about.

"Stupid—that driver—som'un awt to giv 'em a good 'iding. They would us if et wur our fault!" cried Ian.

"Yes," answered Anthony, laconically.

"Hey, let's go down the pond, see if there are any frogs yet," said Paul.

"There should be, it's getting on for the end of April," Anthony added.

"That decides it then," Ian said crisply as he slapped his hands together.

"I won't get wet, will I?" asked David.

They filed along the edge of the land, then scrambled through the hedgerow and then continued down the grass bank between two holdings that Mr. Phipps had introduced them to.

"Hey what about Karen, d'you hear what happened to 'er uncle?" shouted Ian as he balanced with his arms flaying out.

"Pardon?" cried Anthony. "Do you mean Karen, you know in McGlinn's class?"

"Yes!" giggled Christine, "Did you hear what her auntie did to him!"

"Yeah, cut off his willy with the garden shears!" interrupted Ian.

Anthony was trying to keep Dominic and Noel well back from the conversation by slowing down and letting the others get ahead.

"He'd been, you know, he'd got other girlfriends, not just her, so she chopped it off in the middle of the night with shears. It killed him!"

Chapter Six, Abuse: Sanity and Dis-ease

"No it didn't, he lost a lot of blood, but that's just made up." Anthony added factually.

By now they had reached the pond. Ian took one look, then pronounced:

"Ain't no tads or frogs, see, told ya!" Ian said, "stupid idea, weren't 'et!"

He threw a stone into the pond, then another, this time trying to make it skim the surface.

"Don't!" cried Paul. "There's things in there. The frogs may have gone, but there's lots in there." He lay down with his head close to the water.

"Well, I'm off; boring down 'ere!" Ian turned and walked back to the others, who had yet to catch up, and persuaded them to go to Fairfield to knock up some other friends. They all started talking again about Karen's uncle—it was the talk of the Vale at the moment, how his wife had found him in bed with a neighbour, then many days later, snipped his manhood away in the middle of the night. By the time the ambulance had come, he had nearly died of blood loss. The incident ensured that this generation of young children would find out very quickly about the facts of life, though on any day they could observe the procreation of nature around them: animal, plant, insect. They observed and talked explicitly on such matters.

"You coming ?" shouted Christine. She ran back to where her brother was by the pond.

"Look! Look, thur be a water boatman, it is!" He whispered animatedly.

"Come on Chris, leave him wi'es pond, he's still showing off 'bout his sweets—scaredy baby Pauly, scaredy pants, scaredy pants, baby Pauly, loopy loo . . ." Ian's voice trailed into the distance. Christine ran to catch up with them.

"Ooooww!"

She kicked Ian in the back of the legs to stop him teasing her brother. Paul stayed and looked into the pond, watched the water boatman, lay riveted as a great pond snail hauled itself up out onto a reed—then a tiny frog jumped across onto the grass, nearly to his face.

"See, thur' 'es frogs 'ere!" he whispered to himself.

Paul regarded this place as special, as precious, like he would if he had a jewel, a big expensive green jewel. He hated being called names; he wished they could see what he saw—if they stopped for just a little while, sat or lay still, then they could have seen what he had. What had now happened, happened often—the others had moved on, he had been left behind. The others often had a feeling that they were dragging him along. Whenever they wanted to make a rope swing across the brook, he objected: thoughts of damaging the trees. When they wanted to steal bird's eggs from nests, he objected. He was becoming more and more absorbed in micro-worlds, absorbed in the landscape, in God's creation.

Paul rolled over onto his back and simply lay, allowing the vibrant, chattering, sun-lit beauty of that spring growth to bombard him: the chatter of sparrows, the flittings of nest-building blue tits, the wriggling, diving, rampaging life in the pond, the struggling, bursting, and unfurling of new leaves on willow, hawthorn, spear-tipped grasses, the early spring flowers forming carpets of white, yellow, and gold around headland and field boundaries, surmounting grass verges and the muddles of sheds, and the crops growing on in ordered beauty and simplicity. Above all the cool spring sun watched and blessed, and gave of its strength. He lay, he knew not for how long. He heard a van drive by; he froze—was it Old Grumpy. He lay still, hidden in the grass as the van spluttered off into the distance. Once all was silent he sat up, gazed around him, and then stumbled to his feet. He felt a wet patch on the side of his trousers. He rummaged in his pocket—and drew out a crumpled, tip-top wrapper that had split and thawed, and spilt its contents in his pocket! He fished it out, washed his hands in the brook, then wiping the polythene wrapper on the grass, placed it inside the paper bag in the other pocket.

So, Paul wandered on, aimlessly. The lane struck out ahead of him: a white, rutted ribbon, navigating through the holdings, sheds, and barrows. The lane then veered away from the brook, by as much as fifty yards. He walked slowly, leisurely—an unhurried ease filled his mind. He walked on in a generally southerly direction till, after about three quarters of a mile, he came to a post, about three feet high. This marked the end of Hampton Charity. He had never gone beyond this—not because anyone had told him not to, but because somehow this felt like the edge of his kingdom, his world. Beyond lay Christchurch Charity. This morning, eight-years of age, fuelled by a sense of adventure he strode on, purposefully, daringly, feeling the blood in his veins, sensing the newness like the spring in the air. After a short distance the lane turned sharp left, climbing up steadily. At the top of the gentle rise, about two hundred yards away, he could see two brothers. He knew them from the market and the railway yard. Harry often talked to them. He could not remember how, but knew they were relatives. They looked busy, unloading wooden boxes from their small pick-up. He stood by the curve in the lane and looked ahead: a rough mud track, a vehicle's width went ahead. He walked along it. The brook was returning along his right side and as the track petered out, he walked along the wide headland that was between the land and the brook. Ahead of him lay the Red Barn. He had noticed it in the distance, from the Cheltenham Road, up by Gypsies' Corner, but it had been too far away to take in. Now it was only twenty or thirty yards ahead of him. He walked on towards it, stopping again to look. Around the barn, the headland seemed to be creeping out even further than was acceptable to most gardeners, with a profusion of butterfly-dancing, grasshopper-infested, insect-biting grasses, and a collar of primrose around the edge next to the brook.

Chapter Six, Abuse: Sanity and Dis-ease

Walking on slowly, taking in the scene, he walked past the holding pond and onto the lane by the barn. He looked over to the west. In the distance were tiny lorries—he thought about it and then realized it was the Cheltenham Road, and that the lane must lead up to Gypsies' Corner. He looked over to the other side of the lane from where he stood. A small wood or copse lay on the other side of the lane. It was surrounded by a barbed-wire fence. He went over to it and lay on the ground, then crawled underneath the fence. There was a small hole through the wire, and by lying on his stomach he could just get through, under the holly bushes and brambles. After a few yards, as the undergrowth thinned he found himself in another world. He clambered further, towards the centre of the copse. He stood and looked around him. He was surrounded by tall beech and ash trees. Light filtered through the crowns of the trees. It was a bright day outside, but in here the light was muted and soft. Near the centre there was thin, pale, grass. A brook tricked over the stony earth, flowing ever northward to the edge of the copse, where it became the Charity Brook. Paul looked around him. A squirrel darted across the thin grass, then scampered up a young beech tree. He sat down by the brook, his mind trying to take it all in. There was a rustle in the branches—he looked and saw the squirrel had jumped across to an ash.

"Sorry," he murmured quietly, "I hope I'm not trespassing in your world."

He had directed his words to the squirrel, which then hopped across to the next tree, and the next. His eyes followed it as it moved down an old ash tree. At the foot of the tree was a shallow pool. It was really no more than the waters from the brook flowing wide in a hollow or shallow depression in the ground. There had been a lot of rain that spring, and the waters lapped around the thin grass—iridescent lime green and yellow—starved as they were of direct sunlight by the canopy above. Walking almost reverently to the pool he lay down by its waters. He felt he was in heaven, the light streaming in shafts through the trees, the secret, silent, almost holy, world of the pool, the animals, the trees—all safely tucked away behind the brambles and holly.

"Maybe it's a door to heaven; maybe I've got through!"

He heard a tractor revving up in the distance—and thought otherwise. He stilled his reverie.

"Oh help! What am I doing—the time . . . dinner!"

He scrambled back through the undergrowth, crawled out through the fence, and stood. He looked up towards the distant road, and ran: he ran and jogged all the way up till he reached Gypsies' Corner, then made his way along the Cheltenham Road. A lorry pulled up on the opposite side. A voice called over to him:

"Ow bist, young Paul, what you doing up here?"

It was Sam, on the back of Harry's lorry. The boy crossed over and climbed into the cab.

"Shouldn't you be back home, for dinner by now Paul?" his father asked.

"Yes, I . . . I," he wanted to share his new found secret, but then he thought, no! Better keep it safe. I don't want the others finding out. "Yes, I lost track of the time, I was walking round the Charity."

"Well, you're in luck, we're just going back to the yard now, your mother's going to be pleased with you!"

The lorry drew down the drive to the sheds. Paul got out and raced into the back passage.

"And where on earth have you been? Christine's been home ages, worried sick I've been . . . oh there's no thinking of me, is there? No I've just got to slave away while you go gallivanting off around, all over the place. . . ."

The child walked in sheepishly and sat down at the dinner table.

That afternoon he was confined to the house. The next day he stayed in and helped his mother: sweeping and washing the concrete out the back; he then tidied up the outhouses. Then it rained. It was the end of the week before he could get out to the Charity again. Christine had gone round to see her school friends so he made his way across his father's land, out through the hedgerow, onto the lane, then made his way round to the Red Barn. This time as he approached the barn, there was someone there. Paul paused in the long grass around the brook watching as a man in his sixties, bent double, carried a crate filled with spring onions. The man put the crate down by the holding pond, placed his hands on his hips, and straightened his back up. Then he took hold of the crate and slid it into the pool. It floated downstream to the neck of the pool, where it joined another crate of onions, pressed against the section of rusty railing. The man cautiously drew out a packet of Woodbines, unhurriedly opening the top and taking out a cigarette. The man looked up and across to where the boy stood amongst the grasses and rushes at the edge of the water, about ten yards away.

"Ow bist?" It was Jim Beason. "Ow bist, young 'un?" He repeated the question. He stilled his reverie, his daydream.

"Oh, I'm alright, thank you," he answered.

"You be 'arry Broadley's little un, baint you? Paul ain't it?"

"Yes."

"And what be a'you doing round 'ere then, having a walk are thee?"

"Yes, I often come down here, well not as far as this, but yes, I like it."

"Shouldn't you be off a causing trouble wi' some other young scallywags? I'm sure I did when I were you'n age?"

"I like looking at things, like the pond back over there."

Chapter Six, Abuse: Sanity and Dis-ease

Paul gestured with his arm, back along the Charity.

"Oh aye, by Cecil Phipp's land—it bain't been used for yearn though!"

He examined the cigarette with minute attention.

"That's why I like it—there's all sort of things in there—little creatures."

"Aye well, I'um sure there ain't much living in here at moment."

He gestured across to the holding pond by his feet into which he had just slid the crates of onions, the murky sand-brown waters swirling around as the crates bobbed in the soup.

"Is this your land?" Paul asked.

"Aye, after a fashion, I rents et."

"Have you worked it for long?

"Ow, let me see, donkey's years . . ."—he tapped the cigarette on the back of the packet, allowing his forefinger and thumb to slide down it, then turned the cigarette over and repeated the process—". . . that is except during the war, then the old 'uman kept it going. That is Doris, my good lady. My name's James. James Beason—that is, they call me Jim, ever since I wern a lad. I remember your grandfather, old Jack Broadley, 'im and me, we was at school together—afore the first lot that is, you know, the first war. How's he getting on? Haven't seen 'im for a while."

"He's alright, thank you. Did you say you had been in the war?"

"Yes, Aircraftsman J. T. Beason at your service . . . ," at which he stood and saluted, touching his outstretched fingers on his forehead, ". . . sir!"

"What aircraft did you work on? Where were you based? Did you go overseas? . . ."

"Hold on a minute young-fellow-me-lad!"

"Sorry, I . . ."

"That's alright, now let me see, I started my apprenticeship on Hurricanes and Blenheims. That was over in Lincolnshire, then I got moved down to Sussex—that was the rough 'un that was—Battle of Britain . . ."

Jim placed the packet of Woodbines back in his pocket, then proceeded to sit down on his side of the bank. Paul was by then stood opposite him on the other side of the bank. Jim gestured to him to sit down: he did so. Jim unhurriedly lit up his cigarette: he lit a match, drew in on his cigarette, let the match drop in the pool, took out the cigarette, then proceeded to explain about the aircraft he had worked on, where he had been, his time in South East Asia. He talked slowly, measuredly, in tired tones, occasionally dragging on his woodbine, sometimes letting it hang off his bottom lip. The boy asked questions about the different aircraft, telling him of the small plastic models he had made of some of the aircraft, and the drawings he had done.

Longman's Charity

"Well, we can us be sittin' around 'ere all day talking, can us?"

At which he straightened his back up and proceeded to turn round towards the Red Barn.

Paul came back the next day to talk to Jim, and the next week; then it was time to go back to school. He visited the Red Barn—often sheltering in it when a shower came. Sometimes he would stop and talk to Jim if he was working the land. Jim shared his memories of aircraft and his years in the war; the boy his detailed knowledge of the aircraft. But Paul always sat on the far side of the brook, Jim sitting on the barn side. They shared observations about the countryside, the seasons, the blossoming of the hawthorn, the trees. But these encounters were only a few—during that summer. Jim grew older and more arthritic and had to give up his holding. So Paul would sit on the far bank of the brook and go through conversations in his mind with Jim even though he was not there. He continued to visit the copse many, many times during evenings, or at the weekend, or in the school holidays, to sit by its secret shallow pool and glade, especially when there had been a row between his parents. No one else ventured there—or so he believed. He would run or walk from the house, wanting the security of this, his secret hideaway. The peace was holy, the stillness complemented by the trickling of the water over the stones, with the light dappling through the branches overhead. No house was near. No other person was in sight. It was his little world, his sanctuary; he was safe. But what was it he believed he was safe from?

Four

Like most children, indeed like most people, Paul's mind had the ability to shut away certain experiences, certain things that were happening to him, not so much to deny but to lock away certain memories as if they did not exist. Sometimes this is the only way people can stay sane and get through life. But this is also a dangerous mechanism because such a one then loses all conscious memory and understanding of what has happened, indeed is happening on a daily basis; that is, experiences that should not be denied.

The boy's health and constitution was what was in those days described as delicate. All his short life he had been suffering from asthma. He clearly had what was to be diagnosed in his adult life as a Ménières related disease (only in adult life would this vertigo, tinnitus, hearing confusion be diagnosed as a Ménières-type condition associated with the inner ears and the hearing centres in the brain—Ménières *type*, or *related*, because children were not supposed to develop Ménières disease). Because the tinnitus and vertigo would often—but not always—oppress him when his parents were rowing and fighting he blocked out

Chapter Six, Abuse: Sanity and Dis-ease

this experience. The condition was terrifying to a small boy: the grating, rasping dizziness, the sense of being sucked down, spinning; of waking in the night to the noise in his head, the sense of the world spinning even with his eyes closed, the conviction he was being dragged down. Was it the attempted abortion that had caused damage to the developing child's brain and hearing in his mother's womb? Many children who were subjected to amateur chemical abortion survived but were brain damaged. Paul appeared to have survived intact—but had he?

The fights between his parents disturbed him profoundly. His parents were like a couple of spoilt kids arguing over their relationship, fighting over the hatred they had for each other, seething with aggressive belligerence over who hated the other the greatest, when all of that should have been put to one side when there were two children to consider. The two Broadley children were turned out proper, as it was said; they were clean, well fed, properly dressed. But was not that a mask, a front? As a child Paul was deeply disturbed, deeply inhibited and frightened, deeply traumatized, quiet, and lonely. On the surface, the rows and violence between his parents cut deeply into him. He vividly remembered waking in the night as a child after tossing and turning for what seemed hours, having seen nothing in his dreams but his mother's bloodied face accompanied by the smashing of objects, plates, and so forth, and his father's violently dreadful voice. The boy still had the habit of nodding his head constantly when in the company of others; this did not endear him to his peer group. But was this a symptom of a deeper malaise?—at night he would toss and turn, he could not keep still, he would get up and walk around the house whilst the others were sleeping, or from around the age of eleven would climb out of his bedroom window, swing onto the flat roof via the cast-iron drainpipe, and walk his dad's land. Was this involuntary head movement related to a form of nervous disorder, a chorea? The violence of the rows, which were near constant, the alienation and trauma cut deep, but there was a far deeper cause for the trauma he exhibited. Yes, depression and inhibition, he was painfully shy and introverted, and he exhibited Ménières disease, and elements of St Vitus's dance. However, there was a much deeper, more corrosive cause that lay with his mother.

Shortly after the death of William, his grandfather, whom he loved more dearly than anything in his world, Paul started to wet the bed. This in itself is not unusual in boys of his age. So his mother would put a nappy on him each night. This phase of bed-wetting was really only whilst he was seven to eight years of age, however, the nightly ritual continued for six years from when he was seven-and-a-half years of age till just after his thirteenth birthday. However, she would spread out a nappy—the traditional sort made from heavy-duty towelling—over the kitchen table. He would meekly lie on the table and she would fold the nappy around him, pinning the sides with those large safety pins that he hated so much—which dug into his sides. Sometimes, if she was tired she would accidentally prick him with one of them, or did she do this on purpose? Then came the plastic pants with elasticated waist and leg bands. He hated them so much, so very much. But most of all, he hated himself, and he feared: he feared if anyone should come past the kitchen window, or even to the back door. Occasionally this would happen. One of his father's work friends, a fellow gardener, would call by, his mother rushing to the door to keep the man in the passageway, or hastily draw the curtains in response to her son's pleading. The boy would close his eyes, hold onto the nappy to make sure it was covering him, screw his eyes up tightly and wish, oh wish, with every fibre of his body that he could just disappear, just fade away! On rare occasions either his mother did not notice, or was too late, and a gardener would look in at the kitchen window and see this small child lying on the table with his knees up in the air and the towelling wrapped around his loins.

However, there was a much more insidious side to this. Most of the time the house was quiet: Harry was over the road at his parents, Christine—now Chris—was listening to pop music, or out at friends' houses, or getting to know "boys." His mother then took an inordinately long time over pinning the garment around him. She would touch and stroke his genitals in ways that were not appropriate, in a manner that no adult should do to a child: for up to twenty minutes each evening. This happened early in the evening, hours before bedtime. He was touched in ways that were totally wrong. However naive or innocent a child is about sexual matters, it can sense when something is wrong or inappropriate. A child can sense intention and purpose even before the touch happens. Paul hated this but his protestations were answered with his mother's complaints about having to clear up if he were to wet the bed. There was minimal risk to the bed as most mornings the nappy was dry—but his protestations went unheeded. His mother would make him feel guilty about the work she had to do and the drudgery of changing the sheets. So he silently acquiesced. This continued for many, many years. If his sister entered the kitchen then the touching stopped immediately and his mother would busy herself with finishing the task. What effect did this sexual abuse have on him? He felt dirty and hated himself. He would lie in bed at night feeling lost and unclean, lonely, as though something was very wrong and that if he let go of himself then he would be sucked into nothingness. Paul would wake in the night with the sensation of a hand touching, peeling back . . . if he passed a mirror, or saw his reflection in a shop window, he was filled with revulsion at the sight of himself; his mother found him one day cutting out his face from photos in the family album. This feeling diminished in adulthood, to be replaced by a sense that he just did not like himself.

Chapter Six, Abuse: Sanity and Dis-ease

So, Paul buried the experience and memories, this abuse; he shut away the memories even when the terror was building up in him as the evening drew on towards the appointed hour. He was to be middle-aged before the memories, deeply buried in his subconscious, gradually resurfaced and he could face what had happened to him. But as a child he lost himself in the Charity, in books, in model aeroplanes, in a child's fantasy world, anything. His father was something of an innocent in this and suspected nothing: besides Harry spent almost every evening over the road at his parent's house, leaving Meg alone with the children. At no time did Harry perpetrate anything resembling sexual abuse on his children, indeed Harry was very distant from them.

But what effect did this have on Paul?

He knew nothing about the birds and the bees, as it was euphemistically referred to in those days, apart from conversation overheard from his sister and her gang, and, of course, what could be observed in nature. But one lunchtime this abuse appeared to promote pre-pubescent promiscuous urges in him—he was brought before the deputy head at Swann Lane Junior School for chasing the girls and trying to kiss them. Was this normal behaviour for a ten year old boy? Yes, if he was part of a peer group or playground gang. But he was in fact a rather sad and solitary individual, and none of the girls liked him. The deputy stood before him flexing the cane—a cane that was the symbol of the worst behaviour, representative of the worst type of bully, toughie, in the playground. Paul stood petrified. He listened and cried. He vowed to himself never to behave like this again. And indeed his vow was true. If anything, the confusion in him caused by the abuse forced any fragile confidence he had to disappear and he became more and more withdrawn.

He started missing school; first a few days, then a week, regularly. Then longer periods—he was not truanting; he stayed at home, feigning illness. His mother acquiesced. But then Mr. Lovatt contacted the parents and expressed his concern. A meeting was held. No, came his answer, nothing was troubling him, nobody was bullying him, no one was getting at him. So Paul returned to school, more frightened, more puzzled at the feelings in him, more lost. And the evening ritual continued: Christine, part of the sixties-pop-culture-evenings-out with her gang; Harry glued to the television in his parent's house. Perhaps staff at school should have been alerted around two years earlier, a matter of months after the abuse started. Stood in the hall during assembly—the last assembly before Christmas—a few weeks before his eighth birthday, Paul broke down into uncontrollable weeping during the singing of the Christmas carol *Away in a Manger*. Why was this? Did the innocence portrayed in the carol upset him compared to the situation he was in at home, the abuse that was preying on him? A teacher took him to one side, took him into an empty classroom and explained that this was not the way to behave in assembly. He tried to speak, but was silenced, he tried to speak of a dirtiness in him, about what his mother was doing, but was firmly silenced. As he returned to the hall the words in the next carol struck him—"*And He leads His children on, to the place where He is gone.*" It was only Jesus who could understand, only Jesus he could talk to....

Why did his mother do this?

Was it Harry's anger and violence that was the cancer in their marriage? In part, yes. What made him so angry, so violent and bad-tempered? Was it the realization that she did not love him? Or was it the influence of his father—who would not allow him to break the apron strings, as Meg claimed. Harry was by nature a red-necked, gregarious, outgoing market gardener and land worker. And there was poverty, which exacerbated the difficult relationship between them—money was always scarce. Harry also had to face the fact that Meg did not really love him. But there was a third factor—sexuality. This was a deeper cancer in their relationship related to the sexual tension between them. Paul had witnessed hushed snippets of conversation between Meg and her mother or between his mother's friends to do with memories of stories about her as a young woman. Stories of her being caught kissing passionately with Susan on the roof of a department store in Worcester while doing fire duty during the war. Memories of her hating and refusing to have Father Christmas deliver presents into her bedroom on Christmas night whilst she was sleeping—for she said she would not have a strange man coming into her bedroom in the middle of the night. Where does a young girl in the 1920s get such ideas? She was living in a nice middle-class home; there was no radio, television, no media or pop culture to swamp her with ideas about sex.

Then there were memories of conversations heard between his parents and grandparents of how she hated a friend, a business associate of her father's, coming to stay when she was a girl. This was a man in the British establishment that William had come to know and work with in colonial West Africa, during the First World War. (A higher ranking lodge member than William? Or outside of the Freemasons, but with power over them because he knew of their sins, thus they had to acquiesce to this powerful aristocrat?) Though from a poor East End dock labouring family, William Riley had risen to work on the Investiture of the Prince of Wales, and for the Bank of England and the colonial authorities along the African Gold Coast; this had brought him into contact with people who were very different from his own background, or the people he later worked and lived amongst in the Vale of Evesham. Was this man one such example?—groomed in an English public school, this man would come to stay with the Rileys for up

Chapter Six, Abuse: Sanity and Dis-ease

to a week at a time, twice a year. Meg became sick with fear for days before this man would come to stay. If she had been threatened with torture, even death, her terror and shock, panic and fear, could not have been worse. Did Meg's parents suspect anything?—perhaps Meg had tried to tell them, but her father had simply sought to smooth over the whole affair.

If William Riley had one weakness, it was that he believed utterly in the goodness of the English establishment; and perhaps it had a hold over him. Edwardian England had thrown up a multitude of Masonic lodges. William had been a member of The Accra Lodge, a Masonic lodge founded in 1905 in Accra, Ghana, in West Africa, by and for colonial expatriates. He had worked with high-ranking members of the establishment in West Africa, and criticism of the brethren, of lodge members, was never to be tolerated. Whatever a member did, it was never to be divulged outside the brethren. But in his middle years did he try to distance himself from certain of his Masonic connections because of what happened to Meg as a girl? Was this why he spent most of his working life from the late-1920s in a relatively obscure job in Evesham, while remaining an active Mason?

As a young woman Meg had nothing to do with men. Yet she hankered after the ideal of a happy married life with children, epitomized by the large detached houses springing-up on the fringes of the town. William and Renée would chide her for being so snobbish about such matters, particularly in front of other people—"We didn't bring you up to be like this," they would say. As their retirement approached, Meg's parents worried about what they would do with her when they retired and moved away. Was it fear of being left on the shelf, as it was termed in those days, that made her marry Harry? Perhaps she felt obliged to marry Harry because of the time their kissing and petting went too far in the woodland skirting the drive leading from Cheltenham Road to Hampton. Why did this abuse of Paul start after William's death and not when he was an infant?—well, the obvious point that he was wetting the bed and a nappy was needed; this gave her the situation, an outlet for her motivation. But also her father's death would have triggered memories in Meg of the abuse she had been subject to by this business associate of her father. Would not William's death also have rekindled memories of attempts to hush the matter up? Whatever the truth, only God knows the whole story.

When Meg touched and stroked Paul, her son, taking an inordinately long time over the extraneous task of pinning the nappy on him, so early in the evening—long before bedtime—she looked distant, preoccupied in her mind as though she was reliving memories, deep, submerged, sublimated memories from her own past, her own childhood. Her eyes would oft-times moisten and fill with tears but she would not allow herself to cry. Was it at times like this that the memories of the abuse to which she was subjected resurfaced in a semi-conscious way? Only to be shut out, slammed down, and hidden deep in her own sub-conscious in the same way that the memory of this abuse visited on Paul was to be locked away deep in his sub-conscious for years, decades, to come. For we live by shadows, we see the superficial, the shadows of this world, this life, and take them for real, for they appear bright and shining: apparent verisimilitude, when the real meaning, the truly real truth lies much deeper and we so rarely allow this truth, this reality about us, to surface. The sins of the father are visited on the children: wilfulness, *fallen* wilfulness, was visited on Meg when she was a girl; was she really conscious of how she was visiting it on her son? Did she really not see how the boy could perceive the intention—for the meaning and purpose of her actions were as corrosive on him as the act of abuse itself? Perhaps if she had stayed single, remained unmarried, Meg could have eventually faced her own abuse, recovered the memories and exorcised them from her subconscious as Paul did many, many, years later.

But she did not.

For she was to die at her own hand.

Chapter Seven

Winter: Christmas and Survival

∼ *"My soul clings to the dust!*
Revive—please!—revive me according to Your word."
PSALM 119:25

One

The snow came early that year. By mid-November the first showers had come, settled, then cleared within a few days. By midday, after overnight snows, the white had turned to brown, and the brown to slush, and the slush to grey puddles. Then the frosts came. They bit hard. Memories were stirred, dates exchanged: muted conversation held by men loitering in the aisles between rows of produce at the Smithfield market filled the empty minutes before the sale reached the desired stacks of leeks, or winter cabbage. Men sat on nets of sprouts, or leant against crates of cabbage; men pushed barrows laden with late-arriving produce, rushing to reach a space in the aisles before the sale started; engines revved, axles moaned as lorries backed to within a hair's breadth of the extremity of the aisles of produce: shouts of recrimination, calls of reassurance, and children playing hide-and-seek amongst the multitudinous store of winter produce, ripe for sale, completed the scene. Amongst the men, arguments ran thick and fast over when the worst winter had been. Some swore blind that it had snowed "afore Chris'mus" in such-and-such a year. Others would curse the stupidity of the rest for not remembering correctly. By consensus the leading contender for the worst and earliest was 1947. Some of the older generation of growers argued that there had not been proper winters since "afor' thee old war" (referring to the First World War), then, it was recalled, there was heavy snow and frost near every winter. But in all cases, memories were fallible, dates varied, recollection was coloured by personal experience and sentiment: there was little consensus or harmony of discussion. As the sale approached, a wave of men, peering and straining to see into the fray, or walking sideways, would descend. Then Richard Moore, the Head Salesman, would come along clapping his hands and calling:

"Come along there then gentlemen, we can't sit around here all day. Now, who'll start me off? What do I hear for these leeks . . . ?"

As the sale approached, those not wishing to take part moved aside, quickly and suddenly, leaving those earnestly bidding to follow, doffing their caps, touching spectacles, or simply calling out. Those loitering would make a hasty retreat to another corner of the market, or withdraw tactically to the aisles of produce already sold. Those waiting for the sale would abandon the conversation, surrendering the point that they had argued so animatedly for just a few seconds earlier. Such abruptness was taken as normal behaviour in the sale.

The market had been built at the turn of the century. Prior to its construction, major sales had taken place in the market place, or in the wide tree-lined High Street. The Smithfield Market (or "top market," as it was to be known) was a large two-storey building—the entire ground floor being open along each of the long sides, only the steel pillars being seen. This created a large open space, near the size of a football pitch, arranged into rows and aisles for produce to be stacked. The upstairs, reached by staircases at each end of the building, which were closed in, was used for storage. The building was clad in corrugated metal sheets, with small windows set in the sides, below a low-pitched roof. A large yard or space surrounded the building, which on one side overlooked the railway embankment to the north, while to the west stood offices and outbuildings, including the cafe.

Richard Moore, as the Head Salesman, had the unenviable task of balancing the often-contradictory demands of different gardeners—either selling or buying—whilst keeping the sale moving fast and swift. John Loman stood and followed the sale, noting down the details of each sale on a clipboard: lot number, quantity and nature of the produce, seller, buyer, price, and so forth. As each sheet was completed he hastily tore it from the pad and gave it to a waiting runner who then took it to the office for processing. In summer months thousands of items of produce would be sold in the space of a couple of hours, each and every day. Many men, women, and children loitered around the sale—it was a daily meeting place, just like the market places of old. Vehicles were parked around the perimeter of the building, and these were where most of those simply watching, gossiping, waiting, or marking time would stand. The cold weather was obviously the key topic of conversation, and was leading to the usual amount of disagreement; however, one fact was agreed—it was *cold*.

Chapter Seven, Winter: Christmas and Survival

Jack Broadley stood, walking-stick in hand, to one side of the sale, watching the proceedings, politely answering in simple monosyllabic terms any enquiry or fact spoken to him about the weather, but remaining eyes fixed on the sale. Those who had crossed the Rubicon from small jobbing gardener to running their own business growing, buying, and selling produce had not done so by spending their time in idle gossip. Jack stood—his thick brown overcoat standing proud of his bulky body, his lovat-green felt hat pulled down firmly at the front—tapping his stick, lifting it a little between each rhythmical tap. Albert Barnsley stood nearby, but over the other side of the nets of sprouts, stacked neatly in a row, about twenty feet in length. Both were dressed in a similar way. Both believed they had a station within the local community to maintain—their clothes were like a badge of office. Neither made a bid for any produce. They had sons to do that for them. To take part in the sale would have lowered their estimation in the eyes of the other market gardeners; however, both followed the sale with the concentration and attentiveness of a hawk. Besides, bidding was a skill—which in the case of Jack Broadley, his son had and displayed commensurately, but the father was significantly lacking in. Jack would not have admitted to this fact. Indeed he had once come to blows with Charlie Barnsley for even hinting at such a widely, but secretly held belief. Such squabbles often ended up in not so much a fight, but a brawl. Richard Moore would raise his powerful voice and with a polite but forceful request bring about order once more:

"Gentlemen, gentlemen, please . . ."

And with his arms held wide like a circus master, he would immediately stop the sale and walk straight for the erring pair. If this was insufficient, then a firm verbal rebuff and a demand that the warring parties leave the sale would follow. All present knew that if the two parties did not leave then the entire remainder of the produce would be unsold. On this occasion Harry Broadley had rubbed up one or two gardeners the wrong way by pushing too hard in the sale, upsetting the delicate natural social movement as the sale moved rapidly along the aisles: such a brawl ensued. The offended gardener gave Harry a firm punch on the shoulder, coupled with the riposte that it was high time "'sum'un giv'ee a good 'idin'!" Others just laughed. Harry was torn—torn between his father's animosity on one side with the gardener's family; his own inability to stand up to old Jack and really have some independence, and the worsening situation at home with Meg. Harry withdrew from the sale and proceeded to load up some nets of sprouts he had bought earlier. On other occasions he would have hit back, and been prepared to give as good as he got—both verbally and physically—but today he did not have the stomach for a fight. Jack Broadley merely stood immutable, his head neither turning to the left or the right, his stick continuing to tap, his eyes watching the sale as it moved from one row to the next.

Sitting in the wooden box that was mounted on the cab roof Paul had seen all. He felt for his father, felt his hurt and bruised pride, felt the embarrassment. However, he could not get over the barrier that was between him and his father, a barrier placed quite effectively by his mother. So he just looked on. The sale moved on, like a wave once it had spent itself on the shore. The sale moved on leaving behind the successful bidders, also those whose ambitions had been thwarted, and those, usually the retired gardeners, who then began to pick over the bones of the bids, analysing what it said about the growing expertise and wealth of one gardener over and against the waning business strengths of another—pure speculation, gossip, scandal mongering!

Paul climbed down from his seat, over the wooden rails between the cab roof and the bed of the lorry, then jumping off the bed started to help his father with the nets of sprouts. He could hold one net and walk, dragging it between his legs towards the lorry, but he did not have the strength to lift the nets onto the bed. Harry continued to clip labels onto the green string of the nets, then throw them up to Sam who stood ready to stack them against the wooden rails behind the cab. Paul clambered up as well and helped Sam with the stacking.

Soon the idle groups of growers turned their attention back to the weather. It was generally agreed that 1947 was the harshest winter in living memory; likewise it had produced the earliest snows. The early sleet and snow this November and the hard-biting northeasterlies were a harbinger of what was to come. The conversations wound on as the sale progressed towards the final rows of produce. The rows and aisles of sold produce were now taken over by men and women in equal numbers clipping labels onto nets and chips, or slipping cards under rubber bands, or behind the wooden slats of crates. These labels boldly declared the owner's name, address, and telegram details. All were then picked up, re-stacked, grouped according to the buyers, and slowly amidst the scurrying of these people, the ordered lines of the rows, prepared from as early as six in the morning for the auction, were lost: the new stacks even breaking through the white lines delineating the rows for stacking produce and the rows for the gardeners to walk along. By eleven-forty-five, most of the men and women had retreated to the cafe in one corner of the market for dinners of steak and kidney puddings, mashed potatoes, peas, cabbage, liver and onion, strong tea, or had moved off down the road from the market to huddle in groups in the Railway Hotel for a liquid dinner. Both parties formed new small groups and exchanged gossip about the various groups of gardeners in the Vale. Now, over pints of best bitter and double whiskies they converged in their overcoats, gradually being enveloped in the smoke-laden atmosphere while talking about the confrontation—or lack of confrontation—between Harry Broadley and the

Chapter Seven, Winter: Christmas and Survival

other gardener. But they soon exhausted this line of discussion and reverted to the weather.

Whilst a heated discussion developed amidst the smoke-filled haze of the Railway Hotel, few noticed the first flakes of fresh snow falling gently around the lorries, pick-ups, and ordered piles of produce: large flakes of snow, borne on the bitter northeasterlies. Sitting on the tail of the lorry Paul was watching: his heart sang and danced with joy. Would there be real snow, lots of it, for weeks, maybe even for Christmas?! He remembered that it had been in such weather that he had been born: he had been told so—William had told him. He moved the thoughts on in his mind, he did not want to dwell on thinking about the past, about happy conversations with William Riley, it hurt too much—if he did then he would feel cheated, robbed, because William had gone, been taken away. Then he felt he had caused William's sufferings, because he had made him live on, because of his longing to see him, because he had prayed and pleaded with God that he might see him once more. So he was afraid to pray about things that really mattered to him. His Sunday School teacher had told them to cast all their worries on God. But he was afraid to, and where would he start, there was so much that was complicated, painful, disturbing in his life, and then there was. . . . These thoughts he had not shared with his parents, or with Christine or with Renée. Paul buried such thoughts.

And the snow fell. It continued gently to fall. Snow fell onto his red hair; snow fell onto and tickled the end of his nose. Sam and his father got into the cab. The lorry moved off. Paul stayed on the back until they had reached the end of the access road from the market to the High Street. Harry stopped, called to his son, who responded by walking along the bed, grasped the rails behind the cab, placed his foot in a metal bracket, opened the cab door and swung himself in without touching the road. Harry then drove down the High Street, turning left into Avon Street and then into the Central Market to collect some leeks that had been bought earlier. Paul could not remember why the school had been closed for the day—something about the pipes going wrong in Mr. McGlinn's class over in the huts! He watched from the cab window in the lorry as the snow danced before his eyes, while the wiper pressed it ever more compactly into a ridge each side of its sweep. He wondered if the snow would last, if there would be more days off!

"I don't fancy getting to the railway through this lot!" said Harry.

"Why don't us take et up thur now, skip dinner, thur'll be a brawl of 'um trying to get there come two o'clock . . ."

"Yes, if you don't mind, we can pick up the cabbage from Taylor's and go straight to there!" interrupted Harry.

" 'ou better drop the boy off first, 'es mother ul be frettin' if e's late."

So Paul was dropped off by the hedge at the front of the drive, while Harry and Sam turned and drove back up to J. G. Taylor's in the High Street. Jim Beason checked the dockets, and although the crates of cabbage Harry had ordered had not arrived from over by Bretforton, he had some he could let him have—as a favour. They were loaded onto the lorry, then, with Sam's guidance, the lorry was backed, gingerly out of the yard, with wheels slithering in the fast falling snow. They continued on up to the railway.

Two

And the snows fell. They stole in like they had done so many years before when Paul had been born. They silently spread during the night, covering the roads, the yard around the market, the land, crops; they covered all. This time with a hard frost the snow stayed. The weather eased a little as December drew on, but the wind, the frost, and the snow hardened and gripped like a vice. Men were laid off, crops stayed where they were, frozen in the ground. Brave men and women wrapped up in thick clothes, with sacks wrapped around them, moved in stilted posture and stood over the icebound soil to shovel the snow away, then to cut and slice crops from the ground. It took two, maybe three, times as long to get a boat of leeks in this weather, by the time they had been dressed, trimmed, prepared for market. Such produce sold for a price.

As Christmas approached fresh snow fell, and the frosts seized like they had never done before. And the river froze. The River Avon froze over. On Saturday afternoons, Christine and Paul would go with their father down to the river, above the weir, accessed from along Common Road. Here, up as far as the railway bridge they could slide and skate and play to their hearts content—so did half the town it would seem. The weather was clear, crisp, bright, but the light did not last long. They would return to hot soup and toast.

One night Paul woke to silence, an unnatural silence: the air in the room was thin, sharp, it cut like a knife; he sat up in bed and pushed his head under the curtains. The window was frosted over with icy condensation. With his finger he cleared a small circular patch, giggling to himself at the squeaky noise his finger made. Then he peered through the windows—outside the snow danced and whirled, large flakes as big, it seemed, as his fist. Not a sound came through the window: the snow swallowed all; nothing could be seen, nothing heard, nothing smelt, nothing lived, nothing breathed, everything was the blizzard: the totality was absolute—the world had ceased, snow was all that was left. In the morning the blizzard had ended, but the sky still threatened. It hung there, like

Chapter Seven, Winter: Christmas and Survival

a mythological army, grey, leaden, waiting to fall once again on the land—the acrid, numbing cut of frost in the air convinced him that the world had changed.

After dinner the children were allowed out by their mother. Paul walked down the drive, which Harry, Sam, and Chas had spent the morning clearing. He waded through drifts up to his chest, but could still not get around the back of the sheds. He stopped and looked. The hedgerow ahead of him was lost in drifts, the blue twinkling curve of the snow being all that was left of the hawthorn, now under the weight of the blizzard's birth. Longdon Hill could not be seen: all had disappeared. Then the vertigo started—the world started to spin, he sat down, shook his head; the noise got loud, really loud in one ear, then the tinnitus arched over the top of his head to his left ear. He giggled, breathed deeply for a moment or two, then got up, surveyed the scene, and took a few seconds to get his bearings in such a changed world. He made his way back to the drive and met up with Christine in the front garden. They proceeded to make a snow fort around the concrete cover over the old well. The walls grew to be as tall as they were: it had an outer wall and an inner sanctuary entered through a strange curving wall that looked like the beginning of a maze. They sat in it, deciding what to do. Paul sat waiting behind the ramparts for marauding invaders—who never came, save for Harry, Sam, and Chas returning in the old Austin lorry having surveyed the damage caused by the blizzard to the top ground and the orchard down Corn Mill Road, after which they had driven through the town and surveyed the small amount of goods being loaded at the railway sidings.

Lying on the settee in the front room Paul pulled the blanket over his shoulder. It was Christmas Eve. He was ill—again. Flu that had turned into a chest infection, which compounded his difficulty in breathing: try as he could, he struggled to get his breath, even when well. Thus he had developed as a walker, not a runner, for he would soon be out of breath, collapse, and be gasping for air. When he was ill with a throat or chest infection the Ménières was worse, but he kept silent about the symptoms. There was no logical decision behind this. The symptoms—the tinnitus, vertigo, pressure in his ears, and straining sometimes to hear—were, by association for him part of the problem of his parents rowing and fighting, and that other thing, the dirty feeling when he went to bed, which he pushed out of his mind. So he lay dozing. He lay on his side, facing in to the back of the settee. His head was dizzy and spinning continuously. He slept fitfully, drifting in and out of dreams. A coal fire burnt in the grate, the orange light flickering and dancing around the room.

He drifted off into a dream where he was in the car with his parents and his sister, driving to Weston to see Renée. A row was going on between his parents. He covered his eyes, then his ears, then pulled his legs up to his head, but it would not shut the violence out: his mother's screaming and shouting, his father's bawling and cursing, his mother slapping his father whilst they drove. Then the scene changed. He was following them, walking along the seafront in Weston, his mother with Renée, then Christine, then his father, all side-by-side. Paul stopped to look at the wall by their left, marking the boundary between the beach and the promenade; it was wide, about two feet wide, and pot-marked with holes, eroded by the salt spray. He poked his finger in and touched the wall, its rough stone, then he turned and saw his parents walking ahead. He turned to run after them. He tried to catch up with them, but he couldn't reach them. His mother and father, and Renée and Christine, were walking ahead. He was striding out, following them, but the space between them grew. Try as hard as he could, he could not keep up, the space widened. He started to walk faster, almost run, but the gap increased, the pavement spread out in front of him; he called out but they could not hear, people filled up the space; he was slowly, inevitably, being left behind. No one could hear him. He woke feeling so sad, so empty, so cold, almost as though he was going to disappear, be sucked in on himself. The orange flames of the fire danced cheekily, impishly, mockingly on the ceiling above him. In the window the coloured tree lights shone out in competition. The house was silent. His mother entered the room, asked him how he was, took his temperature, and held his hand to reassure him.

"Your father's over the road, has been all day—don't ask me when he'll be back."

Meg turned away. The boy could see tears welling up in her eyes.

"I'm just preparing the turkey—Christine's helping me, she's mixing the stuffing, I must go."

He let his mother's hand slip. He tried to get up.

"No, you stay put there, it's warm here. They say there is more snow to come."

Meg returned to the kitchen.

He lay feeling very unwell, his chest hurting, trying desperately to get his breath but feeling so thin, so weak. He dozed off again. That afternoon Meg called out Doctor Appely, who gave him some medicine, enough to get Paul over the holiday.

Harry did not return that night but slept over at his parents. The row the day before Christmas Eve had started, as usual, over something trivial but had been brooding for days, weeks. Most work had ground to a halt due to the snow, and Harry was forced to spend much of the time at home. Being forced together was too much for Meg and Harry—they needed space apart from each other, and they were not getting it. On Christmas morning Meg wished the children a Happy Christmas, and opened her presents as they pounced on theirs. She made excuses

Chapter Seven, Winter: Christmas and Survival

for Harry being out when her mother phoned from Weston with greetings, then set to preparing the dinner. Once it was nearly ready she phoned across to Harry's parents to see if he was coming over. He came over, carved the turkey, and they all sat down to Christmas dinner. The meal was silent, that is, empty of joy, of happiness, of festive conversation: but the atmosphere was loaded. Paul ate little. His mother scowled at Harry. Harry sat proud with arrogance. He stopped to do the washing up, then returned across the road to his parents. Paul slept on the settee in the front room, with the fire sending its flames dancing on the walls again, the Christmas tree lights glistening through the dark green needles. Harry returned later that evening after the two children had gone to bed.

Paul woke the next morning to the usual sounds from the kitchen: muffled voices, a few muted words, indiscernible, but the tone said all, then as restraint went, they rowed. He then felt fear. Fear rising in him, the sickly tight feeling in his throat, a throbbing in his head; the coughing came back, his sickness pinned him to the bed, while from the kitchen hatred came, cold antagonism came, the obsession by both warring parties that each was infallible in its claim to rightness. He lay in bed, the cold sweat of fear, the dry suffocating hand creeping through him, in him. He sank into the pillows to escape. Christine came in from her bedroom to see if he was alright. She saw and knew of the terrors in her brother. Their parent's arguments did not affect her in quite the same way, however she could see the horror, the dread and panic, that these fights caused in him. She felt powerless. She did not know how to help him; she could not do anything. It was not just this powerlessness that perturbed her; there was a feeling of anguish and of wanting to flee from these terrors in the boy that was natural to her age—she had neither the experience nor the maturity to know how to deal with the problem.

And the light reflected from the frost-hardened snow onto the walls of the back bedroom as the two children tried to find comfort in each other's company, while the parents argued their points, storming and shouting: and the house was surrounded by a frozen stillness as the faintest swirls of fresh snow danced in the silence of the frost-charged air.

Three

The earth was reluctant to thaw, for water to trickle once again. The frost held well into March, but eventually, inevitably, the snow and ice so dominant, present for so long, lost its grip, and simply melted away: by which time it was April. The land, now brown and rich and soft once again, stood proudly with rivulets of water flowing, or lying amidst furrows: the loam could now move and breathe again. The rains came and added to the thaw, the air smelled fresh and soft. The spring finally reclaimed its kingdom from the snow and ice and breathed a new warm whisper onto the earth: the faintest green dusting appeared—lime and avocado, jade and emerald, khaki and yellow-green shoots dared to break forth set-off against the rich dark soil. As the spring drew into summer, the memories of the winter's freeze-up began to dim, and the Vale began reaping the bounty of one of the best growing seasons for years. By now the cherry blossom on the trees had gone and the leaves were putting on a distinctly mature brightness—ready for the worst the summer could throw at them.

Paul, in the junior playground, was playing on the double bars, set about three feet high; he slipped and sprained his ankle. This was straightforward enough for a nine-year-old boy, a common occurrence one could even say. The ankle was x-rayed to see that nothing was broken. The resulting photographs revealed a patch on the anklebone. Subsequent x-rays showed it just as clearly, from different angles. He was ordered not to stand or put any weight on this, his right leg, and in consequence he spent many weeks that spring in bed, or resting on the settee. He was referred to a specialist in Worcester. The foot was examined by many medical experts, who looked at the x-rays, analysed the blood tests, talked in hushed muted tones with colleagues: the word cancer was discernable under their breath, also leukaemia. The boy was ushered away for more tests. He was guided along corridors with white walls and gleaming floors and eventually to a room where someone tried in vain to take yet another blood sample to be minutely analysed. The tension and stress were bad enough without this—it was obviously an inexperienced student. He was ushered by a more experienced man (dressed in a suit, not in a white coat) to another room—containing tanks with insects in, and all sorts of other creatures, and an aquarium to try to make him relax and take his mind off what was happening. Here the man successfully took the samples. Subsequent x-rays confirmed the patch was still there—indeed was growing. Paul ended up missing most of the first half of the summer term of second year juniors with Mr. McGowan: he was not allowed to put any weight on the affected joint.

During this time he continued to bury himself in books, in model making, and pined for walks around Longman's Charity. Models were made from using cardboard covers, surreptitiously gleaned from the sheds, corrugated card scrounged by Harry as off-cuts from Sharp the Printers and by saving up pocket money to buy balsa wood planes to craft and fly, or Airfix plastic model kits. He was developing ability in drawing and painting, confirmed by his school reports. In addition, he had developed a passion for history, therefore, when not out walking the land and discovering that kingdom, he had worlds of his own

Chapter Seven, Winter: Christmas and Survival

built around different aspects of history (often medieval), or aircraft (particularly from the Second World War), model making relating to both areas, or drawing. Hours and hours were spent drawing: sometimes imaginary scenes related to these interests, especially the land—Longman's Charity; other times detailed drawings of planes and so forth. Paul was developing alone. He blocked out the violence of home and hid in these worlds, but they were not a fantasy, they were in some instances defined by academic interest. These worlds had to conform to the real world!

After two months of not walking on the ankle, of the hushed reverence of a generation that would not speak the word "cancer," and despite the positive blood tests, and just as they were planning aggressive anti-cancer treatment, the x-rayed patch on his ankle bone disappeared leaving medical experts puzzled. But then this was not the first time that Paul had survived against the odds: he survived the abortions when assaulted in his mother's womb, and now this. But he was not consciously aware of the divine subtlety of his miraculous survival, he was just thankful to be back on his two feet and out-and-about again. A child from a Christian family may have made the connection, particularly if his parents had prayed for healing. But, regardless of prayer—or perhaps because of the prayers of people unknown to Paul and his parents—and despite the diagnosis, he seemed to have been healed, when there had been no medical intervention.

Christine by now was preparing to move up to Four Pools—the large County Secondary Modern School. The disability with her leg, the malformed hip joint from earliest days, now left her with a left leg over an inch shorter than her right. In consequence she wore built-up shoes. This predictably led to teasing—particularly from the boys. Remarks like "peg leg" cut deep; however, she had inherited her father's ability to fight back, she gave as good as she was given: a well-aimed swipe with her satchel would soon put paid to a carelessly placed gibe from a classmate. There was, at this time, no pain, but she still had to take things carefully—to avoid dislocating the left hip, which was a considerable risk. She no longer travelled to the Birmingham Children's Hospital, but to Worcester to see a specialist. Soon there were discussions about what to do—especially as the difference in length between the two legs was becoming more noticeable. It was suggested that an operation on the right leg—the good leg—to attempt to slow down its growth would be an idea. Thus began the first of many operations over the next ten or so years to try to solve the problem, eventually ending up at the Nuffield Orthopaedic Hospital in Oxford.

Four

Paul sat and watched. In the hedgerow a chaffinch called; answered, or so it seemed, by a sparrow further across in a different hedgerow. It was a still, silent August evening. Earlier that day it had rained continuously for four hours, steadily, relentlessly, then slowly easing off, taking a full half hour to stop. Gradually, imperceptibly, the downpour eased. Minute by minute less rain fell, slowly turning from heavy to a steady rain, from light rain to a shower, then the shower eased to a drizzle, then the mizzle hung: a dampness appeared suspended as mist in the air. Drip, drip, the rainwater was slowly, almost reluctantly, shed from trees, outbuildings, and the old brown Austin lorry. Though the sun was now dipping below the cloud layer over to the west, now a full two hours after the rain had finally ceased, the slow drip, drip, continued, while a faint evening mist rose from the land further over towards the Charity Brook. If he closed his eyes he could hear, first in one direction, then another, then behind, then afore, as water dripped from the corrugated tin above him, each corrugation lazily letting slip its load, channelling the water down onto the crates and boxes, themselves still sodden from the rain. Gently the evening mist crept over and around the foot of the two apple trees to the side of the sheds, infiltrating the open slated side of the grey wooden crates. All was still. A damp chill hung in the air, calling to and hastening in an early autumn. The ground was dark, soaked through by the rain. Young cabbage plants, put in over winter, competed with the weeds to drink in thirstily the water.

Sitting on a low extension of the main sheds, wooden-framed and clad ubiquitously in corrugated tin sheets, he looked over to the telegraph wires, where perched along at regular intervals were starlings, all part of a flock. They sat still, watching. The boy watched, still and silent. Then they flew. At least, one decided to, then, by what seemed some sort of magical telepathy, its decision was accepted by the mass, which followed. They flew down, swooped and swerved, each miraculously keeping the same distance from its neighbour. They flew close to the ground, seeming that they would land, then flew majestically up again, banked over to the right and swooped down again past the same patch of ground, then glided on a further twenty or thirty yards, finally alighting. Atop the dark soil they were lost. He could no longer pick them out: he was transfixed at the way they flew as a flock. Again, one had made the decision to land, or hinted somehow to the others the possibility that this was a good site, then by the same sort of sixth sense they signalled their agreement, and there they were . . . on land—not all on the same spot, but exactly beneath where they were last flying, so that the pattern of the birds on the ground was a replica of the flight pattern, the moment the decision had been made to land. Or so it seemed to him. He was fascinated by their flight, the sense of space, the movement, the timing. He could not vocalize such thoughts; he stumbled when he tried to put into words what he felt or thought.

At school he was slow, ham-fisted at writing, at a loss for words, always sat near the back, was considered a slow learner. Paul watched. Already at this tender age he was becoming one of life's observers: he watched—and felt. The flock of starlings rose, swept over the ground, climbed, banked, turned, swept again, this time landing near the spot originally rejected. Once again they were lost to sight against the sodden dark brown soil. Then, after a few seconds—or was it half a minute, or longer, one could not tell, time seemed to have stood still on that damp August evening — the flock rose again, flew, banked smoothly round, and this time swept right across the land, rising to clear the hedgerow marking the border between his father's land and the lane leading down to the Charity, then flew high and wide. This time the flock became more dissipated as it flew, finally to disappear over the Fairfield Estate.

"Paul, Paul!"

The child stilled his reverie

"Paul, Paul, where are you?" It was his mother's voice. "Christine's in the bath and it's time you were washed and ready for bed."

His mother's words drifted back as she walked into the house, not turning to see him. He paused for a moment for a further look skywards. Then, as if to close the book which was this outside world, he gently waved across to the Charity, turned and walked across and up the passage and in through the back door. Oh, how he wished she would let him wash himself. He wished she would let him sort himself out for bed. But even though he asked, he knew she would not. His mother would not let go. She controlled totally the care of these two children. Partly to give her credibility, and leave no room for criticism, partly to exclude any influence Harry (or his parents—who were strangers) might have on the children, partly to leave no scope for questions of the nature of "can't you just help with the onion tying for half an hour, we can't get the women." If she was constantly busy with the house and the children, then there was no spare time. Paul's head was bent over the sink, his face washed, then behind his ears, while he stood naked. Then the humiliation as she would spread out a nappy on the kitchen table and he was subjected. . . .

Once he was in bed, he would often slip off the nappy, then settle down to reliving in his mind the day's sights and experiences, blocking out all that made him feel so dirty and unclean, cuddle up with his panda bear, with Timmy rattling with purrs at the end of the bed, and try to drift off to sleep. Sometimes if he woke in the night he somehow sensed it in the air—a tension from the previous day's row, which evoked a sadness in him, a deep sense of loss, a deep sense that something was not right. Often, as he slept, the sounds of a row would enter his brain and affect his sleep, his dreams. Waking then was painful—a cold dry sense of death pervaded his body, his throat was dry, he felt wrong, dirty, felt that something was bad, or that he had missed something, an opportunity overlooked: all this led to a profound sadness and isolation in the child.

Five

Paul woke early, loved the morning—particularly the early morning, always had. First he would look out to the garden, his eyes lighting on the flower border, and the swing his father had made from pieces of the telegraph pole timber left over from the building of the main sheds, then his eyes moved down to the fruit bushes and apple trees nearer the bottom of the garden, often halting on a blue tit sitting in the branches gently nodding its head from side to side, hopping and moving its feet rhythmically. The bird flew off, sweeping over the raspberry bushes, then up to the water tank that stood on a platform high up to the left of the lorry shed. Then his gaze would move up above the sheds, above the hedgerow marking the eastern boundary of the smallholding, finally to fix on Longdon Hill, with the Cotswold escarpment rising behind.

Something did not feel right—the sense of dirty emptiness was in him; he could never work out what it was he had done wrong. Then he would remember the last row between his parents: that usually was grabbed-on for the answer. The previous day they had rowed about Harry being up early, and Meg not helping on the land. That had been the start of the row yesterday dinner time. Soon the start of the row was forgotten and it was onto "him" not taking time off to take her down to see her mother in Weston, he complaining how she didn't do this and didn't do that. So he quietly slipped off, out the back door, down the garden, across the land, quietly pottering through the Charity, following the small turfed ridges separating different holdings, down to the brook. He then followed the lane and the brook upstream as they snaked their way to the Red Barn and the copse. With a stick and string he sat patiently for an hour seeing if he could catch any minnows or sticklebacks in the brook. Then, as the rain came on, he climbed in through the broken and weathered door of the Red Barn, busied himself at making a fort or den amongst the trays—carefully putting them all back into place when he had grown tired; then winding his way up the lane, past the pigsty to Gypsies' Corner, and so home along the Cheltenham Road. He wandered slowly, aimlessly, despite the pouring rain, reluctant to return as if he had to savour each

Chapter Seven, Winter: Christmas and Survival

step, holding on to the time lest it should fly away before he had finished with his afternoon. He sat quietly during tea, having been chastised for getting his clothes wet in the rain. Chris was at a school friend's for tea, having spent the day there. Paul sat silently with his mother over tea. His mother had cleared the tea things away, then set up for "his" tea (her husband would eat separately). The rain continued to pour down in torrents.

The next day was brighter. Paul stood. Breakfast was over. He stood by the four bricks that made a small path across the border at the bottom of the garden. To his right were the main sheds, but in front of them stood the old Austin lorry. Trays of freshly tied and cleaned onions were being loaded onto the lorry. Over to one side stood crates full of onions pulled the day before—fifteen in all. Harry Broadley was beginning to specialize in onions and leeks. The freshly pulled onions were carried into the new shed specially built for storing onions. The new shed was also to be used for onion tie-ers. Normally the tie-ers were women. Many of the women who worked for the Broadleys came from the Fairfield Estate. Usually they would sit in a field, surrounded by onions. Men would pull the onions, lay them in a crate and then, having cleared their lot with the charge hand, stack then neatly to the side of the women who would work their way through them. If times were good and not enough women could be found to tie, then Harry would take crates of onions round to where they lived, allowing the women to tie at home, at least in the passageway or garden.

The Robertons—grandmother, daughters, and cousins—were a family who had tied for the Broadleys since the First World War: year in, year out. Most of the time they walked the short distance from the Fairfield Estate where they lived to tie in the field. Often if Harry was not around they would stand or sit around the sheds waiting. Meg would not let them in the house or garden for fear "they would muck-up the place." Often their conversation was about the marriage between Harry and Meg; one sister would comment how on earth Harry put up with her; another would wonder how she came to land herself with him. All in all, it was agreed they were an odd couple, and although young Christine seemed right enough, the boy—or "Harry Broadley's little 'un" as he was called—was a weird one: all silent and moody, not so much grumpy as distant. But then they had been used to seeing the lad from a very young age overwhelmed with the terror of his parent's fighting. And anyhow, he didn't have many friends—or at least no one wanted to be friends with him. The two young Roberton grandchildren, both girls, had been very rude to Paul, teasing him, pushing him, generally trying to make him feel as small as possible. Therefore, when Harry and old Jean Roberton (the grandmother and matriarch of the family) suggested they go off to play together, Paul's indignation was such that he said they were not worth playing with, and if they were to be like they were the last time, so nasty and horrible, he did not wish to play with them! Such comments were true, and to a degree justified, but the girl's mother saw red—and hated Paul Broadley as a result.

Old Jean Roberton just held her peace, smiled laconically and tut-tuted under her breath as she shook her head, knowing full well how proud this one of her daughters could be, and how it had rubbed off on the two girls. Old Jean Roberton was not sure about having a special shed built, it was all a bit luxurious, and then there was her independence. It made her feel somehow beholden to the Broadleys; it would prevent them going off to some other grower as the wont was (which was, of course, part of old Jack Broadley's thinking!).

Paul was leaning on the onion tank looking at the layer of silt that remained after the wooden bung had been removed allowing the water to run out. What was left was a thick layer of fine silt that stank of onions, with tiny rivulets of water still running through, slowly trickling to the hole left by the removal of the bung. In places whole river systems remained—tiny streams joining together to make small rivers—then draining into "inland" lakes. He would dig a small canal through the high ground and thus allow the lake to drain across the silt to the hole: the water that was left was a miniature river system following the same rules as full size terrestrial drainage. He was fascinated: he observed, took it all in, understood implicitly, but could not communicate his fascination and understanding.

"Why down't 'ee clear it out?"

The boy looked up—it was Sam.

"'Ere, come on, I'ull elp 'ou!" turning to Paul's father he said, "Okay 'arry? It needs doing."

"Yes go ahead," came the reply.

So, with his wellies on, he clambered over the side into the tank, and armed with a coal shovel proceeded to help Sam clear the silt from the tank. Each shovelful was deposited with care over the side, for it was worth its weight in gold such was the fertility of this mixture of onion detritus, fine top soil, minerals, and sheer goodness—despite the smell! Later it would be spread over the ground. He was loving every minute: carefully shovelling up a load then carefully depositing the mixture over the side onto the ever-growing pile. He loved the sound, the sharp metallic rasping of the shovel on the base of the metal tank. It was a sound he had grown up with—waking early in the morning to the rasp, rasp, rasp of each stroke of the shovel or spade scraping along the tank, with the occasional clunk as it caught one of the large rivets that held the galvanized steel plates together; then came the sound of the shovel being knocked up and down to clear it of the thick mud that had accumulated at the base of the handle. Then came

Chapter Seven, Winter: Christmas and Survival

the rasp, rasp, rasp, again and again. It was a familiar and reassuring sound, along with the sight and smell of the onion silt with it pungent aromatic odour! His attention was caught with a sudden jolt:

"Paul! What do you think you are doing?"

It was his mother's voice. The boy froze. He looked down—his Wellington boots were muddy, his hands were a little bit, but his clothes were spotlessly clean. He was being careful; besides Sam was keeping a close eye on him.

"Of course, *you* don't care, do you!"

The remark was thrown out towards her husband.

"I suppose you all think I'm made to wash and scrub for you all the time. Look at the state you'll be in! Don't you ever think!

"Anyway," she pointed at Sam, "he's paid to do this."

This last remark was uncalled for.

"Come here now, and put that shovel down!"

The child quietly, obediently, climbed out of the tank. Meg took the child's hand, walked him across the lawn, sitting him down on the concrete outside the back door. She pulled off the boots, while he protested that he could do it himself, he was old enough. But she persisted:

"You don't really care for me, do you!"

Her annoyance was now fuelled by getting mud and silt on her hands and up the sleeves of the checkered bri-nylon overall coat she was wearing.

"You don't ever think, do you! What with his work, his market gardening cronies, and all this mess, and Christine to think of, and this house to keep clean!"

Paul felt guilty. At least he felt he should feel guilty. He bowed his head. Quietly, submissively, he went up to his room.

Six

Paul sat on his bed thinking. At times like this he always thought back to a few years earlier, wishing he was back in previous times and experiences. It would be wrong to say happier times, for most of his life he had not been that happy, whether at school or here at home with his parents. Somehow he was regretting growing up, but he wasn't looking back to a mythical, happy period. The more he lived the less happy he was with life. He would often think back to times when he knew William Riley, had sat with him, shared books with him. But such thoughts hurt. Hurt in a different way to the hurt he felt now at home. It was a missing sort of hurt—like a hole in him.

He shook his head to clear these thoughts away, climbed off the bed and opened the doors to the built-in cupboard at the foot of the bed, and got out a book. Paul had a few books. He read the Bible his maternal grandmother had given him, and the book he had been given in confirmation classes—*The Sanctuary of God*. He loved the Bible stories he heard in Sunday School, particularly about the ancient Hebrews. The Bible he had been given was initially difficult because it was in what he thought of as funny language (the King James Bible), and more often than not he got lost in the pictures, especially those of Jesus—teaching, preaching, healing people, stilling the waves—and he wished, he so wished, and then there was what he was afraid to admit was happening to him. . . . He had a book of legends and myths—Greek mythology, Celtic sagas, ancient tales, retold in the language of modern-day adventure stories. His track-record at school was poor, very poor, yet how many of his peers sought out the Song of Roland to read? His interest in history led him to ask for a volume of Shakespeare's histories, which one of Meg's friends duly bought him for his birthday. The language was difficult at first, but he soon got into the plays. How many of his peers were reading Shakespeare—of their own initiative—while still at primary school?

This book of legends and myths he had spotted in a jumble sale at church, and despite all protests his parents would not buy it, so he secretly took it, tucking it under his jumper. Before leaving he felt so guilty that he went over and showed it to the priest-in-charge, who just laughed, rubbed him on the head and said he could have it—as a present from him! The little red-headed boy thanked him, thanked him till it was almost becoming embarrassing. But as he left, he was puzzled at the sad look in the priest's eyes as he looked at Paul, then to his mum and dad, then back to the boy. He had two other precious books—*The World of Science* and R. J. Unstead's *Looking at History*. Roughly half of the latter book was pictures—hundreds of line drawings illustrating the text: high kings, queens, and nobles, lowly peasants about their daily tasks, ox carts struggling through muddy tracks, Viking ships prowling the coast of Ireland, monks in their cells writing and painting illuminated manuscripts, H.M.S Victory battling the French.

All such pictures were, as he lay on his bed, an inspiration. He would look at an illustration, noting all the details, then imagine himself into the picture—what had happened before the picture, and what was to happen after. He would weave stories in his imagination about these events and others: a fantasy world peopled by knights, kings and queens, friars, Saxon villagers standing up to the Vikings, Sir Gawain battling against monstrous beasts and demons, Greek travellers struggling against the elements—all these fantasies were battles of good against evil. What was more, he would spend hours drawing such scenes, or pictures of part of a story: draw, draw, draw. These invented worlds slipped smoothly, effortlessly, in and out of fantasy and reality. At times he would spend an hour drawing a scene that had been described in a history lesson at school—at others

Chapter Seven, Winter: Christmas and Survival

weave a story before and after the reality, in his mind, then draw different parts of the story. Whether historical, medieval, pagan, Christian, Greek, or fighters in the Battle of Britain, the treatment was the same.

That August morning, Christine had once again gone off with school friends, so Paul settled down with a picture of Irish monks. In his mind he was off—the monks launching out in their coracles from the safety of their monastery on the west coast of Ireland into the unknown, to bring the story of Christ to some far flung northern islands. Just as they were battling with a sea monster, having successfully dodged some Viking pirates; he drifted off to sleep. He woke. His chest was bad—the soaking he had got the day before. He looked out of the window. There was a fine drizzle on the pane. He coughed, a slow, dry tight cough that misted up the window. He cleared the condensation. Longdon Hill was wreathed in a fine blue-grey mist. It had rained while he slept. The long shallow hill was carpeted with orchards across this its northern slope, some in straight lines running from top to bottom, others running at angles to the line of the hill. On the southwestern corner, as the hill fell away, stood a field of wheat. The boundary with the orchards was a sharply angled line, thus creating a triangular shaped creamy-beige wedge. On this the southern corner of the hill, the composition was perfect—at least so he thought; he sensed the aesthetic, but could not express it in his mind, or in words. But soon would come the time when he would paint such a scene.

The boy got to know Longdon Hill from this view in all its moods, all the weather patterns that enveloped it, the gentle shift in colour, clarity, atmosphere. Spread at its feet was the Hampton Charity. In the foreground was the Roberton family; Old Jean Roberton looked up at the house, saw the Broadley boy at the window and thought, "What is that 'ooman doing to that boy, what is her doin' to 'im?" She saw and understood how Meg Broadley was using the boy, indeed both the children, as weapons against Harry, but there was something wrong with this one. Not the boy in himself, but something about how Meg was bringing him up that was not right, puzzling, "sumit up thur, sumit not right, but I'ul be damned if I can work eet owt" she thought to herself. She was right. And this wrongness reached a depth each evening when it came to Paul lying on the kitchen table. . . .

He could not decide what to do. His mother kept him away, physically and emotionally, from his father. Paul did not trust her, could sense she was no more right than his father. Puzzled, perturbed, as any shy withdrawn child would be, young for his age, he withdrew even further. His mother was succeeding in teaching him how not to love. When conflict started he would run upstairs, run into his room, quickly shut the door and rub the wall three times, with a circular movement of his hand—three times, it had to be three, any less and "they," the spirits, would get him—then he was safe! He was learning to manage without his sister now that she was moving up to Four Pools School, her allegiance developing away from her little brother towards her small group of friends who lived in Hampton and up Bengeworth. The younger children around the Fairfield Estate and Cheltenham Road were in the past—she looked towards her teenage pals and the world they inhabited. Although she still spent time with Paul, her loyalties were now divided. She no longer played down the Charity.

The first Monday in September saw Christine proudly leaving for Four Pools in her new uniform—but looking every part a cool, fashionable "mod" from a television program about pop culture—and her little brother returning to Swann Lane. At Swann Lane, Paul had a new teacher, Mr. Lovatt, who was new to the school and therefore an unknown quantity. However, there was no need for his apprehension—he liked, almost loved, his new teacher who was to take him for the remaining two years at Swann Lane. He noticed differences straight away. The desks were no longer in rows facing the front, they were turned in—two sets of rows facing into a large central space, and children did not have to sit in ability rows like before. He sat near a window, but also near to the front—because of his eyesight. Mr. Lovatt was thin, lively, wore glasses (which Paul liked to identify with), made lessons exciting, and made sure the bullies and toughies were kept in their place. He also moved around the classroom a lot—instead of staying behind a desk at the front all the time. Paul liked his teacher intensely, and responded to the variety, the excitement, and the spark he put into teaching. Paul's learning improved immeasurably: his writing, reading, and maths were now average, but in addition Mr. Lovatt actively supported and encouraged his drawing, painting, and model-making. He soon became known as one of the best at drawing in the class, and later in the year was in charge of a group making a large model of a dockyard using wood, papier-mâché, and plasticine—Paul was in charge of painting the model and in getting everything to the right scale.

Meg and Harry did not like Mr. Lovatt—he was too informal and friendly with the children. However, the real reason was that he saw through Meg and Harry; he realized, to a degree, what was going on at home—and his parents did not like this. The boy's attendance began to fall off. And the nervous involuntary nodding of his head was becoming more and more noticeable at school. In the mornings he would lie in bed, feeling cold to the core, even on a summer's day, feeling dirty, feeling wrong, and somehow blaming himself, not liking himself.

Old Jean Roberton was right—"What is that 'ooman doing to that boy, what is she doing to him?"

She was not alone in her concerns.

Chapter Eight
Realization: Fear and Depression

> ~ *"I am a reproach among all my adversaries,*
> *but especially among my neighbours,*
> *and am repulsive to my acquaintances;*
> *those who see me outside flee from me."*
> PSALM 31:11

One

They tore down the hill, one following the other. At the bottom, there was a mad squeal of brakes, a skidding back wheel, dirt and grit being thrown sideways in an arc, then the bike collapsed. Paul found himself crumpled in a heap with the front wheel spinning above his head. Christine followed—but she had been applying her brakes whilst freewheeling down the hill and so came to a more controlled stop. He disentangled himself from the wheels and surveyed the damage: handle bars twisted out of line, mudguard forced up onto the wheel, and blood oozing from the grit-studded knee, the folds of skin wrinkled up like a prune, revealing moist red flesh, now open to the April sunshine.

"Good job you had shorts on—mum would 'ave killed you! You alright are you? Anyway, what about the bike?"

"Yeah—I'm alright." He answered his sister. Wrestling with the bicycle till it was upright he then stood examining it with a ponderous look on his face. He spread his legs over the front wheel, gripping it tight between his knees, then wrenched hard on the handle bars to straighten them up—he was now an accustomed craftsman at on-the-spot repairs to his battered old blue and white bike. It was becoming too small for him, and he had been promised a new bike in eighteen months, ready for when he was to move on to the secondary school. He got on the bike and freewheeled it a few yards: thud, thud, thud, rhythmically the back wheel caught on the forks of the frame on which it was mounted. He applied the brakes with a squeal, jumped off, and gave the rear wheel a tremendous kick, whilst holding on to the handlebars and the saddle, thus realigning the wheel with somewhat pedestrian precision so that it would run smoothly without the buckle scraping on the forks.

"That'll do!" he pronounced proudly.

"What about your knee!" replied Christine.

"Yeah, it's beginning to sting a bit!"

"Come here, let me have a look."

Upon which he sat down on the curb, and Christine proceeded to wipe the graze with her handkerchief.

"Yowwe!"

Her brother flinched and kicked out his leg. Christine was holding the leg behind the knee with the other hand.

"It's alright, I know what I'm doing: they taught us this at Red Cross," she said proudly, wiping the knee in a downward direction, gently removing the embedded grit.

Net curtains began to move and flicker in the houses.

Christine hastily looked up, stopped her tending, and said, "Come on you, let's get out of here, quick before they recognize us!"

A few days earlier, a week after Easter Sunday, the two had been confirmed at St Richard's church—it would not do for them to be seen by the respectable church-going classes, here in the same parish!

Two

The next day they were grounded: they had been seen—disturbing the peace said one elderly lady who saw the accident. Christine and Paul spent the next few days doing jobs around the house and the garden.

Come Friday they were forgiven. Harry had already eaten his dinner at eleven-thirty, having been up since five-thirty, collected produce from gardeners around Offenham, Littleton, Bretforton, and over Weston-sub-Edge, then gone to the sale at the top market, back for dinner, then off to the railway. The family sat down to smoked haddock, scrambled eggs, and asparagus.

"Oh, not asparagus again," moaned Christine.

"Yes: it's cheap, your dad's got plenty of it, and you'll eat it!" replied Meg jokingly.

"But, do I have to, Mum?"

"No 'buts', Paul will eat it if you don't like it. The fish I got special—Mrs. Rogers put it by for me."

"Yeah, I'll eat it." Paul had already eaten half his asparagus and was eyeing Christine's.

"Stop staring," giggled Christine, "you're putting me off!"

Asparagus was a luxury vegetable, served expensively at all the best hotels and dinner parties, and should have been out of the reach of most ordinary people. But the Broadleys, like many other market gardening families, lived off it in season: leeks almost every day in the winter (along with cabbage), peas and plums in August—and for about five weeks in the spring, asparagus, or 'gras. Each morning the spears would be freshly cut by the growers and bundled up—the best made into "an 'undred," bound with willow. However, there were spears that were thin, straggly, curved, or bent, or with tips that had prematurely splayed open. Such 'gras was no good for selling as first- or second-class. Sometimes it could be picked up as a special in the market: Richard Moore would leave a small stack till last, making sure the word had gone out, then gathering the interested group who would buy and split the stack; he would then push for as high a price for the 'gras as he would with all growers. But the trick was to know an asparagus grower, and buy this 'gras off them. About five acres of land near the Broadley smallholding was laid to asparagus. Harry had an arrangement with one grower: he would ferry Chowskie's produce to market in his Austin lorry two or three times per week all year; in exchange, he was given the curved 'gras, or stems with splayed buds each day, in season.

"Tastes as good as the proper stuff," Harry would say, as he slid a spear into his mouth, the butter and water oozing and dribbling down from his lips.

"Can't you eat properly; look its dribbling down onto the table cloth!" cried Meg—and the seed would then have been sown for another row.

Three

After dinner the two children set off on their bikes again, Paul with a knapsack containing orange squash, sandwiches, cake, and biscuits on his back: a picnic tea. They cycled slowly down Cheltenham Road, Christine leading the way, the pair of them pulling in whenever a large lorry came past. When they got to Hinton Cross they stopped and waited for a complete absence of traffic before crossing the road. Once over, they were on country lanes. Christine was now approaching her twelfth birthday, her brother proud to be nearly ten and a half, and confirmed at church with his sister only a few days earlier. So they were deemed responsible enough to tackle the main road alone, having lived near it all their lives. They could cycle in a more relaxed manner along the lane, past Narrow Meadow Farm, then pause for a rest after the slow, strenuous climb along the shallow but drawn-out gradient of Haselor Hill. They would stop at the top of the rise to get their breath back, lie in the grass verge, allowing the gentle spring sun to stroke their faces while the acrid tang of wood smoke folded around them from a small gypsy encampment spread out on the wide grass verge a little way back along the lane. Sparrows chattered and argued in the trees; insects crawled and hopped and explored the myriad of grasses and undergrowth—and bit!

"Come on, let's get going!" said Christine, slapping the insects on her legs.

From the top of the rise they could see the object of their expedition: ahead of them Bredon Hill lay basking like a giant grass-covered whale, or a sleeping king clothed in luscious green apparel, waiting for the day when he must wake, like King Arthur, to reign again. Before them lay another couple of miles of the Vale, with Elmley Castle nestling in the foot of Bredon Hill, which filled their vision with its thousand-foot-high gentle curve.

"Come on, see if you can catch me!" Christine was off—freewheeling down the far side of Haselor Hill, lowering her bike into the curves of the lane as it snaked around towards Netherton.

Paul pedalled furiously to catch her, and tried to overtake, but the bends in the road prevented him. Breathless they entered Elmley Castle, a small ancient village of half-timbered cottages, standing on timeworn footings of limestone, with, in the main street, an open culvert where rain water mingled with spring water from the hill, lined with beautifully eroded slabs of limestone, set into the side of the road. Tiny bridges took pedestrians from the road, over this conduit and into cottage gardens humming with insects dancing in the stillness of the April sun around thrusting young spikes of hollyhocks and lavatera with flowers tightly curled and wrapped in buds. The main street rose gently—already they were on the lower slopes of Bredon. They were in another world—not so much a different world, but an older one. There were market gardens around them still, but intermingled with fields of young wheat. Spreading around the lower slopes were dairy cattle and sheep in pasture, along with ancient woods climbing up around the promontory of Even Hill on the northern slope of Bredon. Paul looked at Christine—and loved her: he did not need friends with her as his best friend and companion, his playmate. He wished they did not have to grow up.

Together just the two of them, or sometimes with Gina or Jane (Christine's friends), they cycled around the southwestern part of the Vale of Evesham. It

Chapter Eight, Realization: Fear and Depression

was bounded by the North Cotswold escarpment, or by outlying hills such as Dumbleton or Bredon. They would cycle through villages—Elmley Castle, Kersoe, Ashton under Hill, Grafton, Beckford—along rough farm tracks with no cars in sight, to Hinton on the Green, Blakes Hill, Aston Somerville, Buckland Fields, Wormington, or over to Childswickham, and finally back via Murcot, Wickhamford, and Bengeworth, stopping off at Jane's house in Lichfield Avenue for long cool glasses of lemon squash. If these journeys were with Christine's friends, then the breathless boy often ended up being left behind. His old small bike, and his panting, compounded by the fact that Chris and her friends were several years older than him, made it difficult for him to keep up.

The kingdom of Longman's Charity was now expanding. Locally, near to home, there was the Corn Mill Road: a narrow access road to allotments, wheat fields, Bert While's yard, and the Broadley's orchard. Here were three acres of fruit trees: plum (Victoria, Purple, and Yellow Egg) and pear trees (Conference). Christine and Paul would help with fruit picking in the late summer, bringing in the harvest, climbing fruit-picking ladders (ladders which tapered as they rose, so as to fit in amongst the branches), with baskets strapped round their waist for the plums to go in. Maybe twenty labourers would be picking at once, bringing in the fruit over a two-week period once it was ready. In spring, Paul would walk around the orchard, voyaging through knee-high grasses, with sheets of brilliant yellow buttercups floating away around the trees, likewise ox-eyed daisy, vetches, military orchids, meadow cranesbills: all would then fall to the mower in late June—no sprays or chemicals were ever used. At the side of the orchard were timber weather-boarded sheds. He would enter the long dark cavern of this shed and find musty leather harnesses and old horse brass from the days before the war, days before Harry and Jack used motorized lorries and tractors.

Beyond the orchard, the Corn Mill Road dropped down towards the River Isbourne. They would cross the river on a narrow footbridge by the old mill, or sometimes if the level was low, wade across the stream—maybe only a foot deep and fifteen wide at the most. Once across they could follow a public right of way across land usually laid to wheat. They met up with a stone track serving yet more market gardening holdings. But here they came across two delights: a ruined tithe barn from the days of much older agricultural use of the land, and the railway. The stone track or lane which they were walking along was an ancient right of way, which was why, a hundred years earlier, the London, Midland and Southern Railway had gone to the expense of raising embankments for the lane to climb up, and constructed a brick arch bridge to span the tracks. The children would climb through the fence by the side of the bridge, and sit on the embankment, buried in the long grasses of lazy September evenings after a day spent picking fruit in the orchard, while the sun drew down in the west, slowly to dissolve amongst the vast expanse of orchards covering Haselor Hill. Paul would clamber down the embankment, place his hand on the track and feel and listen for a train. After the railway bridge, the track met a more substantial lane that ran from Hampton, linking up with Pewitt Lane.

Retracing their steps along the track in the other direction, past the collapsing walls of the tithe barn, they would re-cross the River Isbourne, walking over a small ancient stone arch bridge, reinforced with red bricks a century earlier, but now crumbling. Often they would wander along the bank of the river, sitting and talking, hiding amongst the weeping willows lining its bank: here although upstream from the mill, the river was narrower (only eight to ten feet) but much, much deeper—a fact he had discovered one afternoon to his dismay when he tried to ford it. Following the track further, after the bridge, brought them to the "top ground"—the five acres or so of sand ground that the Broadleys rented—which was now almost exclusively laid to onions in the spring and leeks in the winter. Here they would often wait for their father to come and give the ground a final look over, which he did each evening—then they could get a lift back home.

Tea finished, they cleared up and packed away the picnic, then mounted their bikes and cycled back into the centre of Elmley.

"I know, let's go along here!" he shouted to his sister.

He then overtook Christine and disappeared down a narrow street by the side of The Queen Elizabeth (a public house), which took them past several houses with deep front gardens. They followed the lane, the stream flowing in the limestone conduit by their sides. They cycled on slowly taking in the scene, then turned sharply to the left. The lane started climbing Bredon in earnest. Soon they had dismounted and were pushing their bikes. The lane climbed up through a shallow valley, past isolated thatched cottages while cows grazed, framed by ancient deciduous trees covering the lower slopes. Soon the tarmac gave out and they were pushing their bikes along rough stone. They had never been this far up the hill before. They had usually turned round by Charlie Edwin's cottage half way up this part of the lane, but today was different. They hid their bikes in a deep gulley, which was obviously an ancient footpath, now overgrown with bushes and briars. They continued on foot, tip-toeing over a cattle grid, swinging on a farm gate. They climbed up the hill, grass gradually becoming thinner as the limestone began to jut awkwardly through the thin beige-green, felt-like covering. They walked along a bare stone track, made simply by scraping away the pitifully thin soil to reveal the rock a few inches beneath. Water from springs trickled across the track. They stopped and collapsed on the ground.

Chapter Eight, Realization: Fear and Depression

Then it happened: they turned round and looked back for the first time. Before them lay the Vale; they had been so busy walking and climbing they had not stopped to realize how high they were. As small as a toy town, Evesham lay beneath them. Around it the fields and trees blended with the heat haze into swathes of blue-green, with the horizon lost in mist—before them hills stood in the distance like jagged blue islands, rising from this mist of land and hedgerows. Around their feet tussocky grass grew, interspersed with late-flowering primrose and cowslip and, scant and thin, the first signs of early flowering harebells, interrupted by tall shabby thistles. Apart from the bleating of sheep, there was silence—nothing but the wide open sky and the land, framed as it was on their left by the Malvern Hills, and their right by the North Cotswold escarpment. A lark soared and dived, played and rode on the cool still air. High above, thin clouds spread, wispy, like a thin veil, the thin, fine, delicate blue of the air becoming richer, more substantial as the horizon approached. Mile upon mile the land flowed away. People seemed so small and insignificant—their activities, even their buildings could barely be seen. Paul sensed his own smallness, his own life as being so tiny and insignificant compared to this vastness. They stood as two small beings, tiny specks on the hillside, scratching about as they had climbed, insignificant and insubstantial. Paul then realized that his parents, their arguments, their quarrels, were likewise small, irrelevant, transitory. This vastness, this wonder, this sky, the permanence of the earth compared to these mere people scurrying about, hidden in the distance like ants, drew over him like a reassurance.

Christine interrupted the silence: "It's pretty good, isn't it! I . . ."

"Yes, yes . . . yes . . ." he was lost for words. He had never felt like this before. There had been hints: walks around the Charity, or in St. Richard's church in the mystery of the service, or more profoundly, when he hid around the shallow pool in the copse by the Red Barn. But *this* . . . . He was overwhelmed by a feeling, no, a *realization* of the vastness of the land, by nature, by the world—by the universe— and by beauty, by the beauty of creation, the created world, God's creation. But more than that, by a tremendous sense that it was holy, precious, and important, that every blade of grass was priceless, that the whole of creation was good. He closed his eyes and the vibrancy of life around him, on that bare windswept hillside, seemed to flow through him. He felt reassured, loved, wanted. It was only a few days since both he and Christine had been confirmed at St. Richard's, and this seemed to be part of it: no, the same thing—he felt blessed. Yet, though he could not conceptualize the truth of it, or speak the words, he was only too aware of the presence of a serpent in this garden. His Sunday School lessons had taught him that. For he was only the creature, a small insignificant creature, yet he knew from his confirmation that God loved him and his sister and his parents, but he realized that there was an insidious evil in this beautiful creation that corrupted all it touched, an evil that coiled and wound slowly, gradually, sinisterly in response to people's behaviour, but all one had to do was resist it. A serpent that had courted, flirted with, his parents till they could no longer break free of its awesome power....

"You alright...?"

"Yes, yes, its, its beautiful, I..."

"I think it's time we started off for home."

Quietly, almost secretively, they retraced their steps, splashing in the spring waters that spilled over the bare, honey-coloured limestone. They retraced their steps to where they had hidden their bikes, then freewheeled down into Elmley, on to Hinton, and so back to Evesham.

That night Paul could not sleep. He lay infatuated by the sense that had touched him, visited him, as he stood on the slopes of Bredon Hill, by a sense, a presence so holy, so unreachable. It made him forget all his troubles.

Over these summer months the two Broadley children, along with Jane and maybe one or two others, cycled and picnicked, toured and explored, in these the last few months before Christine and her friends grew up, for they were fast approaching adolescence. The two children often went to Elmley, to the slopes of Bredon. They would return again.

But Paul would return, to come, as if in pilgrimage, again and again—eventually to climb to the top.

Four

Paul woke early. It was still dark. The room was damp and chilly. He lay still, thinking, feeling depressed and worrying. For the previous few days his parents had been rowing. It had been going on since the weekend. Such quarrels were worse during the short days and the long cold nights of late winter. Outside in the Vale there were signs of an early spring, but the damp grey chill remained. The boy lived on memories of the previous summer, of cycle rides, of the villages they rode through, of his sister, of the times together, the beautiful Indian summer in the autumn as he returned to Swann Lane in top juniors for his final year, of plum and pear picking in the orchard. He lay: still and alone in the dark. A fusty, airless, staleness seemed to pervade the house after they had been rowing. The original cause for the quarrel had been forgotten, lost, but whatever it was, it ignited the smouldering pile of indignities that had accumulated over the previous couple of weeks: Meg claiming magnanimity; Harry seeing red at her pride. Harry

Chapter Eight, Realization: Fear and Depression

stormed out of the living room, cursing and swearing, kicking the living room door violently. Meg threw out sharp remarks about his temper, his manners, and running away over the road to his parents, so he stopped just short of the back door and a full-blown row ensued. Plates were smashed, saucepans flung, the poker from the fire was waved under Meg's face, she wrenched the glasses from his face and flung them out of the kitchen window. Meg received a black eye by the end of the evening; Harry, his shirt ripped and stained with blood from the scratch marks down his right cheek. Christine and Paul knew not to interfere, or they would end up punished, hit.

Then the worst part came. The insidious hours, days, that followed, when neither party spoke to each other, save a short mealy-mouthed shot to remind the other that the row had not been forgotten. Harry ate by himself, the children with their mother. Harry would return from his parent's house after all lights had gone out, would rise in the morning, sort out the kitchen fire, get out his own breakfast, then Meg would rise after he had left. One of them would eventually ask how long this was going on for, which re-opened wounds that had been festering for the last couple of days, and they would be off again. This time the second bout was more restrained, due to comments from Meg about Paul's exam coming up, though they were both still prepared to throw inflammatory remarks at each other and expect no reply. Both believed that whoever had the last word had won. Both accused the other of this indiscretion, but both wanted satisfaction.

So, Paul lay, not wanting to move, not wanting to get up. It was early. He looked at his watch: five-twenty. A chill, a damp mist hung indifferently around the house and the land: a cold, suffocating fog born from the mild, early spring, witness to the balmy westerlies funnelling up the Severn Estuary, bringing rain to the land, but leaving in their wake a chill, damp murkiness that filled his chest, suffocated his breathing, that ate into his bones. It was Wednesday morning. He felt dirty and violated by the row, by the animosity that had been festering, and by . . . what was it? . . . it was as if there was something he could not remember; something that reached its worst when he went to bed each evening, or before he went to bed each night. . . .

He lay not wanting to move, not wanting to face the day. Everyone had been telling him it was the most important day of his life, not only him, but all the children in his class. He lay there, closed his eyes, and started to doze. The terrors returned. A cold suffocating fear gripped his mind, he forced his eyes open but the room started to bend at the edges, appear different, subtly different. A thin ghostliness came over him, he felt he was being sucked in and would disappear. He shook himself, but merely pushed the attack into a cave in his mind from which it lurked. He rolled over and grabbed a book from the wicker bedside chair. With a small plastic torch he pulled the sheets over him and started to read. Harry started coughing, then the landing light went on, just briefly, then it went off to reveal a dimmer light beneath his bedroom door: the hall light downstairs. Then he heard his mother rise: first the quiet shuffle on the landing, then the creak of the stairs. Harry rattled the poker in the kitchen grate, raked out the firebox. Muffled sounds indicated they were talking, a few whispered exchanges, words indiscernible, but the tone of the voices said all; "sshhh" sounds, probably about Paul doing the eleven-plus exam or waking the children, then as if neither could restrain themselves, they would be quarrelling again, but this time whispered, muted, followed by a short silence, then more exchanges, for neither could let pass mockery and derision, ridicule and sarcasm, jeer, sneer, or taunt. They were trying to restrain themselves, believing their son was asleep. Paul lay. Fear welled up in him, creating a sickly tight feeling in his throat: it chilled him to the core, and the terrors returned.

He did not want to get up, did not want to go to school to face the exam, he did not feel ready for such a step. Harry and Meg continued their quiet cold-war bickering until he heard his father leave through the back door. This was followed shortly by sounds from the sheds. Through the damp fog he could hear the curses and mutterings as his father cranked the lorry, trying to coax it into life: dank wet air permeated the old engine. So Paul lay still, returned to the world in his book, but could not summon up interest in the story. He felt dejected, depressed, weighed down, and lost. He simply lay, fighting off the terrors, as he did so often, then feigning sleep when his mother came to wake him. He then rose, dressed and went down stairs for breakfast, but ate little. At ten past eight, his father returned.

"You ready then? Come on, let's get going!"

"You remembered—I . . ."

"Come on, we haven't got all day." His father hurried him along.

Normally Paul walked to school, or got the bus on a wet day. Today his father had offered to give him a lift.

He followed him out to the lorry and jumped in. He had suspected that his father would have forgotten amidst the argument of the last few days, and the pressures of work. He had been explaining to him about what was happening in the story about Dan Dare in the comic, *The Eagle*. His father promised that he would take him on the Wednesday morning to the newsagents in Bridge Street to get the latest edition—early. Harry pulled up outside the newsagents, Paul dashed in feverishly clutching the shilling coin in his hand.

"*Eagle* please!"

He took it and started rushing out, forgetting about his change.

Chapter Eight, Realization: Fear and Depression

"Excuse me, young man!" the newsagent called after him.

"Oh sorry." The boy removed his head from the comic and went back in to the shop to collect his change.

Harry drove him round to Swann Lane School.

"You're a bit early, but there are others; anyway, you've got that to read!"

Paul got out of the lorry.

"Good luck, all the best."

Paul walked into the playground and sat down against the wall by the fire escape, immersing himself in the exploits of Dan Dare, and examining in minute detail the cut away diagram of a submarine in the centre pages. The playground filled up with children, many with parents who called out encouragement from the gates. Just before nine the bell was rung and he folded the comic and put it away in his pocket, then lined up.

Paul performed badly in the exam: his teacher had hoped for better, but knew the boy would lack confidence. He sat for most of the eleven-plus examination thinking about the developments in the Dan Dare story.

As far as schooling went, Paul Broadley was happy at Swann Lane. His class work was average for his age, likewise his ability. There were moments where he really excelled—his art work, drawing, painting, and model making, his history, geography, and his beautifully presented and completed visit books. His basic skills were average, though his handwriting was not as neat as it could have been. He was a late developer, or slow learner; under pressure he struggled: it was simple—add more pressure onto the difficulties at home and it caused him to struggle; not to give up, just to take longer.

Maths was always a stumbling point for him—his performance in class was below average, however, this did not take into account his innate sense of space, or direction, or of practical maths. For example, when the top ground had been ploughed, his father always trampled down a line through the overturned clods of soil diagonally from the first gate in, to within twenty yards of the far corner of the field—a distance of about a quarter of a mile: the public right of way on foot. Harry Broadley's son and heir was perfect at judging the direction, the correct angle to take the path across the field to where it met and went through the hedgerow.

Loading the lorry with an assortment of different containers—chips, trays, nets, and so forth—was a problem of mathematical proportions: how to fit them all in the space, yet have them overlapping so as to bind the stack on the bed of the lorry in order to make it strong (like brickwork): he was a master at loading the lorry by the age of nine, particularly with chips—a double width row to start, nine chips with one at right angles in the centre, the outer ones raised up by the metal lip of the edge of the lorry bed, then the second, alternate layer of nine, with the two outer ones at right angles to bind the stack, then parallel rows, with a final chip at right angles in the centre, off set. This pattern repeated itself as the stack rose. Trays were simpler, but trickier to get balanced on their raised corners; sprouts in nets, troublesome until you sensed where the centre dead weight was, and used that to bind and balance the stack: such a minor rural art involved basic number skills, geometry, spatial awareness, shapes, tessellation, and (when counting the layers of a stack) multiplication, or conversely, when transferring a lorry load into a goods van at the railway (which was a different shape and size, so the stacking pattern could not be repeated), division, or subtraction of elements from the multiplied figure! He explained and drew diagrams about the loading for his teacher, who was very impressed.

Reckoned to be the best painter and drawer in the class—this was acknowledged by all, despite Paul's shyness, reserve, and his place as the odd ball—Paul's final year at Swann Lane coincided with the seven hundredth anniversary of the Battle of Evesham (1265): Simon de Montfort and his barons fighting the king for parliamentary rights, and although defeated finally at the bloody Battle of Evesham, the principles they fought for lived on to fruition. It was the sort of medieval history the boy loved—his imagination could run wild. He made books at school about it, wrote a story about a young knight who had to leave his family to go and fight for Simon de Montfort, he made cut-away diagrams of a castle, and painted a large picture—a close up of a group of knights on horseback in armour riding slowly along the road going to meet their fate. He spent many hours out in the top hall working on this painting. It was entered for a local art competition—part of the anniversary celebrations. Paul won the first prize for the junior age range. The prize was a small set of oil paints. He proudly walked up when his name was called out to receive his prize. He walked onto the stage of the Jubilee Hall in front of the whole school: pupils, teachers, most of the parents, and other important local dignitaries. He was nervous, but it was worth it. He was red in the face, his head nodded involuntarily, continuously, but he felt nine miles high.

When the results of the eleven-plus were published, Paul, predictably, had not passed; he had failed miserably.

Before any of them knew where they were, the end of term was approaching fast. It was then the last week—the very last week at Swann Lane after more than six years! Then it was the last day, the last assembly. Mr. Dutton wished them well. Mr. Lovatt wished everyone well in the future and asked them to come back and see him and so did many other teachers. Mr. Dutton sought Paul out and said how he was sorry that both Broadleys had now left. He made a particular

Chapter Eight, Realization: Fear and Depression

point of telling the Broadley boy that he had been a good influence in the school, a good influence on other children. Paul did not know what he meant, just went red and offered to shake the Head's hand, as he twitched his eyes and nodded his head. And so he left.

That evening he walked slowly along a well-trodden course: across his father's land, down the Charity lane, along past Ol' Grumpy's shed, the pond, slowly out along the lane till he came to the Red Barn. There was no one else around. Behind the barn Bredon Hill rose in all its glory, its silhouette firmly etched on his mind. He sat on the bank opposite the barn and imagined talking to Jim Beason about his feelings (though in very truth, he was subconsciously talking to William). He sat talking quietly putting his feelings into words—without another soul in sight. And so it was over. Term had finished, he had left Swann Lane. There had been difficulties, but there had been challenges, there had been support, and there had been moments to cherish, and moments when he was so proud to have achieved. But above all he did not want to leave. He was not ready for Four Pools. He knew not what class he would be in, did not know whom he would be with. He wished that older children could go to Swann Lane. Paul felt angry—he was not sure why, or with what, but he felt angry. He dare not think about home, about his mother and father, he dare not think about the future—he did not want to grow up. He felt frightened: frightened and very, very alone.

Five

"You can stop looking in the mirror like that all the time, I know what you're doing, I know what you're thinking—you just look in there to look at me, I . . ."

"Oh for . . ." Harry paused: "Look . . . woman, what's the matter with you, what do you expect me to look in? I'm driving . . . you . . . !" Harry's language now descended into the vernacular commonly observed in the top market.

"Don't you swear at me, Harry Broadley, I won't have it, I . . ."

"You're the one who started, woman, you . . ."

"Oh, oh, and here we are going to see my mother; oh I've just about had enough . . ."

"Had enough! God almighty woman! I give you a good living; if that's not good enough for 'ee, I don't know what is!"

"Good enough! All you do is spend your time with those market gardening cronies, all you do is sit over at your father's running me down, all you do . . ."

Harry's riposte, his language, descended into the blasphemous combined with the graphically vernacular.

At this Harry pulled the car up sharply.

"Get out 'ooman, go on get out! I've l had my belly full, I've had it up to here with you, go on, get out if it's not good enough for you . . ."

"Oh, you can be so cruel, you can, you, oh, just because we're going to see my mother, you . . . and I've said before about using that language in front of the children; I was not brought up to it, and I won't have it."

Harry interrupted her by leaning over and opening the front passenger door.

"Well, get out and you won't have it—are you gettin' out or not?"

"Don't you touch me Harry Broadley, don't you touch me—you're all the same you Broadleys, my mother warned me about you, all the same!"

"I didn't touch you; I'm only opening the door for you . . ."

"Oh you, you . . ."—here Meg searched in her mind for suitable invectives to attack him with, not wishing to swear in front of the children—"you swine! I, I . . ."

At which point she pulled at his glasses and threw them into the foot well, scratching his head as she did so.

"Oh you . . . , you. . . , you, you just can't stand not to have a row, look at me, look at me—bleeding!"

Harry's forehead had been scratched, only superficially, but the blood was streaming down. He got out of the car and walked to the grass verge. The traffic continued to stream past on the dual carriageway. Harry leant against a signpost: A38: BRISTOL 7 MILES. Gradually, mopping the wound with his handkerchief, the flow was staunched. Meg meanwhile was sitting firmly in the front passenger seat with the door ajar, just as Harry left it once he had released the catch. After a few minutes he walked back to the car, got in, and without a word started the engine.

"Wait for me, wait a minute!"

Meg hastily slammed the door.

"That's it, drive off with my door open, get me to fall out, oh I know you all right Harry Broadley!" The car re-joined the carriageway, Harry not even pausing for her to finish her tirade. He said not a word but gripped the wheel even tighter and continued to accelerate. He looked in the rear view mirror. Meg saw him. She put out her hand and was just about to move the mirror so he could not see her by looking in it when he moved his left hand, struck out at her arm and knocked it back.

"Oh, you, you . . ." Meg writhed about in the seat, "you can't stop can you!"

Harry struggled with the wheel and the car slurred out to the middle of the carriageway, then back towards the verge. Harry pulled the car up with the brakes juddering, the left wheels rising up on the verge.

"Now are you going to stop! Are you going to . . . well stop?"

Chapter Eight, Realization: Fear and Depression

Harry stared her in the face, firmly. He continued:

"If not, we turn back here, right now, we'll turn and go home."

Meg did not want to turn back. This mid-August Saturday was a rare opportunity to see her mother—the opportunities to visit were rare enough as Harry, through his job, was wedded to the land. Meg was silent. Harry was silent. He now stared forward through the windscreen, his knuckles white with the pressure of gripping the wheel so firmly. The journey was restarted. Both parties were now silent. The remainder of the journey was calm, but the atmosphere was thick with animosity.

Christine and Paul sat in the back of the car. At times like this, Christine just got angry: how dare he speak like that! Why can't they just stop arguing? Therefore Christine got angry and would scream at them. She would join in, on her mother's side, sometimes coolly admonishing her father, sometimes directing direct her anger at him. But Paul just sat still. Christine moved around in her seat, as if she wanted to join the confrontation in the front of the car. But her brother just sat. He sat in his corner of the rear seat. He sat still. Outwardly it would appear that he was less perturbed, less involved than his sister. But for all his stillness this was not so. A coldness came over him. A dryness formed in the back of his throat. He would sometimes clench his fists; his knuckles would turn white as his nails dug into the palms of his hands: that is, what nails he had after he had bitten them; likewise the skin around his nails was chewed and torn back. The anger grew and grew in him: anger at his parents, anger at himself—anger because of the way he felt when they argued and fought, anger that they did not think of him and his sister, that they did not think of him. In his mind he screamed: stop it, stop it, stop it . . . stop it . . . stop. But he was silent. The tinnitus would be screaming in his head, the pressure building in his ear. If he opened his eyes then he became frightened by the tunnel vision: around the periphery of his eyes a dark, changing pattern formed, almost like the pattern of bright sunlight on water. This gradually grew till the circle narrowed his vision down to a small tunnel—in each eye. If he closed his eyes, he was overwhelmed: a dark, suffocating, almost enveloping quality.

So Paul sat on the back seat, his head in his arms. His sister tried to hold his arm. He felt himself slowly, smoothly, being sucked into himself. Gradually he lost the sense of meaning in the words, he could still hear the violent ripostes, but it was as though a wall of glass slowly appeared around him. He was slowly suffocating with feelings of dizziness, nausea, vertigo—a dark grating numbness took over. All Christine could hear were the muffled sobs disguising the battle within; a battle Paul fought as he seemed to be being sucked into a suffocating, rasping, darkness. He was fighting desperately to keep hold of himself, not to recede, or disappear. He crouched there, wishing his ears could stop hearing, wishing he was not there, wishing he had never been born—not suicidal thoughts: no, wishing, even praying that he had never been born, never even started on this life. Meg would then blame Harry for the boy's reaction. Harry would blame her; or the boy—for being weak! And then there was Paul. He just kept all of this to himself: told no one, not a living soul. And he hated himself. The journey was continued. Every few minutes there were sullen exchanges between Meg and Harry.

The car slowly pulled into Shaftesbury Avenue, then to a halt to the sound of loose chippings being squeezed, crunched and sent sideways from the tyres. The day was hot, the road was hot, everyone was hot. By the time they arrived at Meg's mother's house in Weston-super-Mare the atmosphere amongst the Broadleys was better, but the tension and animosity was still very, very, noticeable. Anyone could have sensed it: enmity, malice, rancour—both parties believed, were convinced, that each was right, that the other was inherently bad, that the other must be treated as contemptible. There was bad blood. Renée could sense it when she came out to meet the car. It had been arranged beforehand that they would go out to dinner. But Renée was not sure. Meg got out of the car and pleaded with her, pleaded that all was alright, that Harry was just worried about trade at the moment—that was what was causing the tension between them. Renée agreed. Reluctantly, suspiciously, she got into the car. She sat in the back with the two children. Not a word was said. Dinner passed peacefully, in a small restaurant behind the seafront, off the main street, the peace only interrupted by Meg muttering at Harry for being friendly and chatting to the waitress. After dinner they drove along the front. They drove onto the sands at Uphill. Harry pulled the car up near the dunes and Paul asked to get out. Christine got out with him and they walked along the sands towards the incoming tide. They talked and shuffled their feet in the sand.

"Do you think they'll ever stop?"

"I don't know," said Christine. She paused, as if gathering her thoughts, as if trying to find the belief in herself that matters were going to be alright, that things would improve, that her parents would stop fighting. She continued:

"If mum left him, just for a little while, and we came down here, you know, maybe lived with Renée, then maybe, I don't know, but just maybe they might miss each other, maybe they might get back together, maybe." Her speech trailed off, wearily and with a sigh, "I don't know. I don't know."

After reflecting for a short while Paul said, "I don't want them to split up. But I wish they would stop fighting. I wish . . . I wish, sometimes, that we could leave home. Couldn't we leave home and live somewhere?"

Chapter Eight, Realization: Fear and Depression

"I'm not leaving mum! And what about my leg, how would we look after that?"

They were interrupted by a car horn. It was Harry. Slowly they turned and walked back to the car. They got into the back.

They drove further along the sand. When they could drive no further, Harry turned the car—slowly in a wide arc. Paul looked through the back window at Brean Down, viewed across the estuary of the River Axe. Boats lay on the mud. The tide was out. Black Rock stood out with its crisp white edges, surrounded by mud, then further to the left the thin, silver trail of the river as it cut its swathe through the oozing sludge and silt. Yachts, cabin cruisers, and fishing smacks lay keeled over at obtuse angles. Above the scene rose Brean Down: rising to over three hundred feet as a rocky outcrop of land, thinly covered with grass and inhabited by a colony of seagulls who fought and squabbled over the wealth of food to be unearthed from the silt around the deep, meandering groove formed by the river as it made its way across the tidal mud flats. The car pulled off the sands and proceeded along the tarmac road through the narrow streets of Uphill, then by way of the Bleadon Road back onto the seafront in Weston. Paul sat, drifting off in his mind, dreaming of living in the scene he had just looked on; dreamed of living in the farm he imagined at the foot of Brean Down, dreamed of spending his time drawing, painting, reading, making models, working from home, dreaming. But he felt frightened by his feeling, by the feelings he had experienced whilst looking at the scene. The joy, the purity, the . . . he did not know how to put it into words, but the experience was so overwhelming, so full of goodness that he was frightened of it. Then he realized—these feelings reminded him of William. William: dear Panty. He quickly changed track in his mind. They had pulled in by the road that ran along the side of the Marine Lake, the road that led to the Knightstone Theatre. Harry was saying that it was no good, there was nowhere to park. The arrangement was that they would all get out and cross the road to Rozell's for tea: Harry would find somewhere to park. He thrust some money into Meg's hand:

"Here, just in case I'm a long time!"

"Oh no, Harry Broadley, you don't get out that easily; we'll be waiting for you."

Meg, Renée, and Christine, with Paul in tow, walked to the edge of the pavement whilst Harry turned the car through one hundred and eighty degrees and drove off towards Worlebury. They crossed the road and walked up the steps into Rozell's. The cafe was spacious and surprisingly empty on that hot Saturday afternoon. The small party walked to the rear of the cafe to the counter, but were interrupted by a young girl who gestured to them with her arm, to sit at the table in the window. They sat and waited: Meg explained to the girl they were waiting for the last member of the party to come. They waited. Still Harry had not come. Eventually after returning a third time, the girl politely pointed out that, as they could see, many were now coming in from the beach, and soon the table would be required. So Renée ordered. Just as the tea, sandwiches, and cakes were arriving, Harry walked in, came over, and sat down. This lateness renewed the enmity between Meg and Harry. Harry clearly did not want to be there and Meg was convinced he had done this on purpose. Renée tried to lighten things a bit, but all attempts at conversation fell flat, save for Christine talking with her about school and pop music. Tea being finished, they walked across the road, and then ambled down the small access road towards the Knightstone Theatre. Harry went off in the other direction to fetch the car. Finally, Harry arrived with the car. Soon they had returned to Shaftesbury Avenue; they settled into the front lounge for the evening—while Paul sat in the back room looking through an aircraft book he had brought with him. This back room, or dining room, had been where he had often sat with Panty. Evening was over. Once all had retired to bed, he lay, awake, listening to the sounds of a strange house, its peculiar smell, the moonlit shape of the window, the thrill of being somewhere different. Strange as it seemed to Paul, his mother brushed aside the need for him to wear a nappy when they stayed at her mother's house . . . .

The Sunday morning was much a repeat of the previous day—except this time they drove up through Worlebury, through Kewstoke, and out to Sand Bay, returning alongside Weston Woods to park opposite Birnbeck Island. Here the two children went off along Birnbeck Pier, while the adults stayed in the car. They walked slowly, ambling along, Paul looked down through the wooden decking at the green sea below the pier. Once they reached the island they stopped, and leaning on the railings, looked down at the rocks below, the sea pitching violently in the wind. To their left was the landing stage, backed by the scaffold-like structure of the pier. Here stood the ferries to Cardiff and Newport, way over across the Bristol Channel. But today, on this Sunday morning, all was stillness and quiet. The ferry had just left. They continued their conversation from the previous day:

"Did you sleep?"

"Yes, in the end," her brother replied.

They both watched the waves breaking on the rocks below. The closeness between them was not as strong as it had been during the earlier years of their childhood. Christine was now growing up. She was thirteen and her interests were decidedly not childish. But there was still a strong bond between them: they both supported each other in facing their life at home.

"Did you hear them in the kitchen?"

Chapter Eight, Realization: Fear and Depression

"What?"

"Did you hear them?" repeated Paul. "I did: they crept down stairs once they thought we were all asleep. They were arguing in the kitchen: whispering!"

Paul paused. His sister did not reply, but was obviously attentive. He continued:

"I don't know what it was they were arguing about, but Renée came down and that was the end of it."

"Are you looking forward to September?" asked Christine.

He was silent.

Their conversation was interrupted by a loud klaxon sounding off. They knew what it was and raced across the pier to the other side. They were fortunate, because within a minute the lifeboat came out of its building, gliding down the steep slipway, then to hit the water with a great surge of spray, finally to power off out to sea. Amidst the excitement they had not noticed Harry coming up behind them. They jumped when they heard their names.

"Where's Renée? Where's mum?" they more or less said in unison.

"They're back in the car, I felt like stretching my legs, so I thought I'd come and join you."

Harry had actually been loitering behind, about halfway along the pier for most of the time. He couldn't stand the thought of staying in the car, and wanted to keep an eye on the two children. He had followed them, walking as they were along the Old Pier as it was affectionately known, but kept his distance. He knew Meg and Renée would be talking about him in the car, and somehow felt better out of it. Together they walked past the buildings on the island, and on to the furthest reach of the pier. Here, jutting out into the Bristol Channel, they could look down and see the powerful waves swell mightily then crash like splintering glass on the rocks below them. They looked up—out to sea was Steep Holm, further out, Flat Holm, further still, the Atlantic Ocean, thought Paul. He smelled the wind, tasted it with his tongue, fantasized about where it had come from, what wonders it had blown past, or through; he thought of the giant Atlantic breakers hurling themselves around the ocean, pitching and rolling into each other, breaking into a million droplets of spray. The wind blew ferociously, stripping their hair back, flattening it to their skulls. All three could taste the salt in the wind. All three became riveted by the slow, almost gentle progress of a large cargo ship as it appeared from behind Steep Holm, steaming on unhurriedly towards Cardiff Docks—which could just be seen through the heat haze on the horizon. He felt happiness, intuited joy, sensed the immensity of the wide, open ocean. He looked up at his father, who likewise was scanning the horizon. The child looked up, and loved him. Then he felt guilt: should he love him?—his mother did not, and he sensed somehow that his mother did not want him to love his father. He was confused. He looked at Christine, who was trying to keep her hair straight, trying to stop it blowing completely out of style, and he loved her. The ship by now was way past Steep Holm and nearing the haze of Cardiff, within which he could just make out diminutive, smoking chimneys around what must have been the docks.

Christine broke the silence: "Can we go now?"

"Er . . . yes, come on!" Harry was stilled from his reverie. Paul looked, and wondered what his father's thoughts had been: he was afraid to ask. Together they walked back to the car. There was silence by the time they arrived. Soon they were back in Renée's house; Sunday dinner was eaten and the washing-up done. Presently they were in the car and driving out of Weston.

Reaching into his jacket pocket, William's grandson drew out a photograph in a mock-brass frame. He gave the glass a wipe—took out his handkerchief, raised the frame to his mouth, breathed on the glass, then polished the surface with his handkerchief. The photograph was precious to him. He had often coveted it: it had stood on the mantelpiece of the rear ground-floor room in Renée's house for as long as he could remember. He had plucked up courage to ask her, fearing she would say no, but she readily gave it to him. And now it was his. He looked on the photograph: William Riley, Panty, stared back from the sepia-brown picture. It had been taken when he was in his thirties: his skin was clear, hair neatly placed, but above all there were his eyes—open, honest, warm, and loving, just as the child always remembered. That was the trouble—remembering. Paul had known him for such a short time; then he was gone. He looked at the photograph. Paul cried. Gently at first, as he tried to hide his tears, but he could not hold back his sadness: he wept. His mother turned round to comfort him.

"What wrong, Paul?" She took his hand.

He did not answer.

"Is it Panty?"

The boy nodded: "I wish I'd known him better. No, I mean, I . . ." he struggled for the words. "I wish I still knew him, I wish he was . . ."

Meg struggled for words too. She held his hand tight.

"You know, I sometimes think how much like him you are; I sometimes think what it would have been like if he had known you."

He did his best to stop the tears, to bury his grief.

"I'm alright," he shrugged off her arm. Meg withdrew her arm, and turned round to face the front.

In his mind, he prayed a simple prayer to William, by saying his name, saying it over and over again, then asking for his help; asking for help for his mother and father. He told William in his mind of the terrible fears he felt, asked why he felt so frightened when they rowed. Paul looked at the photograph and joy filled him.

Chapter Eight, Realization: Fear and Depression

Instinctively he leant forward and tapped his father on the shoulder:

"Dad, Dad, look!"

He gave him the photograph.

Harry took it, and looked at it.

"It's younger than I remember him, but I can tell it's him. It's a nice photo."

He handed it back without taking his eyes from the road. The boy stayed where he was, sat forward of the rear seat, half pressing himself through the gap between the two front seats.

"What about the life boat then, wasn't it good!"

"You know they can do over thirty knots," replied his father, "but only in the right weather conditions, of course."

"Oh stop it!" shouted his mother, interrupting the conversation: "I see you have lost all your tears now haven't you, all that sadness? You don't seem to care about my father now!"

The boy drew back into his seat. Meg had been jealous. She sat stock still, facing the front, not looking at Harry, not looking to the left or right. She still harboured a grudge against Harry for the row on the previous day. What was more, she was not going to have her son being friendly and talking with him, and she was not going to have her father's name in one breath from the boy and then all this frivolous chat in the next. What was worse was the subliminal intentions of Meg of keeping her son and Harry Broadley apart. Harry for peace acquiesced. Christine sat with her teenage magazine—bored. And Paul, he simply sat and buried his feelings deep, back where they had been: deep, hidden. He placed the photograph back in his jacket pocket and tried to forget.

The remainder of the journey was uneventful. They stopped in Gloucester, in a car park near the cathedral, to allow everyone to go to the toilet. Then, as dusk gathered, they continued through to Cheltenham and on up the A435 to home. Soon they had unpacked the car, and were ready for bed. Harry went over to see his mother and father, then stayed over there, downstairs, doing the books (going through some business paperwork). The nightly ritual on the kitchen table was repeated as it had been for the previous four years, the nappy spread out, the touching and stroking as the boy lay there and wished he could simply disappear.

Paul settled down in bed—reading. Christine and Meg slept together in the double bed in the front bedroom—they had done for over a year—ever since a stormy night when, during a blazing row, Harry had charged out of the front bedroom, into Christine's room to scoop her up in his arms, carry her through, and deposit her in the front room and in bed with Meg, then to storm back, slam the door of the rear bedroom, and thereafter did not sleep in his wife's bed again.

Six

Evesham County Secondary School had only recently been constructed. The school stood in Four Pools Road. This new road was an extension of Fairfield Road. The school consisted of three blocks, plus several smaller ancillary buildings, and was backed by large playing fields—at least three football pitches and a hockey pitch surrounded the modern buildings containing over fifteen hundred pupils. Walkways and small grass areas connected the three main teaching blocks. Paul wandered around on the first morning, trying to take it all in. The site was large and complex; however, unlike other children who were getting lost, he found it easy to orientate, to navigate. He was, however, overwhelmed by the sheer number of children, by their size, by their loudness! He met up with and talked to two boys who had been in his class at Swann Lane.

The school building and its site were typical of a technical secondary modern school: a post-war, system-designed, flat-roofed, concrete and brick, steel and glass, functionalist complex. About two miles away lay Prince Henry's Grammar School, an ancient foundation, north of the railway in Greenhill. It was by contrast a much more traditional building, with no more than a few hundred pupils. Because of its size not all who passed the eleven-plus examination could be accommodated: those who could not be accommodated came to Four Pools—but were in a special stream, apart from the rest of each year. Within a few weeks children in the year had come to realize that those in this special stream had the best teachers, the best rooms and equipment, and were to a degree separate from the rest of the school (many adults would have perceived this as a sort of educational apartheid).

The school had started out as a technical secondary modern, planned in keeping with the spirit of the Butler Act to provide a technical, vocation-based education for the toiling masses of market gardening children. However, by the mid-1960s change was evident. The school was getting a good set of O-level results each year, and had a small but keen sixth form. In essence, it was an early form of comprehensive, taking a wide range of ability, reflected in the sixth form entry each year: Form "A" (those who had passed the eleven-plus, and who followed more or less the same curriculum as those at Prince Henry's), then Alpha, B, C, D, E, according to ability (sometimes a year contained an F-stream such was the pressure from the post-war baby boom). This way children could get the right curriculum to stretch them without leaving them languishing with work that was too difficult, or too easy. Many people—both parents and teachers—were realizing that this system was clumsy and rudimentary.

Paul found himself in 1D—a class of thirty-seven pupils—he had been put

Chapter Eight, Realization: Fear and Depression

there on the basis of his atrocious performance in the eleven-plus. The difference in classes was soon realized by the other children—1A were the best, and literally did not come into contact with most of the other children in the year; 1alpha and 1B were the clever ones, 1C average—(children who wished they were up amongst the others, but prided themselves that they were not "thickos" like the kids in 1D and 1E, who were no good at anything). It soon became a set idea in the playground culture that 1D were quiet and well behaved, while 1E were the toughies, the badly behaved ones: they were regarded by the rest of the year as sheep and goats—the tame thickies and the tough thickies, the two classes being perceived as of equal ability. Paul found himself in with the tame thickies—the sheep of 1D (nearly all the rest of his class from Swann Lane were in 1B). Their form teacher was Miss White—a thin, nervous, teacher whose tiny metal-framed glasses seemed to move up and down when she was trying to get authoritative, such was the change in her facial muscles. The boy had an eye for detail and he noticed many things about the teachers, so much so that he could soon work out which were the new, young teachers, and which were the more experienced. He considered Miss White very new!

Lessons were insultingly easy. He was redoing work he had done at Swann Lane, work he had done with Mr. McGlinn three years earlier! He was bored; little challenged him. At playtime the children he was with were shunned by the rest of the year. In lessons, the young, inexperienced staff struggled to keep control. Paul would complete work during lessons and then sit, bored, trying to look occupied so as to avoid trouble. He was regarded as a thicko in the playground by other children from other classes, and as a creep in his class, for always getting work finished in record time. In the playground he tried to team up with his sister, but she was now nearly fourteen and wanted to be with her friends, though she supported her brother as much as she could.

Then there were the playground bullies. The school was large and spread out with plenty of corners for illicit smoking, for extortion, and for bullying. Paul was a prime target: sweets, money, all went, to the extent that he pleaded with his mother not to give him some to take to school, but he dare not tell her why. If she insisted, he threw whatever it was away, then when he was frisked he genuinely had nothing, but would get roughed over for having nothing: no visible damage, nothing that would be seen by the teachers; no, merely threatened, punched, and kicked, generally roughed up.

The PE changing rooms were the worst for this. He was naturally shy and quiet, at Swann Lane he had been described as "a sensitive little thing," who never got into trouble; at Four Pools he was lost, even more alone. He would stand outside classrooms during play—lining up early, so as to avoid other children, or stopping behind to tidy up. Most teachers just wanted to get out of the rooms as soon as possible, but a small number of the good teachers did take the lower forms—Miss Wilberforce was one, who encouraged Paul's love of geography, of mapping skills, by looking at the maps he brought in from home: invented worlds he had made up and drawn; he had spent hours on them. Art, which should have been the saving grace for Paul on the timetable, was an abject horror. Mr. Ladge was famous throughout the school for being a "good 'un," his art room was alive, vibrant, creative, so was the work produced. But Paul did not have him as his art teacher. He had an elderly lady art teacher, over in the Large Block, who did not like little children who were good at art—"you are all the same, and you will all learn the same, and you will all be good at it," she declared. Every lesson was spent drawing from objects, copying from pictures of fusty old statues with broken arms. No creativity, no spark, no vitality—no paint! It appeared that she was afraid of the children, afraid to let them be good, it was as if she feared creativity. If he did a good drawing, even under these circumstances, it was torn up as not good enough. He hated her. He had a strong streak in him of justice, of righteousness, possibly bred by his parent's quarrels and rows.

However, he was naive and innocent, and on one occasion was set up by two toughies in the metalwork room. While clearing up, he was given some small pieces of metal by one boy and asked if he knew where they went. He did. Just at that moment the teacher screamed and yelled for order, wanting to know who had been making a noise with some small pieces of metal. All was silent. Paul was seen holding them, was deemed guilty, and immediately given a detention. He politely asked the teacher if he could say anything. He was refused. Angry with the injustice, he stopped behind to speak to the teacher, but he would hear nothing, his decision had been made. Paul then committed the cardinal sin. He said that the teacher was not a good teacher because he had not bothered to find out what really happened, that he should not be so cruel and dishonest—and he used the word "unjust." This was like waving a red rag to a mad bull. The teacher was old, thin, wiry, and although he knew something of metalwork, had clearly never been trained as a teacher, and believed his word was law, regardless of justice and honesty. Paul Broadley was given a second detention for daring to challenge him.

When in form, after the register on Monday morning, when the name of that week's detainees were read out, the others in his form laughed and teased him. Miss White, Paul's form teacher, tried vainly to control them, but was ineffective, even with the so-called sheep of 1D. Paul went to the detentions, but sat doing nothing, desperately trying to fight back tears. Mr. Hill, the poor young wretch of a maths teacher, whose voice fluttered with nerves when he was challenged by

Chapter Eight, Realization: Fear and Depression

the toughies, took the detention. He was surprised and shocked to see Paul there. The boy simply took it all in, and remembered. He did not like the sheer size and scale and impersonality of the school, he disliked the lack of knowing—few teachers, including those who taught his class, knew the names of their charges. Although the school provided well for the most able, in particular the A stream, at the other end it was a rough and ready rural secondary modern, with all the grace and charm of a bad tempered goat. He wished he was back in the security of Swann Lane.

He withdrew further into himself and began to take time off. His health was still not good—mostly chest problems. Then there were the terrors, which scared and frightened him. The attacks were more frequent now, not just when his parents were rowing, and they left him feeling so empty, so depressed, so useless and afraid. So he would feign illness—colds, coughs, chest problems, and convince his mother he needed a week off school. Paul's nervousness and fear now showed at school: other children started calling him strange, mental, do-lally; this was compounded by bullying, and the problems at home. However, during the summer term his attendance improved. He tried his hardest to ignore all the problems, but this only masked them—the cause was still there.

Paul worked hard—school work became a form of escapism. During the end of year exams he did really well; it was his way of proving to himself that the work had been insultingly easy, that he was not as the others said. His end-of-year report spoke of him as a quiet member of the class, who seemed to lack confidence, but that he had ability and the right attitude to work. He found himself moved up for the next year into class 2B! But the situation continued into the autumn term: the teasing, the bullying, the intimidation. He was considered an outsider by the children in 2B (a class of nearly forty) because he had not been with them from the start and because he came from 1D/1E; and the situation at home was becoming diabolical. His health deteriorated, both his breathing and the attacks of Ménières; the terrors continued to plague him, though he had lost all control over his memory of the nightly abuse on the kitchen table—when he went to bed he would feel cold, thin, almost transparent, lost and dirty, but unknowing, oh so unknowing, and he could not pin down what was wrong with him. He put this down to the belief that he just did not like himself, that he had never liked himself. His attendance fell away, first a few days off, then a week, then periods of two weeks.

Despite the promotion into class 2B, the pattern of events had got out of hand. His Christmas report indicated he had the ability, and a good approach to his work, but absence had held up progress. Paul worried too much; he worried about little things, not the school work; other factors seemed to prey on him so

173

easily. Form 2B was given a talk about careers, jobs, education, work, their future. He became worried: he did not want to grow up. It preyed on his mind as he walked into assembly the next day; he couldn't face the thought of what was to happen in the future, how he would cope, what was to become of him. Paul stood stock still in the throng of over one thousand five hundred pupils in the large hall, nodding his head nervously, repeatedly, not listening, worrying, just worrying, not wanting to face the future: shunned by his peers: the mark of Abel.

By now he had become afraid of other people. It was a bizarre situation: the other children, even some adults, would shy away from him, feel uncomfortable with him, and were at times irritated with him. He was nervous, afraid, like he did not fit in with them; he could sense their feelings towards him, which made things worse; he was even more out of touch with them, and then they sensed he was even more an outsider. This was not helped by his habit—the outward manifestation of a nervous disorder?—of involuntarily nodding his head, and screwing his eyes up. He began to withdraw from human society—from his peers, the other children around him, from school, from the congregation round at Saint Richard's. The reaction in him to his parents' rowing, the terror, was as severe as ever: the cold suffocating fear gripping his mind, the visual distortions if he tried to force the attack away, the thin, ghostliness which came over him, the sense that if he did not fight and struggle against these sensations he would be sucked in on himself and would disappear; the fear, the deep-seated nausea, the sickly tight feeling in his throat, being chilled to the core, the thin grey fog that took over his mind before he would lose consciousness, sometimes only for a second or two. He tried to tell his parents about this, but could not get the words.

Often now, these terrors induced a panic attack, where he simply had to get out, where he could not keep still, so much so that now he simply had to get away when his parents were quarrelling. When such a panic attack struck, he would run out into the passageway or to the sheds at the bottom of the garden; if he was upstairs, he could climb out of his bedroom window and swing by way of the drainpipe onto the brick parapet of the flat roof over the outhouses or, once it had been added to the house, the lean-to type of veranda at the back, then swing across, stepping carefully onto the joists, rather than the clear, corrugated, plastic sheets that covered it, then onto the flat roof over the outhouses. He would go out across the back garden and escape into the Charity, maybe even the shallow pool in the copse by the Red Barn. This became a habit so that even if there had been no quarrels and rows, he would have used such stealth and secrecy. Whatever the weather, he would spend time wandering around the Charity. And then there was Timmy, his cat, whom he could love and withdraw to. And so gradually the occasional week off became more than occasional through feigning physical

Chapter Eight, Realization: Fear and Depression

illness, though his mother could see that he was suffering, was not fitting in, that he was not getting on well at school with other children and was distressed at home.

On more than one occasion Meg's mother would look at her and ask her, piercingly, "What are you doing to him, what are you doing to that boy?" Meg would simply raise her head, turn away, and not answer, busy herself with something. What understanding did she have of the nightly ritualized abuse when the nappy was pinned around him? Did she mentally block out what had happened to her as a girl, allowing it to surface when her son lay on the table, only to block it out again afterwards?

Seven

Outside it was raining—heavily. Paul sat at the dining table, in the living room. The table lived in a side-bay window and overlooked the driveway leading from the Cheltenham Road down to the sheds. With his head resting on his hand, with the fingers curled into a relaxed fist, supporting his chin, he gazed at the window. The rain came down heavily; it hit the metal-framed glass pane, smacking and slurring as the wind caught it. Drops of water trickled just a short distance from Paul's nose. He watched as they scurried downward, abruptly changed for a few millimetres and went sideways, then continued their downward path. He was puzzled—why did they not run straight down, why did they zigzag left and right while on their downward course? He thought about the glass, thought about why this was happening, thought about the surface tension on the water and how it might affect the way the water was dripping. He examined the glass carefully and wondered if there might be traces of dirt or grease that made the water behave the way it did. He allowed his eyes to see beyond the pane of glass. He watched as two rain drops ran in this higgledy-piggledy manner down the pane of glass then merged: two rain drops joining, he thought—one add one makes one (in this case) he thought. So why is the new drop not wider—it looks the same. Then he realized that the new drop was probably travelling faster, so that was why it looked the same as the other two drops; still it's a funny way to do an addition sum—one add one equals one—he thought.

The rain was coming down in sheets now. It bounced off the gravel drive, smacking with vengeance against the fence put up by Miss Blunt to hide the view of the side of her house. The downpour rattled with a metallic ring off the cab of the lorry as its brown bulk slowly reversed past the window, the gravel crunching under the weight of the wheels, the bed of the lorry burdened with nearly three tons of winter produce: nets of sprouts piled high behind the cab, boats of leeks, the rain dribbling off the white roots that had squeezed through the side of the containers, crates of cabbage, then Alan sitting on the tail of the lorry, oblivious to the rain trickling down and around the features of his face, soaking ever more into his jacket and running off his boots. In the cab Sam and Chas sat next to Harry who meticulously reversed the lorry down the drive into the shed. In the distance Paul could hear the chatter and tone of different voices calling, laughing, exchanging banter.

Alan appeared, walking back up the driveway with a plastic sheet wrapped around him and over his head. In the distance, over and above, the slow growling rumble of thunder grew through the blueness of the darkening sky. The magical blue light which pervaded the scene gave it an awesome air. Alan, having spent the day batting with the elements, pulling eighty boats of leeks at the top ground, having abandoned his raincoat once it had become soaked through, strove along, kicking the gravel from under his feet, while the baptism of thunder and water smote him. The thunder growled and rumbled, the clouds belched and spewed, drenching the land and all that grew.

The boy sat resting his head on his hand, gazing through the window, through the rain, through the mist in his mind, through his isolation. It was now early January. He had not returned to school with his sister. He was off sick. Admittedly his chest, throat, and breathing had been bad, but this was not the primary reason. It had become more and more the norm towards the end of the autumn term for him to be at home, not at school: a fortnight off, then back for a few days, or a week at the most, then off again. He was thought of in this way by the rest of his class, as the "sicky," who was off school more than he attended, he was "do-lally," not to be played with, or befriended, or sat by, and certainly not touched: the mark of Abel. His father did not have patience with him, referred to him as a namby-pamby, saying he should pull himself together, while his mother was distressed and distraught, wondering what to do. Meg would chastise Harry for shouting, implying that it was his actions alone that cased the rows, caused the fights, caused the boy's traumas. Harry would retort by denigrating both Meg and Paul—adding that the boy was a baby, not fit to be his son.

The rain continued. The darkness grew. It was only half past one in the afternoon, but already the light was failing, the land smothered as it was by the dense, heavy bank of cloud. Dusk was premature, unnaturally so as the clouds thundered and tore themselves apart above the Vale, the rain drowning out all sound from the road, as Alan turned and walked down along the Cheltenham Road, back towards the town.

Paul slowly turned his head, pivoting it on his hand, and returned his attention to the book that lay in front of him, the sketch pad and the pencils, and

Chapter Eight, Realization: Fear and Depression

the drawing of a large overburdened wagon, bogged down in the mud of a rutted eighteenth-century track, while peasants fought to push its great bulk clear of the mire, and gentry stood and watched: a day like this one, he thought, as his pencil returned to shading the detail on the tails of the coat of a fine gentleman, stood with buckled shoes, stockinged legs, and fine lace cuffs wrinkling beneath the sleeves of his tightly fitting jacket. He put some mud splashes on the man's stockings, and smiled as he did.

Meg was aware of how withdrawn the boy was, and was at her wit's end. She had taken him to the doctor several times over the last year with various chest complaints, coughs, and colds, breathing difficulties, and because the school was expressing concern about his absence. Doctor Appely wanted Paul to see an expert—a social psychiatrist, or something of the kind, at a clinic around at Briar Close Hospital. Social workers were alerted and were involved; though in a small rural community, these were people who were known to the Broadleys. Mr. Able (head of social services in Evesham) had been a friend of William Riley's, before Meg's parents had retired to Weston, so the situation was partly known already. This was a difficult situation for him, knowing the Broadleys in the way a doctor knows all his or her patients in a small rural community. He could see the state Paul was in. He was taken by his mother to see Doctor Cheen, in a clinic at Briar Close, on several occasions. He was given little white tablets to take—it was said they would make him feel better. They were tranquillizers, though he was not told so. They did not make him better. If anything they made him feel funny. So he pretended to take them then discarded them.

Paul Broadley had been in the habit of creeping out of his first floor bedroom window very early in the morning to go for a walk around parts of the Charity. He could no longer go during the day, as he was off school. His mother caught him, in a distressed state, trying to escape out of his bedroom window one evening while a row was in progress: she feared for his safety, feared his motives. He would not tell her what he was doing—these walks were his secret. Meg therefore feared for his wellbeing, his sanity. Mr. Thomas, a social worker, came every now and then to see Paul, to see his parents, and to observe and assess if Paul was alright, to see if he was safe. Meg and especially Harry regarded this as interfering. Eventually the idea was raised that maybe it would do the boy good to get away for a while. Dr Cheen had stated openly to Meg that he believed it was necessary to separate the boy and his mother, that he was not happy with the influence she had on the boy.

The rain continued to fall. Paul continued with his drawing, working detail into the old covered cart with its wide, mud-encrusted wheels. He sat watching the downpour as it persisted, smacking the window pane again and again as the wind ordered it. In the distance the thunder rumbled as the torrent drove, bouncing small fragments of gravel from the drive onto the lawn. He turned his head round and gazed onto the window again, resting his chin once more on his hand. Just how much water had run down the pane since he had watched the raindrops merge—maybe he would set up something to measure, possibly use a Smarties tube, but no—that would be no good, it would go soggy! The light was now fading, fast. The January dusk was closing in, while from the sheds, he could hear his father, Chas, and old Sam stapling covers onto boats of leeks and crates of cabbage, already with the electric lights on in the shed, even though it was only half past two.

Longman's Charity

Part Three
Through Fire and Water

*". . . if I make my bed in hell,
You are there*

*. . . even there Your hand shall lead me,
and Your right hand shall hold me."*

PSALM 139:8b & 10

Chapter Nine
Captivity: Sanctity and Sanctuary

> ～ *"You make us a reproach to our neighbours,*
> *a scorn and a derision to those all around us.*
> *You make us a byword among the heathen,*
> *they shake their heads at us in scorn.*
> *All day long my disgrace is before me,*
> *and shame has covered my face,*
> *because of the words of those who taunt and revile me,*
> *because of the looks from my adversaries and those who hate me."*
> PSALM 44:13–16

One

A new group of adults now pressed on Paul Broadley. Unlike the adults who had made up his life so far, whether relatives, other market gardeners, teachers, or priests, these professionals, this new group of adults, had one thing the others did not have: power—power in some measurable quantity to impact on his life. This group of experts were concerned: he did not want to go to school! He was very good at art, interested in reading and finding out, but he spent very little of his time playing with other children. He seemed to be quite happy inhabiting a small child's world. This was acceptable for a seven year old, but not a boy of twelve—after all, he was now nearly an adult. When his mother dressed him up, took him to see these various adults, the child in some ways enjoyed the trip out. These concerned adults would talk to him; try to get him to talk back. But he said very little. They would ask him what was wrong, what was troubling him. He could not answer—he knew there was something, but he could not remember. So he remained silent. If he was pressed—and pressed he was by this massed rank of experts—his answer focused on the rows and violence at home. And because of the loudness, the violence, the use of his fists, and the effect on him of the blood pouring forth from his mother's wounds, his answer focused on his father, a father who had exhibited violence and an uncontrolled temper towards the boy's mother, and of whom the boy was frightened, petrified. And Harry? Harry was ashamed of this scrap of a child for his son. And he took pride in reminding the boy that they had tried but failed to abort him on two occasions—that he had wasted good money on medicines to get rid of him. The effect on Paul of these comments was corrosive. Harry now spent virtually every evening across the road with his parents, returning to sleep in the back bedroom after all had gone to bed, whilst Christine slept with her mother. The boy saw his father as the catalyst of whatever troubles these experts perceived in the child, so they suspected Harry of . . . of what?

One day the police came to ask his father to accompany them to the police station—just to discuss, simply an interview. Meg told the children, the neighbours, that it was to do with a break-in at the top ground; they needed Harry as a witness and for a statement. But he was gone all day, hours. Harry, meanwhile, received the third degree in an interview—was he interfering with the boy? Was he molesting him? Harry told the truth—and made sure he gave them what for. Besides, his movements (which they had observed) confirmed his distance from his family and the house: apart from meal times he was now a virtual stranger in the house during the daytime. And Paul had blurted out to these experts about the sleeping arrangements. Yes, the police, these so-called experts, were correct to assume the child was being interfered with but they could not see past their own prejudices: men bad, women good; rural working-class father bad, middle-class mother good. Paul was a child, young for his age, naive and ignorant, still living in a child's small world: should he have been able to recall the memories and put them right? Or were these experts failing him? After many months these concerned adults decided it would be better if he were away from home. The boy did not really understand what these concerns were about, why they kept asking him so many questions, why they kept wanting to see him, why could they not just leave him alone. His ability to withdraw was his way of keeping himself safe, of coping. Ironically the more these concerned adults expressed their concern the more it pushed him deeper and deeper into a hole.

Chapter Nine, Captivity: Sanctity and Sanctuary

Two

So, on a bright February morning, only a week or so after his thirteenth birthday, Paul was driven through some tall black-painted gates in a car—municipal-looking gates, official-looking gates. He was driven into a group of serious and right-looking buildings. The car drove across a tarmac forecourt and through a gap between other buildings into a smaller courtyard. The buildings were a mixture of 1940s prefabricated army Nissen huts, an old Victorian hospital building, and an immaculately kept Georgian entrance. As they got out of the car a man in a white coat greeted them. They were ushered through several corridors, through a pair of doors with neat circular windows set high up in them. They entered a ward. They were invited—authoritatively—to sit in the conservatory. At the end of a corridor was a large open area with beds, hidden below high windows. Too high really to see out of, but through one a tall tree—just the top of it—could just be seen. There were beds, many of them—about twenty-five. His mother was trying to choke back the tears. His sister was at school. His father was working. The man in the white coat asked him some questions. His mother hugged the boy tightly; she didn't want to leave. As screens were drawn around the bed he undressed; slowly he put on his pyjamas. For a second time the staff asked his mother to leave. The child lay there in the bed. He lay very still, very quiet: the sheets pulled up to cover his mouth. In the stillness, with the screens still around the bed he lay, wondering, pondering, questioning. What had he done? What had he done wrong? He was only scared; oh so fearful! *Here* of all places.

Three

For four long months he was to stay in that unit, that ward, in that hospital: Powick Hospital, Powick Mental Hospital. The name had only recently been changed. Founded by the Victorians as The Worcester City and County Pauper and Lunatic Asylum, its only claim to fame was that Edward Elgar had been the bandmaster there at the age of twenty-two years. It was built in the village of Powick a few miles outside of Worcester on the Malvern Road. As Paul entered its walls, its gates, its security, such cultural details were meaningless.

He lay in bed. He lay still. He dare not move; he didn't know the rules, what he should and should not do. He lay there, vulnerable, puzzled, waiting. After a while he was processed: various adults, one at a time, came to check everything about him, to look him over; then there were questions. A tray of food was brought for his dinner, but he did not eat; more people came to see him in the afternoon, then it was tea time. He did not eat. He was taken to the bathroom. Finally he drifted off to sleep—fitfully dozing. He woke to find the screens removed and other people milling around. He started to doze off again—*they* must have given him something. Sleeping fitfully, he woke again to find it is dark, silent, still. Finally he slept.

Waking early the next morning, he lay still, frightened, wondering whether to move. The sky was clear, the air thick with the smell of floor polish. Without sitting up he looked around. The unit or ward was square, with windows and beds around three sides. The fourth side was open, indeed formed a corridor that extended beyond the square, or the central part of the ward. The ward was light and airy. There were about ten beds in the square, central part of the ward, each bed having a large sash window rising behind it. Paul was in a bed on the left-hand side of the square, as entered from the wide corridor; the corridor itself having beds along one side of its length. Opening out from the central corridor were several small rooms with a single bed behind each closed door. In all, the unit could accommodate about twenty-five men, occasionally, a child—like Paul. For child he still was. He may have just turned thirteen, but he was young for his age; he was not yet pubescent. He was, however, overwhelmed by feelings of weakness, insecurity, of being unwanted; racked by suffocating fear and anxiety, almost depression—he had been so since he was about seven. When he was younger, his parents had found him screaming and kicking at them, crying out that they should stop. But in these later years, he would not interfere, just try to ignore them, try to quash the fears inside him, try to smother the terrible sense of lostness.

Although he looked and was young for his age, emotionally he had experienced a darker side of life that many adults never saw. But these feelings of loss, aloneness, alienation, had a deeper root: the nightly ritual his mother subjected him to. Feelings associated with this abuse rose in him when these concerned professionals talked to him, asked him what was troubling him, but the memory was simply not there, was firmly shut away. He knew the associated feelings but could not remember the why. He had long been categorized at school and by his peers as different, not one of them. As he grew older he began to fear these confrontations with his peers; they, like all supposedly good humans, felt a natural inclination to despise the underdog, that which was different: the mark of Abel. He tried to hide in himself at these times, ignore the taunts and jibes. The very act of ignoring them, hiding, set him further apart. Thus his social education was affected, stunted.

Paul lay still and silent. He looked around him. He was glad in some ways to be away from home. Away from his parents for the first time really. Over to the

Chapter Nine, Captivity: Sanctity and Sanctuary

far side of the square, just beyond a well-polished table with some flowers in a glass jug placed in the centre, were two cleaners. Dressed in faded blue-green overalls they both rhythmically swayed from side to side as they swung the mops across the floor, polishing to a shine the pale grey-green tiles. The air smelled rich with the scent of polish.

Still firmly glued to the mattress with the bedclothes pulled up to his nose, so it was barely discernible that the bed was occupied, he became aware of someone standing at the bottom of the bed. It was a man, about fifty, but looking older, dressed in thick, striped pyjamas, with a red and black dressing gown on top, the gown's cord pulled and knotted tightly around his waist, indeed nearly around his chest. The gown was old, faded in places, and worn almost threadbare at the elbow and the end of the sleeves. With his left hand he methodically stroked, lovingly stroked, the piping around the lapel. So much so, it seemed, that here the material was at its most threadbare. He continued rolling the piping around his fingers, gradually working from the shoulder down to the tightly knotted waist cord, then his hand would glide back to the shoulder and start again, rolling and stroking the edge of the lapel. His mouth opened, revealing broken, yellow teeth, then his mouth would close, with nothing to break the dead pan, grey stubble of his gaunt expressionless face. He stood at the corner of the foot of the bed, methodically stroking the lapel, every few minutes opening his mouth, with a faint grunt, possibly feigning a smile, only to return to the same blank expression. Paul watched him, afraid to move a muscle, afraid to breath. The man just stood there. After about half an hour a nursing orderly came in, clapping his hands and calling:

"Come on then, wake up, time to rise and shine. Here we are then, wake up time; let's be having you!"

The man at the foot of the boy's bed did not move, did not change his expression, did not cease the methodical stroking of the dressing gown lapel. The nursing orderly came across.

"Come on Jack, let's be having you!"

Jack did nothing, just stood and stared, continued his staring at the child. The orderly returned, his arms full of crisp white sheets, his head down, counting and fingering them. He checked himself by Paul's bed.

"Now Jack, come on, what's the matter? Off you go, come on, we've got a lot to do."

Without waiting to see if Jack would answer, he carefully placed his arm around his shoulder and escorted him back across the square to the small room he lived in. After closing the door on Jack, the orderly stopped for a moment to speak to one of the cleaners now polishing the floor in the main corridor, then crossed to tidy the flowers.

Men gradually rose from their beds: a motley assortment of humanity, old and young alike. Paul stayed put. Gradually, amongst the grunts, shuffles, and moans, these men disappeared, one by one, along the main corridor, clutching toilet bags, either under their arms or trailing them from forefinger and thumb. Unsure what to think, how to react—he had been unnerved by Jack's early morning vigil by the foot of his bed—he stayed still.

The orderly returned, several other staff, nursing staff were appearing now. One came over to him.

"Hi! My name's Brian; you're Paul aren't you?"

He proceeded to sit down on the bed.

"I'm not supposed to do this you know, sit on the bed that is, but anyway, how are you? It's time you were getting up you know."

The boy did not move a muscle, still with the white sheets pulled up to partly cover his face, the bed looking unslept in, such was the stillness of his night's sleep.

"Tell, you what," said Brian, sensing Paul's wish for privacy. "I've got a couple of jobs to do, anyway most of the men have gone off to the bathrooms, you quietly get up and I'll be back in a couple of minutes."

Brian got up, he disappeared into one of the small rooms off the corridor.

Paul slipped from between the sheets, looked around him, quickly got his clothes out of the locker, then looking around again, quickly dressed. He was thankful that the two beds either side of him were unoccupied at this time. He quickly shoved his pyjamas under the pillow and sat dutifully on the bed, and waited. It was a quarter to seven in the morning.

Four

Accessible along its length from the main corridor was a large conservatory-type annexe, about eighteen feet deep, by forty long. This provided sitting space by day, though each chair, arranged around the sides, was earmarked by particular patients. At meal times three or sometimes four large round tables were put out in this conservatory. Paul sat, not looking either to his left or to his right, just looking at his bowl or plate, and obediently eating. But not much passed his lips; he was not hungry. Breakfast over, the various men disappeared into corners, rooms, beds, or out into the grounds to walk and smoke. He returned to his bed.

By now he was feeling choked by the lump in his throat; he tried desperately to fight the stinging in his eyes, trying not to look around at what was going on in the ward or to be seen. He lay down on his bed and quietly sobbed. What had he done wrong? Why was he here? When would he go home? But he didn't

Chapter Nine, Captivity: Sanctity and Sanctuary

want to go home. But yes he did, he missed Christine, he missed Timmy. He missed his mum and his dad—though he did not miss them together. He missed the familiar sights and smells of the house, the garden, the smallholding, the hedgerows bounding the Charity. The Charity—in many ways, above all he missed Longman's Charity, the freedom to roam, to walk, to explore his world. He most definitely did not miss school. He lay on his stomach sobbing—but as silently as possible. His thoughts returned again and again to why. Why was he here? Why? What had he done? Why? It must have been to do with the empty, dirty feeling that threatened to overwhelm him when he went to bed at night. It must be because he just did not like himself, never had. He raised himself up, and as surreptitiously as possible, disappeared down the main corridor towards the bathrooms. He walked as quietly and softly as he possibly could, as if he was walking on a thin film of sand, and wished to leave no trace of his passing. As he passed the conservatory, many were sitting with glazed expressions. By the entrance staff were busying themselves, looking efficient. He turned right down the narrow dark corridor that led to the toilets and bathrooms. Finding one cubicle that was empty he washed his face of the salt tears, then drying and looking in the mirror—he hated himself. Hated himself for whatever he had done. He was not sure what it was, but he was here, and the sense of failure, of utter failure and dejection was too much. He started weeping again. But the sound of his sobbing was drowned by the grunts and cramped movement of other men in the bathrooms and toilets.

Returning to his bedside he found Brian making the bed. He smiled, and enquired where Paul had been. The boy answered factually: he had been to the bathroom. Brian smiled and commented he was sure things would soon be sorted out, that things were going to be alright.

Later that first morning when the ward was quite empty, most of the men being out at occupational therapy, or gardening in the grounds, and most of the staff having a coffee break, Paul ventured from his bed to explore. The main corridor was about twenty feet wide and about one hundred and fifty in length. The building was Victorian, with high ceilings. Running along the entirety of one length were doors into small rooms. He did not dare venture into any of these. Some were patient's rooms, others consulting rooms, plate stores, pharmacy, or staff offices. At the end was a pair of double doors—the entrance. Opposite the entrance the narrow corridor leading to the bathrooms led off at right angles to the main corridor, the end of the corridor being simply a blank wall, then a length of wall with a window, and a public phone. Then the "day time" conservatory, a further length of wall, and the main square ward with beds all around, finally a length of wall with windows in it, and several beds, lengthways along the side. At the far end, the furthest from the main entrance the corridor ended with a pair of solid wooden doors that were always locked, padlocked with a chain, never opened—he never learned what was beyond.

Through dinner the boy sat nervously watching the faces of men jealously guarding their little patch of table, or scowling across at him.

"If you're going to eat at our table, you can damn well put that sauce bottle back!" grumbled one man haughtily, throwing the long quiff of grey black hair back behind his ear, then scratching the short stubble at the back of his neck, then pulling at the frayed collar with his forefinger, finally to try to winkle out something from between two side teeth with the same finger.

Paul spent most of the rest of that day sitting on his bed, or walking around trying not to be noticed. At night time, once the lights were out, he watched, as by the dim pale glow of the night light, he could see shadowy shapes, of men lying in bed, the shape of the iron bed frames, clouds scurrying across the moon, through the top of one window, the shuffling of one man as he went across the main ward, probably to disappear down the main corridor on his way to the toilet. All was now still, but his mind was racing. He fought sleep, afraid to lose his guard amongst so many strange people. The sights and smells were different, alien; he was lost and unsure.

He fought sleep, long into the night. He heard the clock strike twelve, quietly, delicately chiming. He thought of home, of his father's anger, his mother's love, however smothering. He thought on Timmy, his Timmy, and longed to cuddle him. He thought of Timmy hunting voles amongst the crates and leek boats stacked around the side of the sheds. He saw himself walking among the sheds, then he found himself sitting amongst the spring onions growing at the bottom of his father's ground—about two hundred yards from the sheds, with the house behind. He sat, near to the deep, wide hedgerow, sat amongst a very thin crop— one that had been picked over once, leaving just a few onions behind. But growing amongst them, spreading about the bare earth on that bright sunny morn, were flowers, wild flowers. Each stood in its own space, about two feet of bare earth around it. Each grew singularly, harebells, a poppy, a corn marigold, mayweed, lots of mayweed. They were magical, it was magical. In the stillness of sitting amidst the most perfectly formed flowers, growing so freely, he felt blessed. He looked closely at a harebell, loved its delicate, blue flowers. He looked around him and all felt right, he even felt good about his parents, about home. He felt happy, secure, warm, loved. Then he woke to the sound of a man coughing. There at the foot of his bed, in the thin light of morning he saw Jack, methodically stroking the piping on the lapel of his dressing gown.

And all the loneliness returned; the emptiness swallowed him. . . .

Chapter Nine, Captivity: Sanctity and Sanctuary

Five

Towards the end of the first week, after the ritualized breakfast was over, Paul was ushered into one of the rooms off the main corridor. There he was informed that the psychiatrist who had seen him in Evesham would see him later that morning and so he was to stay in the ward. He nearly said that he always stayed in the ward, that he didn't know he could go anywhere else, but he thought better of it. He sat quietly on his bed, trying not to be seen, and trying not to see. He was afraid to be caught looking at anyone. He was tired, and once the ward had emptied with men going off to their morning tasks, he lay down and slept, making up for the disturbed night. A nurse woke him about half past ten,

"Doctor Cheen wants to see you, Paul, Paul, wake up, Paul, its time..."

Obediently he sat up, rubbed his eyes.

"Can I go to the toilet, please?" he said.

After the nurse had escorted him to the bathroom, he was shown into a room, opposite the daytime conservatory. There sat three men in very important looking suits, and two nurses, one was Brian, the other was a young woman whom he had not seen before. Doctor Cheen was sitting in the middle; all three doctors wore suits. Doctor Cheen was wearing a pink carnation in his lapel:

"Well Paul, and how are you?"

He did not answer.

"What have you been doing with yourself then?" asks another.

"Nothing," the boy quietly answers.

"Is there anything you would like to do?" asks another.

He nearly said "go home," but stopped himself. He was not sure whether he wanted to go home, but then he did not want to stay here, and there are things at home he liked. More than anything his tiny immature mind wanted just to be. That is, to be left alone. Indeed, he did not really know what he wanted, all he did know was that he had this big empty hole in the middle of himself, not in his body, but in him. And it wouldn't go away. Paul found he'd been saying this and the room was silent.

Brian broke the silence,

"You like painting don't you?"

"Yes."

He was annoyed with himself for having said so much.

"Would you like to do some, painting, here that is?" offered Doctor Cheen.

"Oh yes!" he became more animated, "Can I?"

"Yes you can, we have an art room."

"But my paints are at home—I've got this set of oil paints...."

"Well we have plenty of paints here I think, do we not?" Doctor Cheen interrupted.

"Yes, err yes, Doctor Cheen, we do. I'm sure it would be alright for Paul to work in the art room," answered one of the other men, dressed in an equally important looking suit.

As he was shown out of the room, he asked Brian "Is it alright if I go for a walk outside, you know, like some of the other men?"

"Yes, I'm sure it is. I'll have to check, but I'm sure it is," Brian replied.

Six

The next day: a Saturday afternoon, Paul carefully opened the metal-framed French windows in the conservatory. Brian closed them behind, once they had stepped down. The two walked across neatly trimmed grass, he stopped to look back to the building he had just left. Brian carefully explaining where they were, what went on in this direction, then that, and so on. But really, he just wanted to be away by himself. The grass sloped down towards a small valley, with a wood on the other side. Paul looked, started to walk, but then realized there was a fence about half way down the slope: the boundary. He looked across the fence, his eyes alighting on a huge ash tree, standing out from among the other trees and shrubs. They walked back towards the ward—or "unit" as the more enlightened amongst his custodians would like to call it. They skirted around the outside of the ward. He found he was looking up at the high windows, then across to the valley, then down to his feet. There were flower borders around, but they were neglected. The soil looked thin, poor, emaciated, the wallflowers looking stunted, starved, struggling as they were in that mild February to produce flowers. Paul continued to look down to his feet. He drifted into a reverie, thinking of the wild flowers in the hedgerows at home.

"I think it's time for tea now."

Brian gently guided the child back towards the conservatory door.

Seven

Tea was baked beans on toast, with bread and butter, jam, and little fairy cakes for afters. Paul Broadley had been allocated a place by the other men. There was a strict hierarchy and rule system in place for mealtimes; not set by the staff, but imposed by the patients. These rules were not taught, but had to be learnt from experience. The men, the other patients, were from widely different backgrounds, widely

Chapter Nine, Captivity: Sanctity and Sanctuary

different social classes, yet the mealtime ritual was ironically like the old fagging system and pecking order in an English public school. This was not because such a system had been initiated by a patient who had experienced an upper-middle-class private education; no, it had evolved naturally—men guarding what little private space they had, claiming just one iota of superiority over the others and thereby having first choice at the cakes, first choice at the slices of bacon: I've been here longest, therefore I get the privileges; I fought at Dunkirk, therefore I get to choose first. The child sat obediently and did as he was told. If he strayed from the rules, if, for instance, he forgot to return the sauce bottle to the exact place it had been allocated in the middle of the table, then there was retribution: smarting sarcasm or bizarre, often violent, spitting abuse. And memories were long—very long. The smallest of indiscretions would be committed to memory and he would find a patient sidling up to him, reminding him what he had done—he had taken a slice of bread before it was his turn. He knew what to expect, he was marked, he would be got. Such intimidations are the stuff on which childish fears grow. But here, such childish fears mushroomed. The society—for a society of such it was here within the confines of the formerly named Worcester City and County Pauper and Lunatic Asylum—was bizarre at best, demonic at worst.

The child had been allocated a space, a chair; this was where he would sit. He was sitting at the second table. Luckily, he was sitting with his back to the corridor, so if he shuffled his chair into the right position, and if the two men opposite were sitting in the right place, he could see between them, through the window in the conservatory and out, out into the surrounding grounds. He could then look at the tall ash tree that stood in the shallow valley beyond the grounds. Each mealtime, if he could sit in the right position, he could watch this tree. He could see it at different times of the day, over the months he could watch it change from the bare dark grey branches and hulk of the winter tree, through to a tree standing proudly, fully clad in its summer foliage. It was tall, strong, magnificent; it became something of an icon for him. No, he did not worship it, but it became a symbol for all that was good, whole, right, and healthy in the world. From now on he could run down the slope, stand, or sit by the fence and look, watch, even talk to it. Early in the morning, or late in the evening, he could climb up on the metal frame of his bed and gaze through the window—and see it! He felt reassured. This reassurance was most valued at meal times, for then he could not avoid the difficulties encountered with other patients. If he saw it, he was safe, he felt protected. The tree could see him, watch over him, protect him. Often Paul felt frightened, even threatened by the men in the unit. But he watched the tree, and not only did it reassure him, but he felt transported—transported to where he felt happiest, to Longman's Charity. Then it didn't matter if he had to wait, what to some would have been an intolerable wait while his turn came around in the mealtime pecking order for his bread or his pudding.

The tree was a means whereby he could achieve some semblance of inner peace amidst the turmoil. He once tried to paint it, but felt it was almost irreverent to do so. Besides there would be questions—why was he painting it, what did it mean? Then he would be exposing what was innermost, what was secret, precious, and tender. They would destroy it, they would soil it—no, he must guard the tree. One day when some foresters were tidying up the undergrowth in the copse, taking out young sycamore saplings that were threatening the older trees, Paul spent the whole morning sat by the fence watching, praying that they would not cut down his tree. He was tense with apprehension. He feared that if he left, they would feel free to damage it, cut it, even fell it. He was called in to dinner by one of the nurses. After dinner it was raining. He did not go down to the fence, but sat on his bed, half climbing, half squeezing, so that he could see the tree through the rain, through his window. The next day, the men did not return. The danger had passed.

So, Paul waited: waited his turn to be given the plate of baked beans on toast. He was naturally last. This he did not mind. Indeed, he did not mind the pecking order and rules, just as long as it did not get him into trouble. He could simply sit, looking at his tree, and wait. His patience actually upset some of the other men who believed him to be aloof, snooty. They did not realize that this was the only way he was able to hang on to his sanity. The baked beans on toast duly arrived. Paul tucked in.

"We ain't told you to eat!" snarled an elderly man. Swearing was against the rules at mealtimes—but rarely enforced by the staff—and others joined in with far more explicit condemnations.

"Oh, leave him alone, let him eat," responded a taller man, James, who was the self-appointed leader of the table.

The other man, now having got into trouble with James, glowered at Paul, looked at him with venom, as if to say it's your fault, you've now got me into trouble, so I shall remember this and I'll get even! The boy sat looking straight ahead, waiting for permission to eat.

"Go on boy," said James, "go on, tuck in!"

Quietly he ate.

He sensed trouble. Often there were rows at meal times. It was something he was used to; after all, did not his parents spend most mealtimes arguing at home? It started this teatime with James, a tall man in his early fifties, an ex-soldier. He passed the plate of fairy cakes to a young man in his twenties—Jeff. In ordinary circumstances this would have been an innocent enough gesture, indeed, almost

Chapter Nine, Captivity: Sanctity and Sanctuary

one of charity, for Jeff was certainly not the first in the pecking order to take his afters. However, the message and symbolism was understood by all at the table. All, that is, except Paul. Jeff sat looking at the plate of fairy cakes placed in front of him. Other men stopped scraping the sauce from the plates, others visibly stopped eating, their jaws frozen. The other men had smiled as James passed the plate over, but now they sensed trouble, they waited, silent. Jeff was now red in the face, his mouth twitched, he made quiet noises, like a hurt mouse. With a single dexterous blow he swept the glass cake stand and its contents off the table, sending it smashing into pieces on the corridor floor. Immediately everyone else, the men at the other tables, stopped eating and paid heed.

"Ohhh! temper, temper!" James said slowly, modulating his voice into a slightly effeminate tone. Jeff stroked his hair, gently, lovingly, brushing his fringe back, raising his head simultaneously in a camp gesture. Then he grabbed his knife and lunged across the table. He stabbed at James' jacket, but the knife failed to penetrate. Jeff rolled immediately, along with the debris of broken plates and scattered food onto the floor, the large round table crashing over onto its side. The other men had all jumped up and moved away in the second or so it took Jeff to hurl himself across the table.

"You, you . . . you were nice enough when it suited you, you . . . you, you . . ." Jeff's words tailed off into sobs as he covered his face, spitting fire and dredging for words to slaughter James with, lying as he was on his back in the broken plates, the spilt tea, the crushed food.

Paul felt sorry for him. However, the image as silence fell was quite, quite pathetic. Jeff lay, amidst the debris of the meal, sobbing, his arms now covering his face. His right leg rose at the knee, which rocked side to side. The table rocked, perched over near to the next table, exposing the rough-cut timber of its underside. Its polished topside now defiled with spilt food and knife scratches. The other men and other chairs were scattered wide, leaving Paul sat in his chair. He had not moved. He sat with his serviette tucked into his collar, his hands gripping onto the underside of the chair—his knuckles turning white with the force with which he now held on. The boy sat—his eyes riveted onto the tree, his tree, his ash. He did not look down, he kept his eyes straight ahead. He did not look as two orderlies came and picked Jeff up from the broken meal. He did not look as Jeff screamed and ranted and was carried away.

"You . . . , you, that's the last time I take you, that's the last time I satisfy you, never, never, never . . ."

Paul felt for him, he did not understand what all this was about, he did not understand what Jeff was saying, but still, he just stared straight ahead, straight to the ash tree. Surrounded by broken plates, food, overturned chairs, Paul simply sat. The table, large enough to sit six of them was now against the metal window frames and structures of the conservatory. He sat, now unaware of what was going on around him. He was unaware of Brian crouching by him, trying to reassure him, trying to get some response from him, trying to break the grip his fingers were now making as they clenched the chair—blood beginning to seep from one finger as the nail was breaking, tearing from the skin under the strain. The boy said nothing, did nothing, simply obediently allowed himself to be carried to his bed. Fixed, nigh burned in his mind, on the back of his eye was the image of the tall ash tree. That evening he lay still. Still and quiet on his bed. He did not move. He did not even raise his head till it was time for lights out. Silently he undressed and got between the sheets. Silently he lay there.

Eight

Paul did not want to sleep that night. He lay watching the ceiling, afraid to let his eyes drop to the ward, afraid of what he might see. He fought sleep, but somehow as the hours drew on he lost consciousness. He dreamt of a tall ash tree with little fairy cakes growing from its branches, each once dancing in the wind. He woke, feeling defiled, feeling his tree was being defiled by the events of teatime. He fought sleep, felt a suffocating nausea coming over him, fought and fought and dozed and fought, but dozed. He slipped once more into unconsciousness. This time he dreamed a dream worse than the nightmares that haunted him. For though nightmares were bad, nightmares could be dismissed.

This dream occurred often, but not so often to become commonplace. Again he saw himself walking among the sheds in Evesham, at his parents'. Timmy was hunting voles amongst the crates and leek boats stacked around the side of the sheds. Again he saw himself walking among the sheds, then he found himself sitting amongst the spring onions growing at the bottom of his father's ground—about two hundred yards from the sheds, with the house behind. He sat, near to the deep, wide hedgerow, sat amongst a very thin crop—one that had been picked over once, with just a few onions left. But growing amongst them, spreading about the bare earth on that bright sunny morn were flowers: wild flowers. Each stood in its own space, about two feet of bare earth. Each grew singularly, harebells, or a poppy, a corn marigold. They were magical. The scene was magical: sitting in the stillness, amidst the most perfectly formed flowers, growing so freely. Paul looked closely at a harebell, loved its delicate blue flowers. He looked around him and all felt right, he even felt good about his parents, about home. He felt happy, secure, warm, loved. He tried to grasp the flower, to pull it closer, but somehow he could not grasp it. His hand would miss; try as he

Chapter Nine, Captivity: Sanctity and Sanctuary

would he could not grasp it. He could not move from the spot he was sat on—this would have enabled him to look at the flower closer. He was not concerned that he could not move, all felt so right, no, it felt as though it could be right. The more he tried to grasp the flower, the more everything seemed less right, less pure, less happy . . . but that it could—or should—be right and pure and happy. But that rightness, that purity, was so unattainable it was painful with a deep aching hurt to even perceive of the possibility . . . .

Then he would wake.

Such a dream was worse than nightmares because it teased, such a dream offered a tantalizing picture of what could be, but was not. It almost mocked him with its purity, its truth, its love. He wanted desperately on waking to get back to the dream. He preferred it to the real world. Everything around him seemed so broken. Yet what he saw in this dream was so real, so good, so pure. He felt worse on waking from such a dream and finding himself in the reality of Powick than from any other waking. And so he lay, thinking about the events of yesterday teatime. He was so puzzled. Why take him away from his home, where his mother and father rowed so violently and bring him to this? Then it occurred to him that this was normal. That all people rowed and tried in devilish ways to destroy each other like his mother and father did to each other. Maybe he was being punished for not being like them, for not taking all this in his stride: a phrase he remembered being used about him. Maybe all this was normal and there really was something wrong with him. He needed curing?

He thought on the frightening, suffocating evil of the many events he had seen. He thought on the words of a young priest visiting the church when he was taking confirmation classes. The young man had spoken calmly, politely, nicely (to an adult listening, the word "patronizing" would have come to mind). He was telling them there was no hell—there really wasn't. People and the world were nice really! That man had lied. Paul knew he lied. He now knew there was a hell. He lay frightened to move, he lay still with the bedclothes as his only defence against this world. He feared sleep, feared the hell in his mind which was in his nightmares, in his dreams. He feared the hell that was in this ward at Powick, he feared the great empty hole that seemed to appear inside him, that suffocating great emptiness. A thin grey whiteness that swallowed him up, then all light went, all sense went, there was nothing but a suffocating nausea as he was sucked in and swallowed up, as the sound of the tinnitus was raised to a crescendo.

Nine

The boy woke with a start. It was morning. The thin grey light of morning surrounded him. The clock struck half-past. He could hear the birds singing. He heard a shuffle. He lowered his eyes. Jack was stood at the bottom of his bed; methodically stroking the lapel of his dressing gown. Jack's behaviour changed. This time his other hand went inside his dressing gown. His arm moved. He stroked. The arm moved rhythmically. He stroked, or so it seemed, the bulge under his dressing gown. His arm moved jerkily, his breath quickened. The child did not know what the man was doing. He was ignorant of the actual danger he was in, but nevertheless he instinctively felt terror. The fear and terror were complete. Jack's breath became calmer, his arm stopped moving, as simultaneously a wet patch appeared on his dressing gown. The man stood illuminated by the thin light of dawn. The sun was beginning to come up now. Jack stood bathed in the gentle early sunlight. The boy felt fear, yet he felt sorry for the man; he could sense he was lonely, but did not know how to cross the void between them. Then a cold fear crept over him. He knew not why, but sensed he was, had been, in danger. Jack turned and slowly shuffled across the floor to his room.

So he lay, looking up at the ceiling, as he had on the kitchen table at home for so many years when his mother. . . . Then after about twenty minutes he slipped out from between the sheets. He looked around to make sure there was no one up or no one looking, then slipped out of his pyjamas and quickly got dressed. He then walked slowly round into the corridor, then into the conservatory. He hid himself behind the curtain. He tried the door handle, but it was still locked—and the key was certainly not in the lock. So he stood there, he stood watching his tree—looking at the tall ash, bathed in the beautiful morning light. He sensed the beauty in the world. But it was so far off, so impossible to reach, to touch. He stood there, in silence, perfectly still. He cried, the tears rolling down his cheeks: but he wept in total silence, totally still, without murmur or movement.

The stillness was absolute.

Chapter Ten
Deception: Terror and Dread

~ *"... if I make my bed in hell,*
You are there ...
even there Your hand shall lead me,
and Your right hand shall hold me."
PSALM 139:8b&10

One

The building was typical of its period. It also reflected the principles of the civilization that had created it. It was constructed out of sound red brick: Midlands red brick—provinciality was pride. The building was topped off with a grey slate roof. The building was tall. However, it consisted of only two floors— each with high ceilings. The windows were long and thin, and for the most part barred. The bars were painted white, to brighten up the place a bit. Each floor housed a ward: it had been built as such. Each ward was long, impersonal, functional. There were several such blocks or ward buildings. Most of the bricks' redness was indiscernible under the thick layer of grime and pollution accumulated over the century since it was built. The main entrance was reached across a courtyard. A courtyard with a neatly planted roundabout in the centre: African marigolds, red geraniums, and bright, crisply manicured grass providing a moat between the tarmac and the flowers. The whole looked neat, ordered, municipal, yet sadly, oddly incongruous, considering the purpose of the building, considering the frayed sanity that existed inside.

The main entrance doors did not give any hint of the nature of the establishment. In addition this entrance was in the older part of the hospital—a Georgian building, formerly a villa for a wealthy family, but taken over, and with Victorian hospital wings added much later. The entrance was therefore more like an old people's home—indeed a home for genteel elderly ladies. The brass plate that used to inform visitors that it was an asylum for paupers and lunatics was no longer screwed to the wall. In its place, a neat, precise notice in municipal sans serif typeface informed that this was Powick Hospital, and that it was run by Worcestershire Heath Authority. Nowadays it was not just the mentally incurable who were housed within its walls, but drug addicts, depressives, alcoholics, social misfits, liars and deceivers, indeed those who simply could not cope with life. This included both men and women, young and old: race, class, wealth, all were no guarantee against such perceived failings, all entered—but rarely children. Then there was Paul Broadley.

This child walked through a courtyard of grey broken tarmac. This courtyard was a canyon formed by two ward buildings rising high on each side. It was a good distance from the main entrance. He walked past barred windows and through a pair of metal-framed glass doors. He walked carefully—always carefully, lest he break some unwritten code of behaviour amongst the patients—carefully down the corridor, out through another door, then turning back and down another long canyon-like courtyard, equally neglected as the first. However, this courtyard opened up into something of a general backyard with pipes and chimneys, an old van parked next to an open cellar, and a tall black metal staircase—a fire escape. He climbed the staircase and opened the door at the top. Inside the scene changed: tables, chairs, easels, cupboards—all at different angles to each other. Tables were covered with paints, with palates, with bottles of turpentine, and bottles of linseed oil, jars of water, and jars with brushes standing in. He looked at cupboards with ill-fitting doors—bursting with boxes and tubes of oil paint, with rolls of canvas, with paper. Wooden frames were stacked against the wall, likewise finished paintings. The walls were covered with drawings and paintings. Easels stood with smears of paint of all colours covering the bare wood. Turpentine-soaked rags—grey with age, yet iridescent with paint—filled the room with their smell.

People were sitting. People were standing. People were talking, huddled in corners around cups of coffee; they stood at easels, absorbed in painting. There were in fact no more than ten people. The boy had been brought here by Brian the previous day. He had introduced him to Michael—a short man with a little goat beard. Michael had fair hair and talked quickly, very quickly. "Welcome," he kept repeating, "welcome"—he was in charge of the art room, he was the teacher. Paul liked him, but he seemed very busy all the time. He wished the boy well, and said

Chapter Ten, Deception: Terror and Dread

he would see him the next morning, about nine o'clock. All this was said whilst he struggled with some canvas he was stretching over a frame. On the way back, Brian explained the route to him—explained how he could use the courtyards and doors and corridors to give him a more direct route to the art room. So Paul did.

This morning he opened the door tentatively and stood on the metal grating just inside the door. He stood still, taking in the chaotic visual excitement of the scene.

"Welcome, welcome, come in!" Michael had spied him. He rushed over to the door.

"Come in, come in, come in!"

Paul noticed how Michael often seemed to say everything two or three times.

"Here, come this way, here, here," pointing to a small space just inside and to the left of the door.

Michael closed the door after him.

"Here you are, here is where you can work. You said you had used oils before, so here you are!"

He looked at the small table covered with tubes of oil paint, some new, some old: most with their labels obscured by smudges and smears of colour. There was a clean rag, a small pot of turpentine, and a board leaning against the table. It was primed white. Paul moved into the space between the table, the wall, and the easel—the forth side of the cubicle being made by the back of a tall cupboard. The space was no more than four feet by three. From it he could view nearly the whole room by looking around the easel; he could not see over the dark brown cupboard to his left, but could take in the whole room otherwise. Over to his immediate right was a clear space—just inside the main door. Then, as his head turned anti-clockwise, he saw several long trestle tables and easels filling up most of the right-hand half of the room. Set in the opposite wall was a row of thin, narrow, high-set windows. The wall behind him had similar metal-framed windows set in it, set high up near the ceiling. The wall over to the left looked different—indeed it was a partition wall, put up in recent years to divide off part of this long upstairs ward to create a self-contained art room. Set in this wall were no windows, but a single substantial wooden door. This door caught his attention for it was locked and bolted, indeed, locked with a substantial padlock. In all the time he was in the art room he never once knew it to be opened. He was to find out that beyond this door was one of the secure units. Looking at that door he feared what the future held.

The board stood as it was against the table: he had used the small set of oil paints he had been given as a prize by his junior school, but this was different—all the colours he could possibly imagine, and a large board. He picked up the board and placed it on the easel, working out how it should go. Then he picked up a brush from the pot. How was he to start?—this was all on a different scale to the efforts he had done painting paper, or card, at home. There, he had been allowed to use the set of paints on occasional Sunday afternoons—sitting at the kitchen table—when the rest of the family watched television, provided he did not make a mess! But here—what was he to paint? He squeezed some paint out—some sap green onto the palate.

He started to paint. He painted what he missed: the landscape around his home—the land, Longman's Charity. He painted in a way he had never painted before. He painted with confidence, with passion, almost with anger. He was different when he was painting. He was calm, he was lost in the activity both physical and mental of what he was doing. He worked wet paint into wet paint without realizing what he was doing. The sky started off light, but as he progressed he worked in more grey, and pure titanium white—somehow he began to build a stormy pathos into the scene. He did not consciously think—if I do this, it will have such and such an effect. He just painted—somehow it reflected how he was feeling. He created. It seemed to say—no, to express—all the frustration he had been feeling, all the terror, all the powerlessness in his life. He darkened the land, he worked yellow ochre and burnt umber into the soil. He felt he could not stop. But eventually he did. Michael, who had been keeping a quiet eye on him, came over to tell him it was dinner time. He did not want to stop painting, but knew he must: he would be in trouble if he failed to return for dinner.

Two

Paul sat still and motionless at dinner. He did not want to eat. He did not want to be sitting with these men. Jeff was still missing. He had been sedated—heavily sedated—and was in one of the small rooms off the corridor. His chair was empty. Somehow the men left it empty—possibly they knew they had gone over the top that afternoon when all hell had broken loose. Maybe it was a sort of atonement, leaving the chair empty. The child sat and did not eat. He could only gaze at his tree, and think on his painting. Eventually dinner was over and he went straight off—starting the journey back to the art room. He had just got outside the ward door when a voice came after him:

"Paul, Paul!"

It was Brian. The boy stopped and turned—obediently.

"I wanted to catch you Paul—are you alright? You did not eat any dinner; why?"

Chapter Ten, Deception: Terror and Dread

"I wasn't hungry."

"How did the morning go? How did you find the art room?"

"It was brilliant!" came the enthusiastic response—then Paul checked himself, fearing that this might be taken from him if he showed too much enthusiasm.

Brian simply smiled. He was impressed by the boy's assertiveness; he also noticed that Paul had stopped the persistent eye twitching and head nodding.

"Go on, off with you, you get back there."

On his return Michael suggested that he might put this painting to one side and give it a chance to breath. Paul did not understand what he meant, but he could see that the paint was thick and wet and that he probably would not be able to do any more to it until it was dry.

"Why don't you start getting another one ready?"

Paul asked for a large board. Michael had the grace and the sense to give him one—a piece of un-primed hardboard four feet by three feet. He spent most of the afternoon sanding its edges, then priming it. While it dried in front of the radiator Michael talked to him, but the child's answers were very noncommittal. He spent some time looking around the room, looking at the other work going on. He looked at the faces of the other people there in the art room. Finally he sanded and gave the board another coat of emulsion. Michael tried talking to him again—this time asking him about the morning's painting. This time he was more fruitful in getting a response. Talking about painting was safe—it was neutral ground. After the board was complete, Paul drew. He was reluctant to talk too much, but he did enjoy the drawing, though he would have preferred to be painting again. The afternoon was soon over. His walk back through the courtyards and corridors was slow: he was reluctant to return. Eventually he did. He arrived just as the other men were sitting down for tea. Brian intercepted him.

"Here, go sit down on your bed—I'll sort out some food for you later."

He could see the boy was exhausted—not just from the day's work, but mentally exhausted. Brian was deeply concerned for the boy. This started a habit of the child missing tea. He would eat enough at breakfast and dinner and miss out on tea. Teatime was the time when there was most tension, the time when squabbles spilled over into rows and occasionally violence. Teatime was also therefore the time he could go to the bathrooms alone, and find no one there. This meant he could wash in peace, without being threatened by others. He did not bathe—simply washed all over. He was afraid to take all his clothes off at once, afraid of being seen. Sometimes one of the men would come down the narrow corridor to the bathrooms, but he had plenty of time to get dressed. Two or three times a week he would wash like this.

The next morning he was outside the art room at eight-fifty waiting for it to open. Hearing noises inside—on the dot of nine—he knocked on the door. Michael opened it.

"Oh! come in, come in, you're early; no, you're on time!"

"Can I start my new painting?"

"Yes of course, everything is just as you left it yesterday. What were you thinking of doing?"

"Well, often, I often, we often go down to gran's in Weston, and I like the sea, and the quayside up by the old pier and Birnbeck Island and . . ."

"Stop, stop a moment," interrupted Michael, "do you have a sketch or something?"

"No. But I know what I want to do."

"Are you going to sketch it first?"

Paul was silent.

"Look, have you used charcoal before."

"No; does that matter?"

"No, not really," Michael continued "look, break off a piece like this. . . ."

Upon which Michael showed the child how to use the charcoal, how to sketch in the bare framework of a picture, explained about putting in the essentials—like a horizon line, like the quay wall and so forth. Paul then did this from the idea he had in his mind for the painting. When he had done this and was happy, he started the painting. Unerringly this time he knew exactly what he wanted to do. He started with the sky—deep Prussian blue and ultramarine, billowing thickly painted white clouds with flecks of orange from the sun; more Prussian blue—dark and deep—some mauve in as well; swirls of pure titanium white in amongst the clouds. And so the painting progressed down from the sky. He altered little, but worked passionately, though slowly and methodically. The painting took nearly a week: he was exhausted when it was finished.

The painting was large, dark, brooding, full of expression: a harbour with a storm gathering in the sky. The horizon line was high up in the painting. The quay wall flowed round in a wide curve from the middle rear of the picture round to the bottom right-hand corner. Boats were anchored in the harbour but were bobbing, almost frightened of the storm to come, as if they could sense the impending deluge in the air. The painting was dominated by deep, rich colours: blue, purple and mauve, pale oranges, ultramarine, blue-greens, burnt ochre, yellow ochre, white, burnt and raw umber, greys. There was also the odd fleck of brightness such as a cottage door or the funnel of a ship. Bright colour seemed almost comical, out of place in this scene. However, the whole painting had a crude naivety. Much of the perspective was wrong, many objects were out of scale, but this did not seem to worry Paul. Despite this Michael was obviously impressed by what the

Chapter Ten, Deception: Terror and Dread

child had done: it had power, it had expression. It compelled him to look further. Michael knew the shrinks would want to get their hands on it, want to analyse it: both the boy and the painting. His fear was that if they poked and questioned too much then this would stop the child painting.

Three

The art room was to be a lifeline for the child. Painting was to be a salvation of sorts. More than that, it was to keep him sane. Ironically, the people, their actions, the environment, the mini-society that was Powick was enough to have broken many fully grown sane men. At times what he encountered in the ward was enough to make him question his own sanity. Why were these people here? Why was he here? Was he being punished? Was he being corrected for not liking school, for not coping better at home with his parents? Was he being punished for being sensitive, weak, and feeble?

The behaviour and the sights were deeply troubling to this small boy. Tuesday mornings were the worst. This was the day many of the "patients" went for electroconvulsive therapy (or ECT as it was known). The patients were given a tranquillizer to help relax and almost anaesthetize them. Then they were led off individually to a distinctive room. Here they would lie down flat and electrodes were placed on their temples, and their head. A special clip was put in their mouth to prevent them swallowing their tongue. Then all was ready. The power was switched on—only for a second or two, or less. The effect was stupefying: all recent memory was erased: this was the aim—that is, to help the patient forget recent events that might be inducing depression, worry, anxiety, paranoia, or one of many socially unacceptable conditions. But it did not stop there. The treatment involved memory loss but also mental confusion. It also induced in some an epileptic seizure. For days afterwards the men walked, or sat in the ward, their faces grey and ashen, their eyes sunken and glazed, their speech incomprehensible. They sat or walked, or moved like they were dead, like they were dead bodies raised from the grave, or so it seemed to Paul: alive, yet empty of all life. These were the men he had seen around the ward during the day, men he was effectively living with; men who were suddenly different, struck down in a second. It took many days if not weeks to recover from the effect.

Tuesday dinner time he would watch them return to the ward, or observe some already sitting in the armchairs around the outer walls of the conservatory. He would watch them shepherded to their beds by nurses or orderlies, he would watch in horror. This then appeared in his dreams—images of men having their brains sucked out using a syringe. Then the skin would dry and crack and flake and fall away leaving nothing, emptiness. Paul would feel himself suffocating and being sucked into a pale, dense emptiness. He would feel himself becoming crushed, crushed screaming into this nausea.

Paul could not bear to look these men in the face again once he had seen them return from the ECT treatment. One dinner time he sat trying to eat his soup when two orderlies shuffled passed him supporting Jeff between their arms. They deposited him in one of the armchairs opposite him. Jeff had returned from ECT treatment. The table was almost empty. All the other occupants of his table were either away for ECT treatment or occupied in some other task or treatment. He sat in his correct place fearing one may return. Opposite him was Jeff, slumped in the armchair. He was dressed in his pyjamas and dressing gown. This was the same Jeff who had lunged across the table at James with a knife barely a fortnight earlier. Now he was quite pathetic: he sat, his left arm twitching, bent as it was at the elbow with the hand vainly trying to support his head, his swollen tongue protruding from his lips, saliva dribbling down his front. His head kept falling to the right, his eyes rolling crazily, searching round the room for something to latch on to. His legs stiffened, he twisted in the chair, arching his back: he started to shake uncontrollably, at the same time making the most inhuman sound. One of the nurses rushed over and pulled him to the floor, placing him on his side, simultaneously pulling his tongue forward to clear an airway. Jeff shook and kicked violently till the seizure had passed. He was even more confused and demented afterwards. Only at tea time, still sitting in the chair, was he visibly calmer. He was sleeping, but would slowly wake, paw the air in front of him as though he was trying to make out what was there. He understood nothing that was said to him.

It took nearly a week for the effects of the ECT to wear off. Much of the confusion was caused by the epileptic seizure: not just the grand mal attack, but the prolonged absences and blanks he experienced afterwards. A few weeks later Jeff did not return from a weekend at home. The answer came from overhearing two orderlies talking. Jeff had slashed his wrists while lying in a bath full of water. He must have lain there watching as the lifeblood drained into the water— becoming drowsier as the colour of the water pinked, then darkened. His mother would have come upstairs, as he had planned, to find him laid out in the bloody bath water, dead. No one took his place at the dining table in the ward for several weeks afterwards. To the men it seemed taboo not only to talk about him, but also to sit in his chair. It was as if he was still alive—or should have been. Such events, such images etched themselves deep into the child's mind.

It was not only observing and witnessing the bizarre often deranged behaviour in the ward that troubled Paul, but at times he was physically at risk: such as most

Chapter Ten, Deception: Terror and Dread

mornings when Jack was standing at the bottom of his bed, fondling himself. Then there was Robert, a man in his late thirties. Robert was convinced that the television was the devil incarnate, that it would poison all those who watched it. Therefore, he had a mission in life: destroy televisions. This was in part fed by his religious convictions—he was of the Plymouth Brethren. Robert smashed television sets. Wherever he could find them he would smash them—by walking into shops, or simply by calling at people's homes, inviting himself in to talk with them about his faith, and then smashing the television set with a hammer he carried with him. The police and the courts decided a spell in Powick was the best thing for him. Within days of him arriving, Paul stood transfixed and horror struck as Robert lifted the old television in the ward and hurled it through the windows of the conservatory. What was worse was that Paul knew Robert had seen him watching the television. Robert told him so. He must be corrected before he was lost forever in the flames of hell! The boy had sinned. Paul could not sleep that night fearing—not hell, least not the hell Robert talked off—but fearing what Robert would do to him.

In the morning he confided in Brian. The next day Robert sat in the chair recovering from ECT treatment. Paul was doubly horrified. The man sat there reaching out with his right hand, his mouth open in an ungainly manner. Paul was racked by guilt—is this what he had done! He had told Brian. In telling him he had caused this! Robert being punished for threatening him. Oh God! He was desperate with guilt! He was not to know: the decision to give Robert ECT treatment had been made before even the incident with the television set. The child was not to know. He did not ask. He dare not ask. He vowed not to speak of any threats again. He vowed to say nothing—how could he live with himself if he caused this degree of suffering in someone? The memory of what happened to Jeff was all too fresh.

Four

Paul wanted to talk with other people, but he was too shy, too inhibited, and too fearful. His questions, his introductions to conversations were wooden, stilted, which in itself reflected his fear, his inhibitions. Trying to converse with people in everyday society would have been bad enough, but to make conversation with the other people in Powick was tortuous. A perfectly sound, normal conversation could turn into something bizarre, abusive, even violent, for no apparent reason. He therefore withdrew further into himself. He had been able to talk with Brian, the nurse who had befriended him, but since the business with Robert, he feared even talking with him.

Gerald was a man in his early thirties. Tall, clean cut, some would have said debonair, but certainly well dressed and well mannered. Gerald would talk to him; at least, Gerald would try to talk to him. They were in the same ward. He had been admitted before Paul had entered and had watched the boy from a distance. He then started to sit by Paul if he was in the conservatory. He would show interest in the book the child was reading. Paul did not want to show him, but did not want to appear rude. Gerald would tease little pieces of information out of the boy. Somehow he would show that he was also interested. Over a period of time Paul began slowly to open up. He would share, he would talk with Gerald. Gerald not only was interested in World War Two aircraft like the boy, but he had flown a Spitfire in the Battle of Britain. Indeed, not only had he flown a Spitfire in the Battle of Britain, but he had been shot down—and had climbed back into a Spittie the very next day. And he had shot down dozens of enemy aircraft. He seemed to share exactly the same interests as Paul, including medieval history and tales of knights. Also, he had grown up in a village on the south side of Bredon Hill, the side the boy had not explored or known because of its distance from Evesham. Paul showed him the few books he had with him in Powick: a book about the Spitfire, a book of Celtic myths, an Enid Blyton Mystery story, and two more aircraft books. Paul kept them safely in his locker by his bedside. Gerald would walk with the boy to the shop and cafe within the hospital.

On occasional Saturdays he would walk into Powick village with him. The odd thing was that Gerald was not at all interested in Paul's painting. But this was something that he just accepted. Brian had invited Gerald to go to see the pictures in the art room, but this was one area where Gerald did not remotely want to share Paul's interests. It was as if there was something too honest, too open, and too immediate in them. Gerald looked shifty when Brian raised the subject. Brian just stared back at him.

The child was becoming fond of Gerald—he enjoyed the friendship and shared interests. He did not realize he was being groomed. At times he accidentally called him dad. He would not admit to anyone that he had formed a close friendship with Gerald; he would not even admit this to himself. Brian tried to get him to talk about the relationship, but Paul refused to take up the leads. Then came the day when Paul found that someone had been into his locker. One of his books was missing—one of his aircraft books. Brian noticed his distress and enquired, then went straight to Gerald's room and returned within three minutes with the book.

"I thought he might have taken it," Brian commented as he handed the book back to the boy.

There was silence; a long silence.

Chapter Ten, Deception: Terror and Dread

"I might have lent it to him and forgotten!"

"Did you? Did you really?" replied Brian.

There was another long silence.

"I know you didn't. You look after you books very well, and you keep the cupboard locked."

The silence now became loaded; loaded with fear on Paul's part, and with urgency on Brian's.

"He took it Paul; he probably broke into your locker and took it."

"No he didn't!" replied Paul, almost before Brian could finish saying his words.

"He took it, Paul, to find out about aircraft. He took it so that he would be able to talk to you about aircraft . . ."

"No! No! He couldn't have. He knew about them already!"

"I've seen him reading it. I've seen him asking other men who have been in the war about these planes. I think he just wanted to share your interests—please, be careful, don't get too close to him."

"Why shouldn't I be friends? You just don't want me to be friends with him!"

"Look, I'm thinking of you. Gerald, well, you see, he tells stories. He loses track of the truth. He's pathological, he's . . . look, it's no secret, I see no reason why you should not know: he's a liar; no, maybe that's too strong a word. He tells stories; he lives a deception."

Paul sat tense, biting his bottom lip. He was not going to put up with this. He was not going to listen to this nonsense. He put his hands over his ears. He was not going to hear this.

"Look!" said Brian, his tone becoming more urgent, "Look, he has three wives, three families, three lives! None of them knew that the others existed. Well, they didn't till a few months ago. Look, he's taken money. He's set up ghost companies, taken money, embezzled. Look, he's here because the courts took pity on him. I think we are all wondering if he took them in with his stories, with his smooth talk!"

"No! No! No!" the child rocked to and fro on the bed, his legs crossed, his hands over his ears. "No! No! No! I won't hear it, you're lying, you're the one making things up. He's nice. He really is. They don't understand him, no . . . no . . ."

"Paul, look! He took the book to find out about the Spitfire, the Hurricane, the Lancaster. Look, I know. How old has he said he is? Come on, how old—thirty-two? How old? If necessary I can prove it."

Brian now talked more slowly. "He is not old enough to have flown in the war. He would have been a child. Maybe he was interested in the planes. Maybe he wasn't. He's making it all up. He's taking you in. He's never flown a Spitfire in his life!"

Longman's Charity

"No! No! No!" the child rocked to and fro. Then he was silent and still. The truth was beginning to sink in. But surely it couldn't be true, he thought to himself. How could it be?

"You may as well know the truth, Paul: he's a con man. His life is one big lie, and what's more he's never been to Bredon Hill in his life. He did not grow up in Kemerton, he grew up in Selly Oak, Birmingham. He probably got the idea from the drawing, you know the picture map, you have made of Bredon and its villages."

This was the final straw. Paul jumped off the bed and ran down the corridor. He went through the conservatory door and ran—ran down to the fence at the bottom of the slope. He sat looking through the wire netting, looking at his tree. He sat and the truth slowly dawned in his mind. He'd been taken in. Oh how stupid he was. How could he have believed Gerald? It all began to fall into place now—he could see now that Gerald was too young to have been in the war. If the truth be known, the child had wondered, even had an inkling of suspicion at one point. But he had dismissed such thoughts completely from his mind. Oh the foolishness, the stupidity; how ashamed he was. He would not be taken in again. He vowed not to. He vowed as strongly as he could in his mind, as strongly as he could through his clenched teeth, through the tears, through the tension and anger: he vowed not to trust anyone again. No one, not one living person: he had trusted Gerald, who had lied and led him on! He had trusted Brian, and look what happened to Robert! He had trusted William. He had trusted that Panty would not die. But he did. He was so foolish—it was no good trusting people, talking with them, being friends with them. You got hurt! You just got hurt too much: too, too much. He had been right those weeks before when he had seen what had happened to Robert once he had told Brian—he now knew he must stay silent, as silent as possible, in his own world.

So Paul withdrew. He withdrew to where he had been prior to Gerald's friendship. He withdrew further, deeper. He recoiled back into himself. He may have been a shy, immature thirteen year old, but he was learning many lessons his fellows at school were not learning. Most of his peers knew little of deceit and hypocrisy, lies and stories, double dealing, power games, back-biting, bitching: the darker side to humanity. He was encountering a dark, bizarre, often irrational, often deranged, but certainly a very sad side to people that many of his peers would not even glimpse in their whole lives. But for now, he simply withdrew. Further, deeper, into a near silent world.

Paul had been trying to find someone since the age of seven and a half to take the place of the love and friendship that had developed with his maternal grandfather—William Riley. He did not realize this. The sense of having been talking with him was still all too fresh in his mind. He was not conscious of this: this search for someone or something to replace the hole left inside him by his love for William. The various psychiatrists and social workers at Powick could not even begin to glimpse this. In all their talks with him, their attempts at analysis, they did not know or understand the almost savage wrench his grandfather's death had been on this child. They did not suspect that it might have been this one event in his young life, experienced as it was against the background of his parents' troubled and violent marriage, that had set in motion the path of isolation, of being withdrawn, of outsidership, that so concerned them. If they asked his parents about the possibility of some event in the past having a traumatic effect on him, this single event, the death of his grandfather nearly six years earlier, would not have been cited by them. They had not noticed how deep the loss went in him at the time, how deep was his sorrow, just how tightly he held on to it. Such an event as the death of a grandparent is not unusual in a child's life. The effect it had on him was also not unusual: it is the stuff of life—the tragedy and pathos that makes us what we are. However, it was the event of his grandfather's death that had triggered the phase of bed-wetting, which in turn had led to the nightly abuse by his mother, which was the real cancer at the heart of his psyche; no one suspected, even Paul had erased the memory, the accumulating memory, out of his mind. But the abuse had not been happening for over a month now, since he had entered Powick. And a change was imperceptibly beginning to happen in him. He was just beginning to gain a little confidence, even beginning to be a little more assertive. The lack of head-nodding was possibly the most visual sign of this improvement.

After about thirty minutes Paul wiped his face on his sleeve, and took one long, last, look at the tall ash tree in the centre of the copse. He could see the foolishness now. He could see so clearly how he had been taken in with Gerald's lies. Gerald had even conned money out of him. When they had gone for a cup of tea and cake in the small cafe within the hospital, he had paid because Gerald had no money. Gerald had even borrowed his meagre pocket money; he had never returned it. He stood up, took a deep breath. Then he turned to return up the slope. There at the top of the slope was Brian. He had obviously been there all the time. He walked up the slope. He stopped before Brian, who had now stood up himself. He looked him straight in the face and spoke quietly.

"I'm sorry, please, I . . ."

"It's alright, it's alright, I understand . . ."

"You are right," the boy interrupted, "you are right, I can see it all now."

"Why don't you come in and have some tea?"

"No, not just now. Can I sit on my bed please?"

"Yes, of course, come on in."

He walked slightly ahead of Brian. The two of them walked the remainder of the grass slope. They could feel the dampness in the air. They walked in through the conservatory doors. The boy held his breath and kept his eyes firmly on the ground as he walked past the other men having tea. He did not look to the left or to the right.

Five

Later that evening, as dusk was fast approaching, Paul walked once again along the grass slope outside the ward. But this time he kept well over to the left. Eventually he reached a small isolated building: a chapel. It was built of red sandstone, the size of an average village church, but without a spire or tower. However, a small pinnacle rose from the centre of the steeply pitched roof. The walls had large buttresses all the way down each side: not for support, but for appearance. Between each buttress was a tall, narrow, pointed window. The sandstone was weathered quite severely in places. The windows themselves were covered by wire grills and with pigeon droppings. Likewise the buttresses were soiled. The whole building was covered in over-fussy crenellations. He knew what a Gothic church from the Middle Ages should look like. This was not one—this seemed to be a mockery of one. It was, in fact, an example of rather excessive nineteenth-century Gothic revival. It was, however, the hospital chapel. There was a full-time chaplain in the hospital and this building was naturally his responsibility. Walking up to the door, Paul tried to lift the latch. He pushed, pushed hard, but there was no response from the heavy wooden door. It was firmly locked. He pushed, and pushed, to no avail. He looked and read a notice nailed to the door, informing him that if anyone wanted to use the chapel then they should contact the Reverend such-and-such (several letters followed the man's name), and a phone number. He did not note the number. He wanted to go in there now. He had not wanted to before. It only occurred to him now, since the events of the afternoon—the conversation with Brian. He just wanted to go in and sit quietly. He would not try to come again. This was obviously not for him.

He turned and walked away; he walked slowly, very slowly, back along the slope in the direction of the ward. He had not really thought of religion, of God, of his faith during the many weeks he had been here. Each day had been too busy, too hectic, too troublesome to stop and take his breath, or so it seemed. But now he needed it, now he was ready to stop, particularly after the truth he had faced up to in the afternoon; now he needed to feel close to what he believed was God.

As he walked back up the slope, he did not so much lose his faith; it was like

Chapter Ten, Deception: Terror and Dread

having to discard an old garment, much loved, which was worn out, was too small. He had been ready to believe a few years earlier that there was a God who could help him, who could be close to him, who could save him. Around the time when he was confirmed he often thought on Chowskie's faith, which though secret had been revealed to him that day many years earlier. But no longer—he was too confused and weighed down by . . . by what? And now he felt abandoned. Abandoned and lost. Here, in Powick, he was lost for all time. Would he ever leave the place? Could he ever face going back to his parents? Could he ever face going back to school—to Evesham County Secondary Modern? What on earth was to become of him? Even if there was a God, this God was too far away, too busy and too distant to help him or to care. He was going to have to face this alone. Yet although his faith was effectively pushed to one side amidst the need to be ever vigilant, literally in order to remain sane, however much he seemed to lose sight of or even abandon Christ, there was something that held on to him, that protected him, truly kept him sane, and despite all that happened and was happening to him, brought him through this ordeal, through fire and water, intact, whole, sane, and never lost. He, however, was now firmly convinced that whatever was to become of him, he was going to have to face it alone. He kept repeating the words to himself as he shuffled, oh so slowly, back up the slope, finally pausing outside the conservatory door in the dim failing light.

There was still a trace of light over to the west, between two large banks of cloud, one obliterating the horizon. He looked and took in the sky, and decided to paint it. He heard a noise from the door and realized it was one of the nurses locking it. Quickly he turned and knocked on the door. The door was unlocked and opened.

"What on earth are you doing out there? You're supposed to be in here! Where have you been?"

"Only for a walk, I sort of lost track of time—I'm sorry." The boy spoke quickly and then pushed through the curtain and walked past the nurse.

The next morning—early—there was Jack, stood at the bottom of the bed. He had been missing for a few mornings. Now he was back. His breath was fast, he was stroking himself. But then a night nurse came round the corner into the square.

"What are you doing there? Come on, who are you? What's your name? Where's your bed?"

The nurse was obviously new. Without waiting for an answer, he guided Jack in the direction he had already set off in. Paul Broadley hated it all, hated the early mornings in the ward, hated being trapped with these men.

He feared most of all ending up like them.

Chapter Eleven
Sanity: Emptiness and Escape

> ~ *"I am forgotten like a dead man, out of mind;*
> *I am like a broken vessel.*
>
> *For my enemies speak against me;*
> *and those who lie in wait for my life take counsel together, saying,*
>
> *'God has forsaken him, pursue and take him!*
> *For there is none to deliver him!'"*
>
> PSALM 31:12 & 71:10–11

One

The ward at night was like a different world; if it had one, then this was its alter ego. Paul Broadley had seen glimpses of it during the day, when the occasional veneer of good manners slipped. But at night the demons that ruled people's fear and longings and troubles were abroad. He slept fitfully; he could not really relax or be off his guard. When he slept he was haunted by images of the scenes he had seen during the day. He could cope with these nightmares; it was the dreams of hope, of beauty, of love, dreams which haunted him, almost mocked him, that he found so difficult to cope with. Such dreams left him feeling empty, sad, lonely, more bereft than any other: the pain of possibility stabbed in through, then left him bereft. He would wake. This yearning emptiness was complete. The sadness was overwhelming. He would listen. He would look around him. The dim night-lights illuminated the scene. He looked at his watch. It was a few minutes past three o'clock. So he got out of bed. He had always been

Chapter Eleven, Sanity: Emptiness and Escape

a light sleeper, but now, with the torment of his dreams, he had taken to getting up and walking at nights: walking the ward. He had realized from when he went to the toilet in the night that the ward was quiet and almost unattended. If he delayed on returning to his bed, no one noticed him, no one ordered him back: he sensed freedom. He had learnt to sleep very quietly and very still. He also learned to apply the same quiet stillness to his movements about the ward at night, to stand and not be noticed. He was not a tall child for his age and he could move silently around the ward without either of the two night nurses, stationed as they were at each end of the ward, noticing him. He would stand by curtains or beside beds or cupboards and look at the faces of the people sleeping in the beds, who were nearly all drugged up with sleeping tablets.

This night he walked, softly and silently, to the two occupied beds in the far end of the corridor, the end furthest away from the conservatory and the ward entrance. Noise was coming from one of the beds. Cautiously he approached. Before him lay Charlie—he had been admitted again. He could see the cot sides raised on the metal-framed bed to prevent the man from falling out. The bed was parallel to the corridor wall and next to the square. Hiding behind a curtain hanging on the corner of the wall, the corner as it turned from the square at right angles into the corridor, he stood and looked and listened to the sight of the man in the bed. Charlie was making the most unearthly guttural sound—his breathing was very difficult, chest, sinus, and passages all were blocked with mucus, thus there was the most horrendous noise when breathing. He was a very large, obese man. Very fat and flabby, his red skin was stretched taut over the flowing, fatty flesh, bloated mainly with drink. Charlie was a perpetual alcoholic: a body diseased and riddled with the stuff. Every couple of weeks he would revert to the whisky—drink a bottle or two and would be rushed by the ambulance here. He lived in a farmhouse overlooking the Malvern Hills. Charlie's frail housekeeper would find him, or a neighbour would hear him crashing about. He had lived there all his life (Gustav Holst had apparently visited the place many, many, years earlier). But now he was a large, drink-sodden man of sixty-nine years, with very little time left to live. And so the boy watched as Charlie breathed in, noisily, and out, with his lips vibrating, causing ripples in the blubber of his neck and cheeks. The man stank of stale sweat and urine, of alcohol. Occasionally he would let loose wind, involuntarily, either through his mouth or his anus. Then he would give a moan and a shuffle and continue to sink into unconsciousness, his delirious mind soaked in the despair of year upon year of loneliness.

Charlie had never married, simply ran the family farm up until, and beyond, his parents' demise. At times he would cry, would moan. Sometimes Paul believed he could hear a name—Betty, Betty—but then maybe not. Each time

Charlie was brought in, the boy would wake and hear him in the night, moaning and crying through the alcoholic haze. Paul would then leave his bed and stand by the curtain and watch. Stand vigil. The fifth time he was brought in in this state there was little crying out. He went to see him: his eyes were grey, the pupils cloudy, every vein in his face stood out. His breathing sounded like sandpaper on a glass window. The breathing became shallower and shallower. There was nothing the staff did for him. They simply gave him the space to dry out. They had long ago ceased to try to tackle his alcoholism. This night he was visibly weaker. So Paul retreated to his bed. In the morning he was gone. He had died in the night. Paul looked at the bed in the morning. It had been stripped and made. The other patients had not even known Charlie had been in that night: they had all been fast asleep. They had not known he had died there whilst they slept their artificially drugged sleep.

Paul would often walk in the ward at night. Often he would stand near a curtain or behind a bed frame. Often staff would attend to a patient without noticing him. He had learnt the art of standing very, very still—more than that, he would somehow deny all thought in him, all will to speak to people, to be part of a scene. So much so that people did not notice him. Certainly during the day he was barely noticed around the ward or grounds. At night he could therefore walk and stand and watch: he observed, and remembered all—all the distorted, tortured, manic faces, distorted and tortured by relations, by work, by pressures, by drink, by drugs, by life. Even in sleep there was no peace for these people: not for them the sleep of angels, but neither the sleep of devils, for none was evil, no, they were simply fallen and broken. However, many of these images now added to the child's dreams to haunt him when he slept: the bloated, broken body of Charlie; or the image of a man who was rushed in with bandaged wrists, bandages stained with blood. Images too of the faces of men he knew, animated by day, but tossing and turning, trying to escape the pain in their minds as they lay under the artificially induced comatose state of tranquillizers and sleeping pills. At night the boy stood, then walked, and stood and watched. He learnt to observe humanity in the raw, with vanity, ego, and illusion stripped away; humanity in all its sadness, all its folly, its fallen wilfulness, prey to and obsessed with all manner of demons, legions of demons.

At night he felt less threatened by the other patients. Less, that is, than during the day. During daylight, when the men had risen and dressed, they spent most of the time trying to protect their own personal patch—their tiny corner, their personal space. This, of course, led to arguments and fights. But it wasn't just finding himself near to potential conflicts that Paul found hard to avoid: often he himself was the focus of threats and intimidation. For example, when Jack stood,

Chapter Eleven, Sanity: Emptiness and Escape

as he did so regularly, at the foot of his bed during the early hours; on several occasions the threat became closer and more real. One afternoon when he was lying on his bed, waiting for tea, a group of three young men came up to him. One was a patient—in for drug abuse—the other two were friends visiting him. They invited themselves to consume his drink of orangeade, then proceeded to stand close to the bed.

"So what are you—a boy or a girl? You seem quite a nice sort of kid, but then you can't be that nice to be in here. What you been doing then? Eh? Eh! Cat got your tongue has it?" said the one of the visitors.

"He don't say much, he don't; weird he is; weird if you ask me. Strange in fact!" said the patient.

"Oh! one of them, eh!" said the second visitor.

Both visitors and the patient were now sitting on the bed. The first visitor continued.

"I tell you what, let's pull his trousers down and have a look—maybe he's a girl; I could do with a bit."

"Or maybe he's both!"

Their language now laced with the graphically vernacular.

"Or maybe he likes both—here give us a hand let's have a look what he's got between his legs," said the patient, upon which he placed his hand firmly over the boy's groin.

"I can't feel nuffing—you're right, this one's strange!"

"Get on with it, get his trousers off!"

At that, the gong sounded for tea. All three jumped and got off the bed.

"We'll be back kid, we'll be back. . . ." The first visitor said to him, pointing and wagging his finger. He came back close and put his head next to Paul's:

"And if you breathe a word of this, just one word of this to anyone, we'll get you; not a squeak or I'll cut your throat from side to side."

He gestured with his finger across his own throat.

"We'll be back; we'll be back!"

With that they left.

The boy lay, petrified: the palms of his hands sweating, cold shivers running down his spine. Slowly his eyes ceased to see, his mind ceased to think. That deep-seated nausea was welling up from his stomach: he fought in his mind to stay conscious, fought and fought with every ounce in his being. The ceiling started to spin, then the thin grey fog took over in his eyes, in his mind. His hands were shaking. He tried to stop then, he fought for breath. Then he was gone.

When he woke it was dark. He found that a blanket had been thrown over him. Men were still moving around the ward—it was not yet time for lights out.

One of the staff must have found him sleeping and thrown the blanket over him. His mind was so confused; he couldn't remember where he was or even, for a few seconds, who he was. He moved his head—ouch! The pain shot through his eyes and down the back of his neck. Everywhere lights were too bright, painfully bright. The noise in his head—the tinnitus—was screaming. It was times like this that the sound of the tinnitus merged imperceptibly with the pain of a migraine, or was it that the pain of the migraine merged imperceptibly with the tinnitus? He lay. Somehow things began to fall into place; somehow, he did not know how, he knew he must get away from here, knew his life was threatened; knew not why, but that he must get away. Brian came up to him.

"Did you have a good sleep?"

"I've got a headache. Please can I have something?"

"I'll bring you an aspirin—I won't be a moment."

Brian disappeared and returned with the aspirin.

"Here take this."

Paul took it, obediently, and upon swallowing the aspirin, asked if Brian could help him get into bed. Brian did. He slept fitfully that night. He woke, as usual, but this night did not walk in the ward. His head still throbbed, likewise the nausea kept him from moving. He could no longer think straight. He could no longer cry. He could no longer remember the past. He could see no future. All he knew was this. The emptiness was complete. The sadness was overwhelming.

And so Paul learnt to hide these feelings. This was the second lesson he had learnt as the end of the second month of his time here approached. He learnt not to show his feelings. Not to show his suffering. He learned to be normal and polite on the outside, to show no emotion, no criticism, only to let people know you were all right. He kept the real self hidden safely away, safely in a box inside where no one could see him, no one could touch him, no one could hurt him. Combined with the first lesson he had learnt (that of trusting no one, not speaking of things that troubled him, of not sharing), these two lessons now were his last and only line of survival. On the surface he would try to be as normal as possible. He gave one of his pictures to Doctor Cheen when he expressed how pleased he was with the boy's paintings. It formed a point of conversation in other meetings in weeks to come. But he kept himself tightly locked away: never trusting, speaking little, showing no fears or feelings. When there were fights at teatime, or when a female patient was found in bed with one of the men from his ward—which almost led to open warfare between several of the men, when they returned from the ECT treatment—he kept himself steely tight, buried deep down; with a neat, polite external veneer to keep all from suspecting. Only in the privacy and solitude of moments alone could he face the pain, the loneliness, the sadness deep down and cry: cry silent, salt tears, which flowed down his cheeks onto his lips. When he was sitting by the fence in the grounds looking at his tree, when he was hiding at night behind the heavy conservatory curtains, looking out, then, in these moments, he would allow himself to cry: with few tears, silently, in absolute stillness, he would weep.

Two

For the first month or two Paul was cut-off from his family. Indeed, it was only when the spring began to manifest itself in the cherry blossom scattered around the grounds that first his mother, then his mother and sister, and then his father as well would come to visit him. Paul would wait with almost tortuous expectation for his mother's arrival. But he was only too aware of the staff in Powick watching him: watching him and trying to predict his reactions, predict his feelings, form ideas about his response, his behaviour. He felt at these times as though he was in prison, worse still, as though he was on show in a glass case, or in a circus. This inhibited him when his mother came in, walking slowly along the corridor towards the square, the boy turned and saw her—she was looking around. He wanted to jump off the bed and rush over to her, rush over and fling his arms around her, but he was only too aware of one nurse who had stopped attending to one old gentleman sitting in the chairs in the centre of the square, to stand and observe. The nurse may simply have been looking up to see if assistance was needed—but Paul's state of mind by now was approaching paranoia. He had to watch himself so carefully, believing himself to be under threat by these people who had taken him from home and kept him in here. It took only a few moments for his mother to look round and see him. She walked over slowly. Unknown to him, she was feeling in the same state that he was—wanting to be private, to have a private talk, to be with her son, but feeling so much under observation.

Their talk was brief at first—they asked about each other's health: Meg asked how he was; he asked how Christine, Timmy, Renée were; he wanted to ask about his father but was scared to. He asked about the blossom on the apple trees in the back garden; was the hawthorn in bloom? She asked whether he was eating enough; was he sleeping well? He wanted to walk in the grounds with his mother, he asked her: she replied that she had been requested to stay there with him. He began to look tearful. The nurse, who had been hovering near-by inanely straightening sheets and rearranging pillows, came over and suggested to Meg that it might be time for her to leave. The boy looked at him, a feeling of sadness, tearfulness, now mixed with feelings of injustice, even anger. But he felt paralyzed—he could not speak. The nurse pointed out that he seemed to be perturbed by her visit. This made him even angrier—it was the interfering ways of this nurse, these doctors, this place, that was upsetting him, not his mother. Or was it? But he could not voice these feelings. He waved goodbye to his mother and started walking past the beds and was about to follow her along the corridor when the nurse caught his arm:

"I'm only looking, only watching, you, you . . . !" spluttered Paul.

He watched as the nurse took out a small notebook and wrote briefly in pencil. By now his mother had left. The boy knew that this would get back to the doctors. He felt almost ashamed of what Brian would think of him. He wanted to ask when his mother could visit again. But he was afraid to—afraid of what they would think. He knew they thought he was too fond of his mother, too close to her. Doctor Cheen had said so. He was therefore very wary of his actions and his speech.

Unknown to Paul, his mother had come over with his father that Tuesday morning. The doctors had specified that only his mother should visit. His father was busy with the height of the spring onion trade, but still took the morning off to drive Meg over. Harry simply sat patiently in the car, watching people come and go, indeed he was amusing himself wondering if there was any difference between the patients and the staff, trying as he was to spot which was which. Harry had a rough and ready approach to these experts: an interfering load of busybodies, living off taxpayers' money!

Meg quietly got back into the car. Harry started the engine and proceeded down the gravel drive towards the main road. Turning right, he passed under the recently constructed footbridge, then towards Worcester. Neither spoke. The silence was not through enmity, it was a silence that came from the fact that neither Meg nor Harry wanted to face what they had just gone through, why their son was there of all places, why the doctors and social workers seemed to have so much power over them, their lives, and their family. Both were silent all the way through the busy traffic in Worcester, all the way along the Worcester Road, through Pershore, finally through Hampton and into the Cheltenham Road. Only whilst driving through Hampton did Meg's head stray from staring forward through the windscreen and momentarily turn to the right to glance at the house she had spent nearly all her childhood and single life in, and then to the left to glance at Hampton Church. Then she resumed her forwards stare.

The next week, on the same day, the Tuesday morning, Meg visited again, but this time she stayed for longer. But there was a barrier between them. Both were aware they were being watched. In addition they sensed that they spoke and behaved as though a glass screen were enveloping them. There was now a distance between them, an independence that was small, subtle, yet growing. In

Chapter Eleven, Sanity: Emptiness and Escape

utter sadness this sense was never to leave Paul. He would never relate to his mother in the same way again—not for as long as she would live. In more normal circumstances this could have been considered as part of growing up. If it was, then the situation he was now in would form this part of growing up to include the perverseness of the conditions he was now living in.

The visits continued. Soon would come the day when his mother and sister would visit. He queried if his father was coming, but he received no reply. He was pleased to see his sister; they talked about her time at school—she was now studying for her CSEs. Paul knew that he could never go back to Four Pools, that he could never face the other children, that there would now be a gulf between them; most of all he feared their knowing: he feared their knowing that he had been *here*, in this place. In addition, he had missed so much schooling now that he feared he could never to catch up with them. So he talked with his sister about pop music—her life interest—though he didn't listen to a radio in Powick. He tried to talk about books, but she did not read for pleasure. Still, at least with these weekly visits he could get his mother to bring in some of his books. After about five of these weekly visits he was allowed to walk in the grounds with them. He felt happier. He still was reticent to talk, but groped for the words. At least he believed that they were not being spied on, that he was not being listened to. Unknown to him there were social workers, or child psychologists, or just plain nurses observing him, measuring his movements and actions and gestures against some textbook model of behaviour. But despite their supposed expertise none could identify the key problem: the six years of abuse at the hands of his mother. There were the traditional, patriarchal, old school experts and there were the fashionable young experts—cool and "fab" (in the sixties jargon), reflecting the liberating pseudo-progress of the year, 1967—but none managed to identify the root problem of the abuse.

Before long Harry was allowed to visit. Paul wanted to express his joy at seeing his father, but then he saw the enmity between his parents, the subtle signs of a cold war. He knew they had been rowing, though they had done everything to conceal it. Others would not have suspected, but he knew. He knew. They sat for a while, the three of them: Paul Broadley, his mother, and his father. Paul wanted to go out in the grounds with them, but no, the social rules imposed by his guardians prevented this. It appeared that the boy had to go through the same ritual of a short meeting in the ward, then a longer session, then after about four or five visits they could go into the grounds; and indeed it was so.

After many more visits, indeed after weeks, there came the Saturday afternoon when the child was allowed to go out with his parents and sister. The four of them drove further west towards the Malvern Hills. After a while they pulled up in a lay-by and ate a few sandwiches, opened a flask of tea, then proceeded back along the road towards Powick. Paul had wanted to drive around and through the Malvern Hills, but time did not allow. Driving back he caught a glimpse of Bredon over to the East. This upset him. He had not seen the hill for over two months. His mother could see he was upset, and feared returning him if he was seen to be perturbed. He wanted to explain why he was troubled, that he was feeling homesick for the land, the smallholding, the Charity, Bredon Hill—but, he could not. Once his mother had returned him to the ward he settled on the bed. Brian came over to talk with him. Brian could sense the hurt, the puzzlement in him.

"I'll bring you some tea round if you would like some."

Paul declined, with a nod. Paul feared that Brian would tell. But it was not his parents that had upset him. No, it was coming back here that had distressed him. But he need not have worried. Brian was as concerned as the boy as to why he was still here. Brian would not tell. Indeed Brian was coming to the point of almost confronting the doctors and social workers. His thoughts were interrupted:

"I saw Bredon."

Brian collected himself—quickly:

"What, this afternoon?"

"Yes. It was lovely. The sun was shining on the tower!"

"That's what upset you—am I right?"

Paul smiled.

Three

The drive back home from the hospital in Powick was uneventful. There was the usual unspoken silent animosity between Meg and Harry. But Christine was growing up. Early in May would be her fifteenth birthday. In arguments she sided with her mother. Harry was just not good enough as a husband to her mother, or for that matter as a father to her. She spent most of her spare time with friends from school—she would be round Gina's house in Hampton, or up Jane's in Bengeworth. There they would listen to Beatles records, chat about teenage interests, talk about boys. When she was with her parents, Christine would often provoke a row by throwing out a sarcastic comment to her father. He would respond: a row would follow. All was hurtful and scathing, but the hurt inflicted had to be brushed away. This was achieved by inflicting a suitable riposte. Meg would rise to her defence. Sharp, bitter, caustic, and cutting remarks would follow. Initially Meg onto Harry and Harry onto Meg: Christine would restrict herself to condemning Harry. To her he was sub-human, beneath contempt, but should always be around to provide.

Chapter Eleven, Sanity: Emptiness and Escape

They piled out of the car once Harry had pulled down the drive.

"Don't bother with tea for me, you . . . ! I'm going up the top ground." And as so often when words failed Harry his language descended into the vernacular, which he knew would exasperate Meg even more.

"What—in those clothes!" came the response from Meg.

Harry didn't answer but drove the car down to the sheds, got out, threw his jacket onto the back seat, slammed and locked the door, then rolling his sleeves up as he walked, went into the next door main shed, and got into the lorry. He backed the lorry up the drive fast—differentials wailing. He slammed on the brakes as he passed the side of the house as Meg called out to him:

"You don't bring my mother into this, she's worth a million of you!"

He thought better of it and put his foot hard down on the accelerator. Harry backed the lorry into the Cheltenham Road, then drove off up to the top ground.

Four

Later, when Christine had gone over to Jane's for the evening and Harry was over at his parents' house, Meg could be seen walking out from the side passage of the house. She walked off along the Cheltenham Road towards the river. She crossed by the New Bridge and immediately descended the steps from the bridge into the Crown Meadows. She paused for the moment to think how this was the way she would come home from shopping on a Tuesday morning—so many Tuesday mornings; it was always a busy day for shopping. Then there was the Tuesday Doctor Cheen suggested—no, insisted—that he take Paul into Powick. It amounted to taking him into care—but he did not use those words. If they had refused then he would have taken somewhat sterner action. A Tuesday morning was the time she had taken her son in to Powick. Tuesday was the day for visiting the boy. Here she was now on a Saturday evening thinking of the times the previous winter that she had walked home through the Crown Meadows, laden with shopping, with Paul in tow. Should she have insisted he go to school, even forced him? What should she have done? If only she was able to talk with Harry about the problem. If only they were able to show a more united front to Mr. Able, to Mr. Thomas, to Doctor Cheen, if only . . . if only. She would not allow her mind to think it. That is, if she had not married him or if she had been sterner with herself when she left him those few months after the marriage; if only she had her mother to talk to more often—if only. By now she had turned and walked under the viaduct that took the road over the Crown Meadows, she walked under and out the other side and along by the riverbank. She walked in the general direction of Hampton, though on the wrong side of the river to get to the village.

Longman's Charity

If only. If only her father had not been so stern, so strict; if only the war had not happened—her life, she firmly believed, would have been so much different, if only . . . if only.

She stood and contemplated the waters. She brooded over the swirling green and black depths. She deliberated on her lot, her fate. She stood on the edge of the bank looking at the waters, and at the soft red-brown soil of the steep bank. It wasn't the first time she had contemplated taking her life. She often walked here and, since the difficult times had set in once Christine had been born, she had often walked the bank—and thought of suicide. She often contemplated the bottle of Valium she kept in the kitchen drawer. She knew it was wrong to consider such things, but she was desperate—she could see no way out, no way forward. She turned as the light was failing and walked slowly back along the bank. She retraced her steps under the viaduct and then across Waterside and up the Cheltenham Road: by the time she had returned it was dark. No one had missed her. No one had known she had gone: Harry was still over at his parents', Christine was still at Jane's, and Paul was locked away. No, she must stop thinking of it like that. She sat down on the stool, her elbows on the kitchen table, her head held in her hands and wept. Times had not changed: she felt cursed—cursed and damned and trapped. As she sat weeping, Timmy came in through the open back door and brushed around her legs. Meg took one hand and reached under the table to stroke the cat as it erupted into purring.

Harry meanwhile was sitting in the faded old leather armchair at his parents—just across the road. He was watching television. His mother stayed in her room, rarely descending the stairs when he was there—indeed, rarely descending the stairs at any time. She had been a recluse for years, seldom speaking, even rarer was the occasion when she would venture out. She no longer wandered off in the way she had done so often as a young married woman, wandering in the Crown Meadows, rambling in both speech and gait. Old Jack Broadley suffered from gout, and from liver and kidney disorders. Harry would sit, watching the television, having done-the-books, as he would say, (the accounts and paper work to do with the business side of market gardening). Harry had for years kept out of the way of Meg. She had her house. Just what she had always wanted: he provided a living—a fairly good one—though there was never much spare money for luxuries. But rarely would two or three days pass without a row. Harry spent as much time as possible either out doing his job, or at his parents' house. However, he slept back with his family, though in a separate bedroom from Meg.

When Harry and Christine were out Meg wept, thinking often of suicide, and where it would all end. She had laid in a store of bottles of tranquillisers and sleeping tablets and would line them up on the kitchen table, examining each

Chapter Eleven, Sanity: Emptiness and Escape

bottle and its contents minutely. She would do this year upon year, for more than quarter of a century, until she gave in and took them. . . .

Christine got in late from Jane's. She had been given a lift back in the family car. Jane's parents declined to come in as the Broadley family was infamous for its troubles. From the age of thirteen-years (two years earlier) Christine had been sleeping in the double bed with her mother. The arrangement of Meg and Christine sleeping together lasted for sixteen years, till Christine was twenty-nine. Meg liked the arrangement; Christine went along with it. Once Paul had grown up and left home there was no excuse for this arrangement to continue as there was the small, third bedroom that he had occupied. Harry was always silent on the arrangement. Perhaps, because of the abuse she was exposed to as a young girl by the visitor to her parent's house, Meg's sexuality was confused and grey. If this was so Christine's was not: while this arrangement lasted she had boyfriends, she rejected proposals of marriage, not to mention a steamy affair with a married taxi driver from Oxford. Meg made no secret—within the family—of often warming her feet on Christine's back at night whilst they slept together. Was Meg using Christine in the same way she had abused Paul?—as an attempt to deal with the tension in her own past without owning up to it? Was this a pseudo-incestuous, pseudo-lesbian relationship? Was it simply that Meg felt more comfortable sleeping with another woman than with a man? Was Meg now channelling her sublimated anger and distortion at what had happened to her, which she would not openly admit to herself had happened, onto this bizarre sleeping relationship with her daughter? When Christine was twenty-nine years of age she broke the relationship very brutally and left home, undergoing a breakdown of sorts in the process.

Five

"So why did you paint this one, eh, Paul?"

The boy was silent.

"We are only interested, Paul. You have spent so much time painting."

The man was persistent. It was almost as though he had a thesis hanging on the boy's reply.

"I'm, I am," he corrected himself, "I am not sure I know."

Another man tried: "This painting Paul, it looks nice, it looks almost as though you could live here doesn't it, eh?"

They didn't seem to be getting anywhere. There were about eight of them—all men, sitting around the room. Some sat, some stood, one leaned against the door. Most wore expensive suits, some wore white coats—the latter were those standing. Brian wore a white coat, and he leaned against the door. All the others were perpendicular, either stood or seated firmly in chairs. At the furthest edge of the circle from the door sat Doctor Cheen. All eyes were deferentially, towards him; some almost reverentially, almost pious or devout in their gaze. All except Brian's: Brian fiddled with the top of a biro, clearing the underside of his finger nails, then folding his arms he would look at the others, but rarely did his eyes give honour to "the Doctor" as the others did. Paul was sitting on a small chair in the centre of the room. His paintings were propped up around the room, some leaning against the legs of some of the doctors, others against the wall, or on a table—but none, ironically, hung! Another man—this time in a white coat had a go:

"I like this one. This is really good! It reminds me of where I used to go when I was a boy, on holiday!"

Paul could see he was going to get nowhere, least not out of this room, or even out of this place until he answered them. So he did. The man was now sat on the floor close to the paintings. So he spoke of how he saw the scene in his mind, so he drew it, then he painted it. The man queried about the hills, the tree, why they were this shape. He said he had seen them like that when he had been driving with his family in South Wales. They had not actually been to South Wales, but the child had realized that this man, these men, wanted something and they would give him no peace till they had it.

"Why is the chimney pot this colour?"

"Maybe it's gone rusty, they could use a different metal but it would get too hot. The paint would flake off from the fire if it was painted."

The man seemed satisfied with the answer. Paul wasn't—he didn't know what he was talking about.

"This seaside picture—I can almost feel the salt spray!" Another man now joined in. He wasn't going to miss out on the act, so he sat on the floor also.

Paul wondered if they were all going to sit on the floor. He wondered if he was supposed to sit on the floor. He stayed put on his chair. Still, he thought, at least they seemed to be more cheerful. By now several of them were talking with each other about the paintings. And so it went on. The boy was feeling rather left out. He almost asked if he could go and walk in the grounds, but thought better of it. So he sat patiently until they had finished. Brian had stood, coolly, almost implacably throughout it all, saying nothing, but thinking a great deal.

Later, after tea, which had been one of the more eventful meal times, with plates of spaghetti in tomato sauce ending up hurled across the conservatory, Brian walked with Paul in the grounds—the gentle slope of the grounds which led down to the fence. Brian had been asked to talk to the boy, to relay some decisions.

Chapter Eleven, Sanity: Emptiness and Escape

"They like your paintings Paul, but they believe that the rest of your schooling is being neglected. They want you to go to the woodwork room—see what else you can do with your hands. Also you are to go to the school room in the mornings."

Paul said nothing.

"I'll take you there tomorrow, for nine-thirty."

Paul Broadley stood placidly looking at his ash tree. He was tempted to tell Brian about it. But feared that if he shared the secret, then somehow the tree would no longer look after him, protect him. No more was said between them that evening. Slowly they walked back up the slope to the French windows.

Six

The next morning he was escorted to the school room by Brian. It was an unpretentious room with little or no display—only posters; no children's work. The teacher was young—Paul thought in her twenties. She was sitting with two other children, and was struggling to get them to write a story between them, but they were having difficulty as neither could spell, and knew very few words from memory. She was trying to sound out the words, trying to coax them into understanding, into learning. He looked at the two pupils—he was certain they were both older than him, by a year or two. The teacher sat him down. She explained to him what she was doing with the other two: a story about a ship that some people were sailing on, a modern ship, a liner. She talked in very slow, measured tones as though she believed he would not understand. Would he like to join them? He replied in the affirmative. She gave him an exercise book and a pencil. He took out his fountain pen and wrote: The Mystery of the SS ORION. He proceeded to write a story about how two men and two women missed getting onto the liner as it was berthed at Southampton—delayed by some strange men in the booking hall. But these men had taken their place on the ship and they were up to no good. They were carrying forged money. Paul included some children on the ship—going out to meet their parents after term had finished (these were ideas he had got partly from reading Enid Blyton). Meanwhile, the teacher, Miss Rose, was still coaxing the two other children into writing—they were now on the fourth line of their story. After twenty minutes she said:

"I really think you could take more interest Paul. Paul . . ."

The boy had moved away to a separate table to concentrate on his story. He was now on his fifth page. She picked up the book, read through the story briefly,

"Yes, er, well, very good, well, I mean, it's a good start; there are quite a few spelling mistakes, and the grammar is in need of improvement, and the

225

characters, well they are a bit old fashioned, why don't you have a pop singer on the ship? Now there's an idea..."

The child drifted off—he ceased paying attention.

"Are you listening to me, Paul, are you listening?"

"Yes, I'm sorry—I was thinking about what you were saying about the story."

Being here in Powick had taught him to lie.

She put the book down, looking at him rather strangely and returned to the two other pupils. Paul worked on the story for another twenty minutes—over ten pages in all—then he found himself cajoled into joining the other two for a glass of orange squash and a biscuit while Miss Rose sipped at a cup of coffee. After the short break they were given a maths sheet to complete. It was simple place value—addition and subtraction, only tens and units. Paul completed it in a matter of minutes while Miss Rose was struggling on the first sum with the other two. Paul sat doodling on the back of the piece of paper, drawing the ship that had been in his earlier story. Miss Rose was too absorbed to notice his boredom.

At dinner time he walked back along the corridors to the ward. For some reason—unknown to him—he was not required to attend the classes again. Next day he reported to the woodwork room. This consisted of a largish room with approximately six wooden workbenches in the centre. There were several men working away—none of them younger than forty. One large man, with an enormous stomach that rested on the bench, was working on a model of a house. Each piece of wood was lovingly cut and sculptured, indeed the entire model must have taken him months. Paul often watched the man as he worked away on the model. When absorbed in his work, this man was totally engrossed in his creation. So, the boy set to making a box for his paints, with a sliding lid, and compartments for all his oil paints—a large one for the tube of titanium white, and smaller ones for the other colours, then along one side of the box, a long compartment for the brushes. It took him about seven mornings to make this. During which time the large man completed one window frame for his house.

Walking along the corridor Paul now noticed this man—he was always accompanied by a nurse or orderly gently shepherding him along as his feet slowly bore his great bulk, as if his joints were prematurely stiffening. His mouth was always open, with phlegm dribbling down from the corners. His eyes did not move, his face was expressionless, his head neither looked to the left or the right. Paul could see why he was accompanied by the nurse. He never knew his name, and by now he was too afraid to enquire, for in asking he would be giving away some of his deeper inner self, which he now knew he must keep locked away, safely protected from other people, from the world. To have enquired would have involved trusting, letting go. This was contrary to the lesson he had

Chapter Eleven, Sanity: Emptiness and Escape

learnt following on from Gerald's deception, and also with what had happened to Robert, and of course Paul's mistaken view that he had caused the man's suffering: therefore he could not show his feelings. Above all else, he must at all costs convince the outside world that he was normal: he must put on a polite exterior, showing no emotion, no criticism, no opinion, and he must give nothing away about inner feelings or interests—to have enquired of the man's name would have been a breach of this commitment to his own sanity.

Paul watched the large man. Although the man's face was expressionless whilst walking along the corridor, he became alive whilst making his model. He did not speak. He did not even communicate through looking at another, through glances, or even a sigh: he was expressionless. However, when he worked on the house, he changed. Most traces of the bizarre, the eccentric, the grotesque had vanished: this was the man's life—working on the model house; it was his love.

One morning, almost the last morning that the boy was working on his paint box, he entered the woodwork room to find the man sitting on a chair holding his head in his hands, a low moan coming from his mouth, his body rocking gently to and fro. A nurse was trying to comfort him, but to no avail. His house lay smashed and wrecked, broken into what seemed a million tiny fragments. At such moments Paul feared for his sanity, his safety, for who could have done such an act? It was clearly not the man, the creator, as Paul had fondly thought of him in his mind. Someone must have come in, maybe forced their way in, it would not have been unusual for one or two patients to have been walking along the corridor during an evening. But why smash this man's model, his work, his love? For indeed, he had realized that this man had indeed loved this house, cherished it, put his energies into it—it gave him a tentative fragile strand of sanity. Paul loved his painting, the act of painting, the finished pictures, planning them, so was this now something else he must give up, to lock away safely, deep inside him? He had known from an early age not to trust love, almost to fear it: the example of his parents was evidence enough. Then there was Panty, he had loved him—and he had gone! He indeed, feared for his sanity and his safety.

Then came the day Brian disappeared. Brian had been the one element of continuity over the last three months. Unknown at the time to him, Brian had become increasingly disillusioned with his role at Powick, and in addition, not only the treatment of many of the patients, but in particular the reasons for them being there. The prime cause for him resigning appeared to have been a confrontation with Doctor Cheen over Paul (the boy overheard a comment to this effect from two staff talking in the corridor). Brian had been strongly of the opinion that the boy should not have been admitted—there was nothing mentally or psychologically wrong with him, or, for that matter, socially: all he suffered from, if suffered was the right word, was having withdrawn from normal boyish activities and social intercourse as a way of coping with the difficulties of his parents' marriage. Doctor Cheen declined to be drawn one way or other: he allowed himself this privilege. In all probability Dr Cheen suspected that it was Meg who was the prime cause of Paul Broadley's traumatic state—leastwise the traumatic state the boy had been in when he had been admitted; however, he had no firm evidence. Brian concluded that both the doctor and all the rest of the team did not really know what they were doing with Paul Broadley: this ranged from why he had been admitted, to where they would go from here. In confronting Doctor Cheen, Brian had cooked his goose, in a manner of speaking, and would have been asked for his resignation if he had not tendered it. All he knew was that Brian was there one day, and gone the next.

So, now Brian had gone. He had been the one person who had understood him, the one person who had helped him: Brian had showed the courage to confront Paul and get him to see Gerald's deception. The doctors had simply stood by and observed. But then this was a reflection of their belief in simply putting all these social outcasts and misfits together and allowing some natural law to take over. What they failed to understand was that left to their own devices the weak withdrew and the strong dominated: the staff did nothing to tackle the anarchic sub-culture that led to intimidation, mental abuse, and violence—however hidden at times it may have been.

Paul missed Brian—deeply. By now the Saturday afternoon excursions continued, and the authorities within the hospital seemed satisfied that he was not in imminent danger. So much so that the suggestion came from Doctor Cheen, flanked by four other lesser doctors, two on his left, two on his right, that it was time for the boy to go back to school, back to his old school: Four Pools. This filled the child with horror: he lay awake at night filled with terror, dread, dismay—he could not go back, how could he face the other children. He resolved to talk to Doctor Cheen. He did so. Doctor Cheen was impressed by Paul's decisiveness, but was dismayed by his fear, by his pleadings. The problem was quite simple really: he feared going back to his old school. He feared the reaction of the other children, the playground teasing, the bullying, the snide remarks, being ostracized. He would be labelled as strange, as looney—after all, he had been in Powick. Doctor Cheen did not see it like this, though he obviously reflected subsequently on what Paul had said. Later, the boy was informed that he would not immediately go back to Four Pools.

That night Paul slept—peaceful and soundly, at least until dawn. He became aware of sounds in the ward. He listened. He could hear an argument. He could

Chapter Eleven, Sanity: Emptiness and Escape

not make out the words, but a nurse was arguing. No, it was a man arguing and the nurse was trying to coax the man back into bed: he drifted off, slowly sleep took hold, but then there were catches of argument lodging in his mind: something about fire, the flames, someone trapped. Sleep took hold. The boy would wake. The emptiness was complete. The sadness was overwhelming. He listened. He looked around him. Now was the loneliest part of the day. He had always woken early, but now he would feel such empty, bitter, loneliness whenever he did so.

Seven

Once all the words had flowed away, once all the frustration and anger had been spent, the queries pondered, power wielded, decisions taken, then, on a cold, drizzly, spring day in late May, Paul stood surveying the ward, a small grey-and-blue plastic bag holding his possessions, wondering if it was really true—finally the ordeal was over, he was leaving.

As he walked down the corridor with his mother, he paused to look through the conservatory windows at his ash tree, and bid it goodbye in his mind. Then with a mixture of relief, trepidation, and also of fear for the future, he walked out through the door of the ward, into the long corridors, and finally out through the main entrance.

His father had already packed his small suitcase and his paintings in the boot of the car, so Paul got into the car and quietly closed the door. There was little said on the journey back. Paul sat wondering how things would be. His mother and father were polite to each other—almost civil. The boy got out of the car on its return to the driveway along the side of the house. He delighted in the feel of the gravel under his feet. He was escorted by his mother into the house, took his bag up to his room. Once he had taken the few books out and put them back onto the window sill, he then went to the end of his bed and gazed fondly out of the window at the land, the smallholding and Longdon Hill.

He rushed down stairs, out of the back door, and into the garden. He went straight to the raspberry bushes at the end of the garden. He disappeared into them, then emerged holding Timmy. He walked around the bushes and down the far side of the sheds, finally to climb up onto the small corrugated tin extension, which was his den. There he sat, with Timmy purring for all he was worth in Paul's arms—hugging and pressing his face close into his fur, whilst he gazed lovingly on his world, Longman's Charity. The May blossom in the hawthorn was nearly over. He guessed it had been a good spring; the density of the remaining blossom was such that the trees must have been covered a few weeks earlier. His eyes followed the line of the spring onions in the field, young, emerging, about six inches tall, green and translucent, flapping wildly in the breeze, with the cool, bright, spring sunshine glowing through the thin growth. He surveyed the crop, following closely the slight irregularities that showed up if you looked at them at this obtuse angle, until his eyes came to the wild grasses, vetches, and cow parsley that formed a moat around the sheds. Timmy struggled in his arms. Paul saw: he released the cat. It leaped, scurried, spread its front legs while glowering from side to side in the grass: it hunted. Success was only a few moments away. He saw only the rump end of his cat—it froze, then the tail started thrashing, then it reversed, jumped with that silky smoothness so impossible for humans, up onto the den roof, and deposited the vole by Paul's left hand. The master had returned. The boy stroked the arching back, purrs erupted, and the cat nuzzled into Paul's left side: peace had returned.

Chapter Twelve
Exile: Desperation and Return

~ *"You brought us into the net.*
You laid affliction on our backs.
You have caused men to ride over our heads!
We went through fire and through water—
but You brought us out to a rich place: to fulfilment!"
PSALM 66:11–12

One

Christine and Paul stood leaning against their bikes, getting their breath back. They looked over to the west, back upon the rise that they had just climbed up. It was only a small hill, no more than a hundred and fifty feet high, although at first it rose calmly, once the lane had left the Cheltenham Road and crossed a little bridge with neat red brick parapets, it then climbed with the most beautiful curve, quite steeply, between hedges marking fields of wheat, till it levelled out among orchards. Christine and Paul had swung their bikes to left and to right to gain that extra pressure on the pedals to get them up the short rise of Blakes Hill. They were standing, half bent over their bikes. Before them, for about five miles lay the Vale of Evesham spread through to Bredon Hill, which rose majestically before their view.

It was a warm, hazy day, early in the summer holiday—Christine's summer holiday, for Paul had not returned to Four Pools since coming back from Powick. Once they had their breath back, they placed their bikes down in the long, rough grass surrounding the dirt track that struck at a tangent from the lane. They sat down in the wide grass verge that merged into the headland surrounding the orchard and the wheat field. It was fast turning into a muggy sort of day: over on the horizon the heat haze hung like a thin layer of cloud and blended with the landscape. Over to their left the numerous small hills that made up Dumbleton floated over the landscape, bathed in the humidity. The river glinted over to the right; around Burlingham, he thought, his eyes trying to pick out the appearance of roofs, spires, and lanes amidst the pale pastel green, yellow, beige, and muted brown—colour fusing together in the advancing summer heat. The sky was a pale white-blue even layer of cloud and sky, as if the two elements had ceased their independent lives and fused into a cover of air and cloud. In a city, it would be declared pollution, smog, but here, the heat haze was pure, refreshed by westerly breezes flowing up the Severn Estuary from the Bristol Channel and the Atlantic Ocean.

They both sat with their arms hooked around their knees, legs drawn up, looking on the scene and thinking their thoughts. Christine was the first to speak:

"Have you got that bottle of squash?"

"Yes." Paul handed her the bottle whilst answering her. "Yes, do you want some?"

She took the bottle and lazily unscrewed the cap, then took a long cool drink, swallowing whilst drinking in more.

Paul spoke: "I put some ice in before we left, it's all gone now, melted, but it does make it nice and cool."

Christine passed the bottle over to her brother, who wiped the top with his hand, then took a long drink himself.

"Do you know Ian? You know, he lives round Briar Close . . ."

Paul interrupted her: "Is he in your class?"

"No," she answered, "4C, well, he was, we're all in the fifth year from September, we're gonna be the best, the cream—we'll be fab!"

"What about him?"

"He wants to go out with me! He keeps asking, he's dead keen." She broke into a giggle as she told her story. "He goes to the 'youff-club,' he must have found out Jane and I went there, and he keeps pestering us!"

Paul said nothing. He listened, but did not know what to say.

Christine continued: "He came and danced with me and Jane the other week, kept edging Jane over so he could just dance with me, he kept wanting to talk to me!"

Paul sat blithely listening, whilst gazing on Bredon, the dark, rich green woods on Even Hill standing boastfully in the August sun as crops all around in the Vale lay at their feet, sweltered and begged rain. He took the top off the bottle of squash.

Chapter Twelve, Exile: Desperation and Return

"I don't mind if he dances with us at the 'youff-club,' but I'm not going to the pictures with him; he's too keen, keeps trying to grab me when he dances."

He slowly removed the hand that covered the open bottle and, placing the opening to his lips, lifted the bottle, slowly letting its liquid flow.

"He keeps writing me notes and giving them to me at the club. He gived one to Gina the other week—it was rude, what he said he was dreaming of!"

Christine looked at her brother: "What you thinking?" she asked.

"Just thinking; just looking. Do you remember the times we rode to Elmley, or that time you had a puncture in Aston Somerville, by the railing round the pond?"

"Yeah, we had to push the bike all the way back!"

They both paused. Then Christine continued:

"Are you looking forward to going to your new school?"

Paul was silent.

"Don't you want to go?"

Her brother looked down. He thought about her question; he did not know. He wasn't sure. He knew everyone wanted him to go to school—indeed, he wanted to: he loved reading, he loved learning, loved finding out, doing school work, likewise painting, drawing, model making, but . . . but where to go? He could not face going back to Four Pools. He had hardly been there in the Autumn Term, and he had not been at all since Christmas, and it was now early August, and he was thirteen and a half, and Christine was talking about pop music and boyfriends, and doing shorthand and typing at school next year, and he did not know what he wanted, apart from disappearing into a hole, and he did not want to grow up. So he simply sat and was quiet.

It had been early summer when he came out of Powick. Much had happened since then, and a lot had not happened. He had been taken by his mother to see Doctor Cheen at Briar Close to try and sort out what was to be done with him. He had lowered his head into his chest as he walked along Bridge Street while teenagers from Four Pools school called and jeered, threw insults at him: bantered and derided, mocked and gibed, heckled and sneered, calling him loopy, mental, strange. These taunts were no isolated occurrences—it was the norm. In addition, this derision was not confined to Four Pools miscreants, but extended to Meg's circle of friends, whom he had to face when he sat with them over coffee in the Vinecroft Cafe up High Street on Tuesday mornings, or people like Harry's market gardening friends, who would whisper about him, go out of their way to avoid him. It was as if parts of the community needed a scapegoat, needed to project their worst fears and prejudices onto one single person, felt they were somehow better for deriding and mocking a lesser mortal. Was this the mark of Abel? Was there at a deep spiritual level in humanity an equivalent to the mark of Cain? Something that draws attacks on a victim, a relative innocent, rather than deflecting attacks from the bad person? Amongst animals the runt in a litter will often be prevented from feeding, or shut out of the group, denied shelter; or the smallest chicken in a brood will often be pecked to death by its brothers and sisters.

Paul Broadley was now officially classified by the local education authority as "Educationally Sub-Normal." He had attended a meeting of experts who were to judge and decide on his educational ability. One of the panel, an elderly gentleman, wanted to pursue the designation of "imbecile"—it had been good enough in his day—but those of a younger generation preferred the new fashionable terminology: "Educationally Sub-Normal." The boy sat and listened whilst they argued about the definition. He was regularly visited at home by a young social worker who was obviously checking that the boy was "alright." However, Meg found the visits wearisome, trying, and soon took to hiding in the larder with Christine and Paul, crouching and lying low, as Mr. Thomas walked around the house peering in through each window, vainly knocking on the door. Meg begged the two children to be quiet, not to move or make a sound.

Paul Broadley's days were ordered that Summer Term in much the same way as they had during the months before he went to Powick: reading, drawing and painting, model making, cycling, and walking. He continued painting, as he had done in Powick, having now built up a considerable collection of oil paints and brushes. However, he was only allowed to paint on certain afternoons, and on the kitchen table or in the outhouses, and nothing too big because of the problems of storage, and he was required to paint special pictures to order for Meg's friends. Most days when the weather was good he would go out walking or cycling, sometimes quite far away. Often he would walk down the Corn Mill Road to the Orchard, although he regularly returned to a well-trodden route down the Charity, quietly, methodically, contemplatively walking to the pond to sit and look, watch and think, then move on toward the Red Barn, and follow the hedgerows further on into farmland. He would lie amongst long grasses looking through their tall slender architecture backed in the distance by the spire of Bengeworth Church, then return and draw or paint the scene from memory. Soon he would take a selections of paints out with him to make small oil sketches on cardbord, out in the field, *en plein air*, notes to work up into paintings at some later date. He would walk to Longdon Hill, looking at its slopes from numerous angles, drawing it from different directions, observing the weather, the cloud patterns: light and shade filled these days. But matters at home had not changed.

Chapter Twelve, Exile: Desperation and Return

Meg and Harry still fought—Harry's temper by now was hot and violent, Meg's contempt of him complete: both reflecting to a degree the failure of their marriage, and the frustration of their middle age, both of them now in their mid to late forties. The suffering, the terrors, continued in Paul. This despite the truce between his parents upon his release from Powick. Soon this truce developed into cold war rumblings in his parents' relationship—the ceasefire was now breaking down. And what of Paul? Paul suffered—the early morning depression, the attacks of panic, of mental torment, of suffocating vertigo, the thinness in his mind, deep within him which threatened to suck him into oblivion, coupled with the onset of migraine, which was to plague him in years to come.

There was, however, one difference. The evening abuse happened no longer. On return from Powick Paul refused to wear a nappy, claiming he had not worn one when he was in Powick and had not wet the bed. Meg refused to believe this at first and tried all sorts of psychological blackmail and pressure, insisting it must continue. But he stood his ground. He had blocked out the memory of the abuse so effectively that he had lost all consciousness of what had happened; this had been the only way he had coped. Indeed, when the various professionals had questioned him in Powick as to what was really troubling him he genuinely could answer that he did not know. He had effectively wiped the memory of all those nights from the age of seven to thirteen years. He would be in his early forties before he would gradually, imperceptibly at first, recover the memories. None of this recovery involved professional help—a counsellor, or a therapist—no, in God's good time, and through what he saw as the influence of the Holy Spirit pressing on his mind, the memories picked themselves up and slowly presented themselves to his conscious mind. But the hurt, the distorted feelings, the sense of a hand touching, feelings that went with the memories had to be handled carefully, unpicking and remembering bit by bit, piece by piece, raised memories and feelings that made him want to get up, move, run, anything to get away from the memory.

But this was in the future. For now, that the abuse was no longer happening had given Paul a confidence, an alertness, a self-assurance and self-belief, that the doctors had seen growing in Powick. But now was the problem of heritage: the heritage of the abuse and how he was stereotyped by the local community—at school and out on the street—and by the so-called experts. So he avoided venturing near the town, simply trod well-worn paths around the Charity, Bredon, and so forth.

Doctor Cheen had suggested he should go away to school—a boarding school. Only it would have to be a different school, a special school, because Paul Broadley had missed out on nearly a year of education, which meant he was not the same as the other children, other normal children. He was therefore less than normal; he was "Educationally Sub-Normal." All this power wielding, all this intellectual vanity from standing committees and sub-committees, from social workers and psychiatrists, from educationalists and social psychologists, and . . . and their neat little aphorisms and definitions, this all meant little to the boy. His only thought was that a boarding school meant the sort of school Fatty, Larry and Daisy, Pip and Bets, in the Enid Blyton books, went to: the sort of school where people were nice, where there was camaraderie and comradeship between children, where they met up in the hols, and had exciting adventures. A rather silly, plump, elderly hospital secretary at Doctor Cheen's clinic seemed to confirm the boy's illusion, as she would recount from her boarding school days about "super teachers, jolly good sports, and sticky buns under the sheets."

Once it had all been arranged, Paul Broadley went to visit the school, but came away with a deep-seated mistrust as to what was being arranged. The day he visited the school, in a far-flung shire, no classes or work were going on; vague excuses seemed to be given as answers to questions. But there seemed no alternative. So he prepared himself in his mind for when he would start—in September. In the meanwhile it was arranged that he would take lessons three mornings a week with a retired teacher living in Bengeworth during the remaining weeks of the Summer Term. He did maths, English, and science. He wrote a long story—several chapters filling three exercise books—about a pilot in the Royal Air Force, during the early years of the Second World War. This story developed over several weeks. Brian, the pilot, fought in France as Hitler's Blitzkrieg steamrollered through Western Europe, then he flew in the Battle of Britain, he was shot down but returned to the air. He wove lots of other threads into the story: the pilot's background, childhood, and family; he created a village near to the airfield in Sussex from which Brian flew in the Battle of Britain; he built into the story the dark, evil side of Nazism—the concentration camps, the annihilation of the Jews, the cruelty of the SS—and the dire situation for Britain as the RAF fought in the skies over Southern England, outnumbered by the German planes, their backs-against-the-wall: the final stand for democracy, freedom, and civilization. Then Paul's mother told him that Doctor Cheen and lots of others were waiting to see what would happen: was the pilot a figure for his father, and was Paul going to have him killed off? So he stopped writing the story—and the expert's theories were confounded, their thesis unprovable, their hopes destroyed.

Paul stretched out his legs and lay down, soaking up the sun as the heat spread around them as the morning drew on.

"What you thinking little bruvv?" asked Christine.

Chapter Twelve, Exile: Desperation and Return

"Nothing much," he replied with a sigh, "just thinking how I'll miss all of this. But then I suppose I've got to leave it sometime."

"Yeah, things are gonna be so different for us, not like the old times—Jane keeps teasing me that Ian's my boyfriend! He's not. I don't want him for my boyfriend. Mind you, I like Steve; he's fab!" She paused and looked across to the orchard.

"What you gonna do when you grow up, have you thought?"

"I don't know," he replied. "I don't really know. I haven't really thought about it." He had: he wanted somehow, however unrealistic it might seem, to spend his life painting and drawing, reading and writing stories, finding out about things, walking and exploring, but he knew that was not possible. Christine continued:

"Dad wants me to marry a market gardener, so as to carry on the family tradition. Either that, or you follow in his footsteps!"

That worried Paul. He did not mind the work—he used to help his father a lot; but not now. He used to travel around with him in the lorry; but not now. If he tried to get involved with his father's work, if he showed interest, his mother criticized. Anyway, his father's violent temper and anger frightened him away. He could love his mother, if his father was not around. He could love his father, if his mother was not around. But he could not cope with them together. No. He firmly believed he would have to leave home, move away when he grew up.

"Anyway, I'm gonna marry who I want—and he's gonna be rich, stinking rich and famous. Hey, do you remember that time when you suggested that when we grew up we could go our separate ways, then meet up when no one knew us, so we could marry!"

Her brother smiled and laughed:

"Yes! I was about eight, and we were walking down the road past the Police Station, towards the New Bridge. It was a silly idea, looking back on it, wasn't it?"

Paul thought on all that had happened over the last year, indeed all that was happening. He thought about days gone by. He thought about bright summer days when they were little, of the afternoon they went with their parents, with Meg's friend Rosemary, with James, and their son Duncan, of how they paddled in a ford on the Cotswolds, somewhere, now forgotten by name, but recorded in a photograph fixed in his parents' album forever, about how happy he felt that day, how his parents could get on, did get on that day. He thought about the early spring expeditions when they were at the junior school, when on a Saturday morning they would walk with their mother down the Cheltenham Rod to cut catkins from the hedgerow, how for a lot of the time his mum and dad got on, though never lovingly, . . . but then although the rows occupied only a small proportion of the time, they were deadly, particularly in their effect on him. He thought about the daytrips with their mother on the train to Worcester as young children, the happy times driving around with their father in the lorry, in the market, at the railway—then he realized that most of the good, happy memories were either with their mother, or with their father, but rarely with them together. At times it was as if his mother had tried to protect them from the influence of their father and his world.

"Do you remember the time we got into trouble for hearing the "eff" word in the market?"

Christine answered,

"Yeah, I don't think I've ever seen mum so angry!"

The two of them had been in the top market one morning in the school holidays, about five years earlier, when a miserable old gardener had grumbled about them blocking the gangway between two rows of produce. He had told them to get out of the 'effing way in a most explicit manner! When they returned home for lunch, Christine told her mother what had happened; she asked her mother what the word meant (though she knew all along!). Meg hit the roof. The two children retreated to the passage between the kitchen and the outhouses, and Meg launched at Harry about how she was trying to bring the children up properly, and how he did not care, and how it was *his* friends, *his* market gardening cronies who were the bad influence. Harry retorted: apart from the fact that the old land worker who had said the remark was not even known to Harry, he was not going to take this sitting down. A long and bitter row ensued. Lunch was hurled across the kitchen, plates smashed, while the children stood transfixed in the passage. Christine seemed to revel in the fact that she had triggered this row; Paul hated the row as the terrors returned. The long, slow antagonism, the cold war, lasted for weeks after this confrontation.

Christine sat up, lazily. By now the heat was building up:

"I suppose we'd better get moving, it's eleven-forty."

They unhurriedly rose, gathered themselves together and wheeled their bikes the short distance to the lane. The sense of an ending had characterized the morning. They would cycle together again this holiday, but they both experienced a feeling that these were the final days of their childhood together. This was unspoken, had probably been brought on by the reminiscences they had indulged in, as well as Christine's enchantment with growing up. They freewheeled slowly down the hill without a word.

That night Paul Broadley was visited by a recurring dream: a nightmare that haunted him persistently, regularly, well into his adult years. The nightmares, these visions of loneliness, had been with him all his life, but now a new vision was added, generated by his experiences in Powick. He dreamt that he was lying

Chapter Twelve, Exile: Desperation and Return

in his bed in Powick, or sometimes he was standing in the wide corridor, between the daytime conservatory and the main square of the ward. In either place he was frozen, rooted to the spot, he could not move away, or for that matter move his arms, legs, head, or even his lips. He could move his eyes, or so it seemed, but he could not cry out, all he could do was see with his eyes—and think. The ward was strangely different. It was tall—taller than he had known it, over twice as high. In the height, near the ceiling, were pipes, lots of them, but they were alive, moving, subtly, not so that they could be noticed, save by him: a faint chattering, muttering, very thin and distant seemed to come from these pipes. The furniture and the doors were the same, the ward, the same, yet different. Then he began to perceive sounds, faint at first. It was as if the souls of all the people who had spent time in this ward were now trapped there—inhabiting, infiltrating the very fabric of the place. And the strangeness was compounded by the colour: everything was cream, absolutely everything, every fitting, every item, everything. This was the standard National Health Service colour at the time (with some fittings picked out in fern green) but the cream colour in his dream—his vision?—was somehow loaded, menacing; he was convinced it was conscious, it knew and controlled. And no one saw him. No one was aware of him. He was frozen to the spot, surrounded by this cream perversion; people were moving around doing whatever passed for everyday normal business, but he was totally ignored. He was trapped; no, worse, he was condemned, contained in this purgatory. Upon waking, the emptiness in his heart was absolute, the barren desolation in him was devastating and silent in its cold chill.

Two

The world Paul had returned to from Powick that summer had changed quite considerably. Chowskie had died—his age still undetermined—peacefully in his bed. Jim Beason had retired; he discovered this when he walked to the Red Barn and was bawled-off by a young gardener and his brother from further afield using Jim's pond to wash their onions in. Sam, faithful Sam, had been rushed to hospital in the spring with pleurisy. Once discharged he retired to his cottage in Cropthorne, only to have to move to live with his sister in Pershore when it was discovered he could not care for himself. That summer he died. The world was changing. Road transport was taking over from the railway. Large articulated lorries that took nearly twice as long to reach their destination as the railway, ran from firms that sprang up all around the town. The lorries would clog up the road network, but it was called progress. Within a few years the railway goods yard would close. Harry Broadley sold the old brown Austin lorry and bought a blue Volkswagen pick-up—he now specialized in onions and leeks alone. Over the next ten years market gardening would be decimated by a younger generation leaving the Vale, by EU regulations, and by supermarkets forcing the closure of the local markets and dictating the condition, quality and price of fruit and vegetables grown in the face of cheap imports.

Three

As August drew into September, after days of cycle rides, or afternoons sat amongst riotous runner bean plants on his father's land, with brilliant scarlet flowers piercing through the cacophony of greens, as the heat of the summer drew inexorably into the damp chill and blood-red sunsets of autumn, Paul Broadley was driven the long distance from his home and the land he knew to a far distant shire, to go to school. On a September morning with drizzle-soaked fields around him he was delivered into a gravel-covered forecourt fronting a redbrick Georgian building, separated by a white fence from the by-road. To the rear was a single-story, wooden-clad building painted dark green. The main building was tall, wide, and built at a right angle to the road, a narrow country lane. To the rear of the main house was a copse, while behind the gravel forecourt were several smaller buildings, workshops and so forth. The house stood proudly in its neat, ordered Georgian red brick, with symmetrical, white, wooden sash windows; the main front entrance framed by carved stone, with a black front door reached by shallow steps where a large old dog lay wheezing and dozing in the failing light. The drizzle baptized the scene, initiating Paul Broadley into this new world.

Paul was escorted in through the front door and straight up the main staircase, along a corridor and thence another small narrow staircase to a largish room with three beds. Having placed his bags down, he stood by the window looking down onto the gravel forecourt. With tears welling in his eyes he watched his mother and sister clamber back into the car, which then drew out into the lane and disappeared behind the lush, dark-green, mature foliage of the hedgerow. He sensed tears running down his cheeks but felt none of the relief of weeping. And so he ceased to cry, ceased to feel the aliveness and relief that should come from crying; stone-cold hardness had taken the place of openness, even humility. The tears trickled, but inside a knotted, twisted hurt simply tightened another degree or two, sealing him in even tighter from his fellow humans. There was no sense of relief now from weeping, however silent and still he was.

Chapter Twelve, Exile: Desperation and Return

Paul Broadley left the window; the drizzle turned into a gentle shower. He descended the staircase—accompanied, of course. He was deprived of the solitude that has kept him sane in the past, though *they* could not accompany him to the worlds he inhabits in his mind. He entered the dining room and sat obediently through supper, eating nothing, but spending time pushing the food around his plate. Afterwards, he returned up the staircase, retraced his steps along the corridor, and up the narrow, enclosed staircase to the room. He undressed, washed, and slipped between the sheets, closing his eyes finally on the world, a strange, alien, unwanted world. He lay dozing, fitfully, until later the two other occupants, both young men of sixteen or seventeen, entered, undressed, and got into their own beds. Finally sleep overtook him.

He woke early, about five-thirty, to the dawn chorus, which inevitably reminded him of home. He rose and dressed before the other two in the room were up. His only excursion was to the bathroom at the foot of the small staircase. He then sat in the chair by his bed waiting for the day to start. The others rose. He followed them, once they were ready, down to breakfast. He ate little, simply watched the others and hoped he would not be noticed; he put all of his being into survival tactics, hoping, against the odds, to survive, not knowing what was to happen or what was to become of him.

After breakfast and after everything had been tidied away, he was told to wait, seated in the hall. Eventually he was seen by the staff—they escorted him into a room and attempted to talk to him. It was reminiscent of the interviews in Powick: earnest, committed professionals desperately seeking reassurance as to the truth or objectivity of their ideas. These people seemed to be measuring him against these theories, their preconceived ideas. Paul's natural caution warned him, instinctively, that he could not vocalize such thoughts, such feelings. He was told he could walk around the building, around the grounds, but must not leave the premises. He asked if he could do some painting—not at the moment was the answer. He asked if he could take books from the library—no, it was for staff, for adults. He did not ask any more questions.

Paul Broadley walked around the building. He discovered over to one side of the ground floor of the main house were additional buildings or extensions: the kitchen and similar rooms. Upstairs in these extensions were dormitories and bedrooms and bathrooms. Outside were two long, low, single-storey, green-painted wooden buildings used as classrooms and workrooms. The grounds extended a little around the buildings, but he soon came to fences. Beyond the landscape was low, undulating farmland, a mixture of arable and dairy pasture. On the horizon, he could see the occasional glimmer of roofs or church spires. It was September, the harvest was in, and the fields lay yellow with stubble. Behind the main house, standing as it did at right angles to the lane, there stretched a long thin copse, a narrow wood consisting of mature oak, beech, elm, with younger hardwoods and bushes growing in amongst them. There appeared to be no boundary, so he assumed that this was acceptable territory for him to wander through. He could always see the house and presumed that others walked in the copse as there were two distinct paths, trodden into the dirt, paths snaking through, running parallel, one close to the lane, and the other near to the metal fence dividing the copse from farmland.

Paul Broadley walked around the buildings, observed the adults, observed the children. The children were aged between ten and eighteen, and from what he could deduce these children and young adults were social misfits, indeed similar to the type of people in Powick. For various reasons, these pupils had fallen through the normal education system. Some had emotional problems, others exhibited behaviour that—put politely—was challenging, many had found they simply did not fit in with the education system as it was then, others were from children's homes, yet more were the children of parents working overseas, for whom no school could be found. Most accepted their lot once they arrived here. Soon he realized he did not fit in, would be unable to fit in, did not want to fit in. Staff were, he considered, too informal with most of the teenagers, lessons were non-existent, behaviour bad. The whole place seemed to teeter on the edge of an abyss: an abyss where a small group of teenagers ruled, and the younger, shyer, and more sensitive individuals withdrew and were dominated by those who were stronger, more arrogant and forthright, anti-social, anti-establishment, and who preyed on the fears of both staff and pupils. It was in some respects a *Lord-of-the-Flies* situation where the dominant personalities and characters amongst the boys would oppress and intimidate, exhort and bully the lesser individuals.

Within the first few weeks, the entire sixty or so boys and young men were assembled in the main "library" room. Two boys who had attempted to run away were paraded before them. Both looked the worse for wear for their attempt—not from the fatigue of being out in the countryside or sleeping rough, but from the way they had been handled since their "capture." The way they were paraded before the assembly, sat and stood as they were around the walls of the room, reminded Paul of a similar situation in a barn, in a little book he had read that summer: *Animal Farm*. From then on he thought of the Principal of the school as Napoleon, and the staff as Napoleon's hounds.

The school seemed to be run under the image of a liberal regime, hence the lack of lessons—children would go along if they wanted to. Only after two weeks, when he enquired, did he find himself directed to one of the classrooms. Paul was shocked by the simplicity of the lessons. He could not believe what was expected

Chapter Twelve, Exile: Desperation and Return

of him: the work was just like he had done in the second and third year at junior school. It was similar, though far simpler, than the thin curriculum he experienced in 1D, his first year at secondary school. The teacher set no boundaries, no rules, expected little from her charges; equipment was scarce, or spoiled and broken.

Paul Broadley spent the evenings walking around the grounds, or doing whatever jobs or chores were required of him around the house. If it was raining, he would sit by his bed or in one of the downstairs rooms, but he avoided certain no-go areas. The main dormitory wing was one such example. He had witnessed a male-on-male rape, and if not penetrative rape, then abuse and harassment of one naked boy of around eleven years old by four youths aged around sixteen, who teased him, interfered with him, humiliated him, gained a perverse pleasure from touching him, exploring him, and threatening him; he had seen one child, naked from the waist down, walking around the corridor between the bedrooms chanting away about self-abuse whilst displaying his genitals; one shy young boy was urinated upon for "telling"; others were "got" whilst in the showers or bathrooms. He feared telling staff as it was common knowledge amongst the children that complaints would not be taken seriously. These actions of gross indecency were passed off as childish pranks by staff. So he steered clear of the bathrooms, save for having a wash early in the morning when no other person was around. Then there was the extortion, the bullying: money was the object, likewise the agreement to do the chores of the one who was threatening in exchange for 'protection.' All of this sub-culture amongst the boys was probably similar to a traditional English public school, but populated by emotional and behaviourally disturbed youths who had fallen through the conventional system, but were not sufficiently criminalized for probation, an approved school, or a borstal.

Paul Broadley hated the school—the regime, the lack of structure, the lack of an education—and feared as profoundly for his safety as he had while in Powick. In Powick most of the men were locked into a world of their own and only clashed when personal territory was invaded. To this extent they were defensive. Here, a large core of youth was aggressively offensive. He hated the school. His only outlet was to write to his mother about the conditions, about the pain he was suffering. However, his mother showed the letters to Dr. Cheen who wrote back to the boy, in very patronizing tones, about having to grow up and face the world, and that he was over-reliant on his mother and so forth. At times he glimpsed an abandonment of all hope. He even received a postcard from one his grandmother's friends in Weston with the advice, "Hope you are keeping your chin up because that's the way to win." Then Paul Broadley found himself summoned to the Head's study. Dr. Cheen had communicated the contents of the letters to the school authorities. Paul Broadley did not keep his chin up, he applied a lesson he had learnt in Powick: silence. He simply withdrew behind a self-imposed hermetic, stone wall. Gradually he became adept at silent non-cooperation, passive, dissociating, non-cooperation. He answered all questions in short, simple tones, but gave nothing away, offered no direct criticism, spoke little to either pupils and staff, kept himself to himself, involved himself with no one: refused to talk, refused to share, refused to be with others, to be involved. Such silent, passive, non-conformity became a characteristic.

The boy asked to be allowed his oil paints, but was refused: the answer given was that they had paints in the classroom (powder paints, or bottles of cheap "ready-mix," or colour blocks, just like any primary school). So Paul ceased to paint. Solitude was his companion, walking in the grounds, small as they were, or along the thin copse (no more than a few hundred yards in length). He felt like a caged animal in a zoo. He needed space, so one Saturday afternoon he left the house, walked out of the gate, and proceeded down the lane towards the crossroads a mile or so away. He stopped by a phone box to phone his parent's home—but no one was in. He discovered a footpath, a right of way that would take him around and through some fields and back to the school. But he was spotted by some of the staff in a car, they had missed him—they must have been watching and observing him. He was bundled into the back of the car. The next day, indeed a Sunday afternoon, the school was assembled in the long, main room. All the pupils were either seated or stood around the perimeter of the room. The Head of the School entered—a very large, obese, middle-aged man, with greasy hair, ill-fitting clothes, and a mid-European accent—and proceeded to tell the assembly about a child in their midst:

"A child who has only recently joined us. A child who is a viper in our midst."

He spoke slowly and left long silent, pauses between each statement:

"He writes to his mother."

Silence.

"He writes complaining about us; about our school."

One or two boys shifted uneasily.

"He has told stories about us."

Some children were surreptitiously looking around to see if any other child was blushing.

"He has been making up stories about us. He has tried to run away from us."

At this point several boys were looking a bit shifty—as if the accusations could apply to any one of them.

"This boy is ungrateful."

Silence followed as the Head allowed his eyes to scan the assembly.

Chapter Twelve, Exile: Desperation and Return

"This boy is ungrateful, is a viper in our midst."

One young boy coughed, cleared his throat, then blushed as he saw the assembly focus their attention on him.

"This boy tried to run away—we found him walking the lane, about to disappear along a footpath across a field."

Silence reigned, though one or two shifted now in their seats.

"We have ways of dealing with such boys. We have ways of dealing with such boys if they will not appreciate what we can offer them."

Paul Broadley knew he was the pupil being referred to, but showed no emotion, no expression on his face, simply fixed his eyes on a bookcase in front of him.

"Such ingratitude should be dealt with, he is a traitor to all of us."

Paul's eyes burned into the bookcase, he cared nothing for the criticisms, for the veiled threats, but pleaded in his heart that he would not be named. He had been forced to witness these mock trials before, these denunciations of those who had challenged the hypocrisy, tokenism, and liberal inconsistency of the establishment in this school.

"This little viper. This traitor . . ."

One small ten year old started crying at this point. Others, notably the sixteen-, seventeen-, and eighteen-year-old youths simply exhibited bravado.

"We have offered our hospitality to this child, but he shown gross ingratitude. This will not be tolerated!"

Only this last remark showed the slightest sign of emotion, inflection, almost of anger.

The assembly was dismissed; they filed out in silence. Paul Broadley was grateful that he was not named. He did not know why, many of the other pupils would have known it was him. Or maybe there were others who were in a similar situation to his. He imagined that there were several lonely and isolated individuals here in this hellhole that, like him, could no longer communicate, were locked into their own isolation, and for whom there was no hope, no future.

So he continued to write letters to his mother. He continued to post them—secretly—continued to complain about the regime, about his unhappiness. It was clear that there were others in the same predicament as he was. There were others who could not speak of the horrors, the sufferings, and were afraid of the large, loutish youths who ruled the place. Children suffered in silence, watched as others, one by one, were abused, physically and mentally, by the older youth, while those in charge, those who were to care for these children, seemed to ignore what was going on, or were blithely unaware of the misery and torment hidden behind the liberal, easy-going organization of the school, or simply did not know how to face it.

Four

And so the days passed into weeks, and as each day started, Paul feared for his sanity, feared for his future. Towards the end of October the frosts began. He minded them not, despite the cold in the attic-level room he slept in. However, the sight of the frost filled him with longing: with the deepest, most profound longing for the Charity, for the Red Barn, the copse, the brook, the hedgerows. He felt his heart wailing deep inside him, but now could not weep, could not explain his feelings, could not speak about the deepest, most important, but most sensitive parts in his life.

Then one Saturday afternoon, beyond all expectation, the nightmare ended.

Paul Broadley watched from the bedroom window as a car drew into the gravel-covered courtyard. It came to a halt. Out of the car stepped his father. He watched as his father walked across the gravel drive and disappeared, he presumed through the main front door. He went back and sat on his bed. He heard voices below. He heard his father's voice raised in confident, almost angry tones. Then there was silence. After a while he heard footsteps on the small staircase. One of the staff, a woman, entered the room, followed closely by his father, who pushed his way passed the woman as she started speaking:

"Paul, your father's here to see you, he, err, he seems to have some idea..."

"Idea my foot; I've got plenty of ideas," his father interrupted. "Come on Paul, I've come to take you home."

The boy was puzzled, transfixed, wondered if he was sleeping, dreaming.

"Well, are you coming or not? Make your mind up, we haven't got all day!"

He hastily grabbed his clothes and threw them into his suitcase, hurriedly gathered his few possessions together, and within five minutes he was walking down the main staircase following his father.

"Mr. Broadley, I beg you to reconsider, I..."

With graphic language and his body shaking with tension and righteous anger Harry turned on the Headmaster—but restraining himself from physical violence spoke loudly, forcefully, but not shouting—

"Reconsider, my aunt fanny," Harry replied, wagging his finger in the Head's face. "And if you start talking about calling the police again, I'll make sure they hear both sides of the story, certainly with what goes on here!"

The head was silent; the other staff moved away or looked sideways.

Paul Broadley followed as his father left the building through the main door leaving the handful of staff and boys who had gathered dumbstruck. Before he could gather his thoughts properly he was sitting in the back of the car and being driven off down the lane and back towards the main road.

Chapter Twelve, Exile: Desperation and Return

Harry had made up his mind earlier that week. He too had read the boy's letters. He had read between the lines, unlike Meg or Dr. Cheen. (Returning very late from his parents'—over the road—he had gone through Meg's correspondence case when the house was in darkness and the others were asleep.) He could tell that this was not just a case of homesickness or a child not wanting to grow up. Regardless of whatever action the authorities wished to take, he was going up to collect his son, if it was the child's will, and he was going to make sure none of these phoney staff stopped him. He did not need to wait for a reply when he had asked Paul, on entering the bedroom, whether he wished to come home or not, the smile on the boy's face was enough. He needed no word of thanks to know he had done the right thing; for once Harry had been decisive and taken control of the situation instead of angrily wiping his hands of his marriage, of Meg, and hiding over the road at his parents' house.

The boy's expression spoke volumes of gratitude.

Epilogue—
A Leave-Taking

~ *"When You give them their needs, they gather!*
You open Your hand, they are filled with good.
You hide Your face, and they are troubled.
You take away their breath: they die!—and return to their dust.
You send forth Your Spirit, they are created.
And You renew the face of the earth.
May the glory of the Lord endure forever,
May the Lord rejoice in all His works!"

PSALM 104:28–31

The lane led down a shallow gradient to the brook, the stone drive rising methodically as it passed over the waters, skirting the edge of the copse. The copse stood dark, grey, brown, hard, and brittle in the depth of its winter hibernation. Crows' nests stood out in the crowns of the trees, stood proudly against the dark steel-grey-night-black of a February sky: black balls of tightly knitted, convoluted twigs, now used up, spent, seemingly dead. But the crows still haunted the land. They flapped ungainly, cawing in the hard, stiff air. They flew around the copse, inelegant, clumsily soaring and climbing. On the land they hopped, staggered, ponderous and awkward, as they fell and scrambled over the rigid, frozen clods of earth. The furrows were frozen, suspended in the ice as if claws held the earth still: immovable, impenetrable. The crows fought in an uncouth manner over whatever insect or morsel they could find wandering the bleak earth. The losers slouched off, their beaks stabbing at the soil, puzzled at its unyielding stubbornness. With clumsy, awkward flapping of wings, beating strenuously against the raw, biting air, they lumbered skywards, their gawky legs,

Epilogue—A Leave-Taking

and necks slamming into the air, feathers furling and flapping in the icy stillness.

The land was frozen, suspended in this world, never again to breathe, never again to live: nothing else moved; nothing else dared to face the sharply cutting, bleak, bitter, wintry indifference. The land was enveloped in the white haze of frost: the earth stood hard and concrete. Grasses bent under the weight of the frost. Stone stood proud, in its element now with a friend in the bitter, unresponsive ice. The brook lurked green beneath the ice sheet, air bubbles frozen into the stiff, glassy membrane, sealing the waters and the myriad of tiny fresh water creatures into their own mini-universe. Tense, sharp diagonal lines shot through the frozen water as plants trapped in the margins were crushed and strangled as the ice gripped tighter and tighter, breaking the lush, joyous growth of the summer's survivors, cutting as effectively as a knife the top growth in the air, while the rest of the plant wallowed beneath in fresh water. The very air seemed to have been taken over by this hoarfrost, as it deposited this coating of rime on all. This new air was weightier, denser, yet more resonant. It carried the faintest sound of traffic from the distant road, half a mile away at Gypsies' Corner.

The steel-grey now lightened with pale hints of cerulean blue, high above the land. It was dawn, with the faintest glimmer of orange penetrating the horizon over towards Longdon Hill. The only sound, bar the faint hum of the traffic, came from the crows. No other bird dared invade this world while these monarchs swooped over the frozen earth. A solitary pair hopped gawkily around the perimeter of the Red Barn: stabbing at loose stones, glowering at grasses clinging desperately to the dusty soil in the crevice between bricks lying forlorn at the foot of the walls.

Paul stood.

He stood passive, quiet, still, observant, reflective. He watched the minimal activity, felt the air as it stung his cheeks, stood and took in this changed world. Like a desert, life was at a minimum, flowing liquid water absent, the atmosphere stricken, sullen, crisp, and violent with cold.

Paul sat.

He sat on a pile of broken bricks. He sat and looked, watched carefully, picking out the traces of movement beneath the sheer, unyielding, green ice covering the waters of the brook. Tiny bubbles hung beneath this glass, tiny signs that life existed. He noted and took heed. He protected himself—like the ice covering the waters, spreading their cold mantle over the land. Likewise he had secured his heart safe, impenetrable, guarded with a mantle of reserve. He raised his head. The light, weak and sullen, began to permeate the steel-grey now steel-blue sky. It offered no warmth. None was taken. The frost ruled absolute. The sky was clear, empty, transparent: no hint or wisp of cloud had dared challenge the ice, dared to penetrate the sheer, absolute, purity, of the morning. It was still early. The sun had still not emerged over the horizon. No other human had dared enter its court. Nothing moved, nothing lived: he sat alone in isolation. Against all the odds he had survived the last year, he was still sane, still whole, inviolate, save for the mental terrors and the torment of memories. Now he was taking one day at a time, he dared not imagine, or even hope as to what the future held. He sat and watched his breath condense in the cold air. Here, at the furthest reach of Longman's Charity, he felt safe, he felt alone, he felt secure. The aloneness was now part of his security. The fewer the people around, the more secure he was: people hurt.

Paul stood up.

He stretched, then walked around an old metal cistern towards the lane where it rose gently to traverse the brook. He walked over this bridge, then into the lane as it became a track, two rutted mud widths with a grass ridge down the centre. He stumbled over the steel-hard petrified mud, so took to walking down the central ridge instead. His journey left a green trail along the ridge as his boots and trousers brushed off the frost. After several hundred yards the track gave out and he was walking along a headland, about two meters wide. This then curved around the top of a field, then went straight on again. He walked on, leaving a green trail in the frozen grass where he had been. Soon he reached a small group of trees; he was surrounded by farmland—bare fields. He sat down on an old log by the trees and looked over and down. He had passed the watershed for the Charity Brook. This was a different kingdom. Over to his left was Longdon Hill, now seen from the end. Over before him the sun just began to appear over the North Cotswold escarpment about two miles away.

The sun rose slowly, feebly—a blood-orange red ball. It pierced this frozen kingdom, but lacked the strength to have any influence. He watched this slow, muted sun rise, shaking his head to clear the memory of the nightmare, the terrors that had woken him early, with their images of a nihilistic purgatory, memories from the last year. Today, a few days after his fourteenth birthday, was the anniversary: one year since he had been admitted to Powick—formerly, the Worcester City and County Pauper and Lunatic Asylum.

Paul Broadley had returned to Evesham, sleeping in his old room, looking from his window to Longdon Hill. A cold, empty peace resonated at his parents' home. Despite all the tension and the terror, he had settled back in at his parents. He then returned to Four Pools, unannounced, though everyone had known where he had been. He walked at playtime through the barrage of sniggers and hatred, intolerance and jibes; he walked as the untouchable, the strange mental one, he who had been away: he who had been *there*, he who was not one of us!

Epilogue—A Leave-Taking

He had returned to class 3B, yet out of all the children in his year, only one spoke to him, Richard, whom he had known at Swann Lane. The head teacher ignored the classification of "Educationally Sub-Normal" and returned him to the stream he had been in a year earlier.

As puberty took hold he was racked even more by self-doubt, by a sense of inferiority. He felt a strong attraction to girls he knew, he would talk to them, sense a mutual friendship, attraction, but always held back. He would always fall short of asking one out, and never allowed a relationship to develop. The sublimated memories of abuse held him tight in his own forsaken world. He knew something was wrong, wrong with him; he wished he had the courage to break out of these inhibitions, but he had lost the key to the memories. He had genuinely and completely lost all knowledge of the years of touching, stroking each night on the kitchen table.

So as the years passed he remained a chaste and celibate bachelor. And hope of a friendship, love, of marriage was totally out of the question. He feared and mistrusted love. The lessons he had learned in Powick, and then away at the special school, were all he had to cling to. He was now convinced of the need to show no feelings, not to show his suffering. He had learnt to be normal and polite on the outside, only to reassure other people that he was no threat. He kept the real self hidden safely away, secure in a box inside him, so no one could touch him, no one could hurt him, for no one could reach him. Likewise he had learnt not to trust anyone, not to speak of the things that troubled him, nor to share with or trust anyone with anything important to his life, his sanity, remaining polite, but distant. If events troubled and threatened to the extent that his very survival was at stake, then passive non-cooperation was the only safe, defensive line: passive, disassociating, non-cooperation (a lesson he had learned away at the special school). He answered questions in short, simple monosyllabic tones, gave nothing away, offered no direct criticism, spoke little to other people, did not talk, did not share, distanced himself.

Such silent, passive, non-conformity characterized him over the coming years, disguised by normal conversation—or what he took to be what the recipient expected as normal conversation. These three lessons were now his last and only line of defence, all he had for survival. They became a thin silver strand that held him above the rend—or fracture—of insanity.

Paul Broadley wanted desperately to be accepted as normal. He did not desire or seek revenge—or retribution—for what had happened to him, but he did long for his situation to return to something past; he wanted to erase what had happened. He desperately thirsted for his situation to develop into a more normal life. He could do nothing about what had happened, about what they said he was—mental. All he could do was to think, to plan eventually to move away.

Longman's Charity

He watched as the sun completed its journey above the horizon, around it a white-orange glow. He stood up from the log and moved back around the group of trees, walking back along the headland. As he walked alongside the hedgerow he saw in the distance someone moving around the Red Barn. This person then sat down where he had sat, overlooking the brook. Paul Broadley stood by a small tree, next to the hedgerow, only thirty or so yards away. Jim Beason sat gazing into the brook's frozen waters. He was alone. Paul knew his wife had died. Jim—now an old man, who had given up his right to the holding, but could not abandon it to its new occupier—sat, forlornly, lost, grieving for Doris. Her loss, her death had sunk into him deeply.

Paul knew.

He also knew that Jim had just returned from Powick. The authorities, those around Jim, were concerned at his grief, concerned that he should have got over it by now—two years on. Maybe they thought he should have snapped out of it, maybe they thought he could not care for himself, old and arthritic as he was. Maybe in years earlier he would have been escorted to the workhouse. He had taken to sleeping overnight in the Red Barn. This did not worry the new holder of the land, but it did those who believed people should not live in sheds anymore. Jim looked up and saw Paul. He raised his hand, beckoning to come over. Paul stayed where he was; he was afraid to move. He did not fear Jim in the way other people did now. But he was afraid to talk to him, he feared Jim's link with Powick. Much from Paul's stay in Powick was now bottled up and buried deep inside him; different feelings and thoughts were in him. He wanted to go over and talk with Jim, yet he felt fear. He could not reconcile these feelings, so he stayed cautious.

Jim sat.

Paul Broadley stood.

He was now no longer a child. After a long while the young man moved away, leaving Jim sitting on the bank. He moved back up towards the hedgerows and retraced his steps round, past a crumbling and collapsing shed, now rotten with neglect, then back to the Charity Lane which he walked—slowly, deliberately—along, scuffing his feet in the crushed limestone. The sun was now climbing above Longdon Hill, however its warmth was only just beginning to change the colour of the tips of the grass from a frosted mint-green, to the rich dark sap-green. But this was to be all: the frost would hold for the day, only the air became less sharp, less fierce, less cold.

Small vans were starting to arrive, parking by the sheds. Men and women emerged, wrapped up tightly against the cold, coughing and spluttering, land workers nodding a greeting to Paul Broadley as he walked. He was now regarded as a man, not as a child. Over on the horizon before him stood the spire of

Epilogue—A Leave-Taking

Bengeworth Church; over to the left stood the Bell Tower, beside it thin wisps of smoke rose from the roofs of houses: Evesham was beginning to wake up.

Jim Beason continued to sit, talking into his overcoat, oblivious to the cold, oblivious to those around him, sitting by the Red Barn, gazing into the brook.

In time Paul Broadley did leave home, move away. He spent time working for the Forestry Commission as a Land Rover driver and woodman on Bredon Hill (Fox Hill Wood, round through the Shawl, Cames Coomb, to Comberton Wood and Far Wood, on the northern slopes of Bredon, around Even Hill) and the North Cotswolds (Half Moon Plantation, Upper Slatepits and the expansive woods south of Bourton Downs towards Hinchwick Hill Barn and west towards Scarborough Farm); he spent time studying at art college, then university; times teaching at a London art college, times returning on a weekend to see his parents and sister—and to walk the land, and revisit the Red Barn, the hedgerows near and around this part of the brook. He would return to climb to the highest part of Bredon Hill, to sit and gaze into the distance, the wide expanse north over the Midland Plain or west to the Malverns and the foothills of the Welsh mountains. He would cycle and walk for miles, losing himself in the North Cotswolds. But his heart lay firmly shut away, firmly sealed in a tightly hermetic box: inviolate, untouchable. Till one spring evening, when sitting alone in his flat in Highbury, North London, he was touched by Love so pure, so gentle and honest, so open and beckoning, that all that had gone before, all that had happened in his childhood, all melted away: *Love bade him welcome*. He wept for the first time in oh so many years: he was twenty-six years old. Love had taken him by the hand and led him, taught him, showed him love's wounds—initially his mind recoiled at the sight of the wounds, the Cross, yet the more he let Christ love him, the more he learned to love Christ, the more he became human, the more life began to make sense. The deeper he drank of the Love of God, the more he could pray, "Thy will be done . . . whatever the consequences." But the full account? That is another story.

Three years after this conversion, Paul Broadley married; and has been happily married ever since, as the decades roll by into their old age. And was there any value to the suffering and traumas of Powick, the terrors, the nihilism of his parents' marriage? Hilary, his wife, suffers from severe epilepsy, and he is now her full-time carer. Paul's childhood experiences have helped him with Hilary's situation in ways that other people—bereft of such experiences—could not begin to conceive of, let alone understand, for there is the often bizarre nature and total unpredictability of Hilary's epilepsy (the distortion of sense perception and accompanying behaviour that temporal-lobe epilepsy can engender) from daily complex partial seizures to several episodes of *status epilepticus* (with the ever present risk of death) . . . but again that is another story.

Gradually, one by one, the old gardeners retired, or died in the job. Holdings were amalgamated, more cars and pick-ups appeared down the Charity; people changed. In the mid-1970s a road was put through between the Cheltenham Road and the Oxford Road. There began nearly twenty years of relentless development. The old sheds were bulldozed, the holdings levelled, the Charity Brook, scoured and culverted; factories built, superstores erected; houses formed a tide of development that flowed to within a couple of hundred yards of the Red Barn. The line of building halted hesitantly behind the tarmac defences of the new ring road, but stood threatening to engulf yet more land.

Christine lived at home sleeping with her mother until she was twenty-nine years of age. Together it was now Meg and Christine on one side when rows erupted, Christine proving she was a match to her father's anger and vitriolic skill in a row. Harry sold most of the Broadley land as development spread, living off the capital until it ran out; then he would work for other gardeners on a casual basis. And what of Meg and Harry? Meg and Harry continued on as they had done for so many years squabbling, rowing, with only age taking the passion out of their arguments until one Sunday afternoon in early October, when aged seventy-five years Harry, getting out of the car, suddenly collapsed on the drive by the house: an abrupt, devastating, and complete stroke.

In the previous three years there had been a renaissance of feeling and understanding between Paul and Harry, between father and son. Both could talk over the old days of Paul's childhood with ease. They could forgive each other for past wrongs, share and begin to grow as father and son. But then came the stroke. He lay, unable to speak, unable to recognize anyone; the mind once so violent in thought now was stilled. Just over two weeks later he died. The ancient Greeks had a saying, that you could not fully understand a person's life until it ended. Further, that the manner of their death was to a degree a measure of their life. Harry died after a violent and destructive stroke that left him stricken for sixteen days, totally incapacitated, still, silent, but with some awareness of sorts, before death took hold. How apposite considering his violent outbursts, the manic, almost evil destruction of the temper he had, a temper he did little to control.

Meg, who for so long had criticized, grumbled, and claimed hatred for him, who said she would rejoice on his death, suddenly realized she had lost the last chance to make peace with him, the last chance for them to forgive each other, to come to terms with all that their stormy forty-two years of marriage had been. Harry had died with very little money; he had been working for a younger gardener earlier in the day when the stroke smote him, working still to make ends meet. The house by then was run down and in need of renovation, a house Meg could not now face leaving. She could not come to terms with what had

Epilogue—A Leave-Taking

happened, with her feelings for Harry: she had not been able to live with him, but she could not live without him.

Meg was indecisive as to what she wanted: to stay in the house, or to move. But then came the afternoon when Christine could get no answer at the house, all the curtains were drawn. Eventually, with the help of a local policeman, they were able to get in: Christine was summoned by the policeman into the living room to see the body.

On a cold February morning, as fresh snow lay on the ground, Meg had finally taken her own life: an overdose of tranquillizers.

Was committing suicide after being addicted to sleeping pills and tranquillizers for twenty-five years a fair reflection of her life? She had talked of this, threatened for twenty-five years that she would do it, one day. How much was this suicide a measure of her refusal to face the truth about her marriage, her life with Harry, and the abuse she was subject to as a girl? When Harry died she could no longer hide in being house-proud; but she also knew with cold certainty the truth that she could no longer live with him but also that she could not live without him. When Paul went with his sister to Worcester to identify, formally, his mother's suicided body, it was the hands that struck Paul—his mother's hands. He recognized them, he knew them so well: it was at this moment that the memories of the abuse he had received started to impinge on his conscious mind, as he stood looking at his dead mother's hands, and he would recover these memories, slowly, painfully, over the next six years.

Once more Christine and Paul sat in the black hearse as it unhurriedly made its way to the crematorium. To Paul in particular, the tragedy of his parents' marriage was overwhelming, likewise the agony of trying to get close to them, though the gulf between them had seemed unbridgeable.

And Christine and Paul stood scattering her ashes on the whiteness of the snow, in the Broadley orchard, on the same spot where Harry's ashes had been spread barely four months earlier.

The story was over.

> *"Let my prayer be set before You as incense, O Lord,*
> *the lifting up of my hands as an evening sacrifice."*
> PSALM 141:2